GOLDEN BOY

Also by Bob Thomas

GOLDEN BOY

The Untold Story
of William Holden

BOB THOMAS

St. Martin's Press
New York

Editor: Toni Lopopolo
Assistant Editor: Karen Johnsen
Design by Manuela Paul
Production Editor: Amelie Littell
Copyeditor: Gregory Weber

Library of Congress Cataloging in Publication Data

Thomas, Bob, 1922–
    Golden boy.

    1. Holden, William, 1918–81.   2. Moving-picture
actors and actresses—United States—Biography.
I. Title.
PN2287.H58T48   1983   791.43'028'0924   [B]   83–2912
ISBN 0–312–33697–7

First Edition
10 9 8 7 6 5 4 3 2 1

To Cynthia and Sam Summerlin

CONTENTS

ACKNOWLEDGMENTS

The author is grateful to many people for sharing their memories of William Holden. Some contributions were extensive, some fragmentary. All were appreciated. A cautionary note: the appearance in an anecdote of a person listed below does not necessarily mean that person was the source of the anecdote. The author is also grateful to Carol and Wayne Warga and Robert Gottlieb for much-needed encouragement. And to Pat Thomas for support above and beyond the call of marriage.

The author is grateful to the following for their recollections of William Holden:

Bernie Abramson
Tony Adams
Edward Albert
Leon Ames
Dana Andrews
Julie Andrews
Irving Asher
Max Arnow
Art Arthur
Lew Ayres
Lucille Ball
Frank Baur
Marilyn Beck
Mary Beedle
Wally Beene
William Bemis
Ben Benjamin
Harvey Bernhard
Jay Bernstein
Jacqueline Bisset

Robert Blumofe
Eddie Bracken
Harry Brand
Robert Butler
Red Buttons
Michael Caine
John Campbell
Teet Carle
Bob Carroll
Richard
   Chamberlain
Jan Clayton
Paul Clemens
Walter Coblenz
Robert Cohn
C. C. Coleman
Mike Connors
Steven Crane
Broderick Crawford
Pat Crowley

George Cukor
Jack Dales
Patti Davis
Chico Day
Frances Dee
Dick Delson
William Demarest
I. A. L. Diamond
Bob Dingilian
Edward Dmytryk
Harlan Eastman
Clint Eastwood
Shirley Eder
Blake Edwards
John Engstead
Jamie Farr
William Feeder
Gail Feingarten
Jean Howard
   Feldman

Phil Feldman
Bob Fender
Jose Ferrer
Mary Fiore
Richard Fleischer
Nina Foch
Glenn Ford
Carl Foreman
John Forsythe
M. J. Frankovich
William Friedkin
Phyllis Gardner
James Garner
Jackie Gleason
James Goldstone
Jack Gordean
Betty Graf
William Graf
William Graham
Bonita Granville
Coleen Gray
Richard Guttman
Paul Harper
Sterling Hayden
Andrew Hickox
Jack Hirschberg
Victor Honig
Bob Hope
Geoffrey Horne
John Houseman
Rock Hudson
Arthur Jacobson
Erskine Johnson
Isabel Johnson
L. Q. Jones
Richard Kahn
Garson Kanin
Arthur Kennedy
Burt Kennedy
Pauline Kessinger

Michael Klassman
Dick Kleiner
Jerzy Kozinski
Norman Krasna
Nancy Kwan
Alan Ladd, Jr.
Dorothy Lamour
Alan Landsburg
John Landis
Evelyn Lane
Ernest Lehman
Kay Lenz
Milt Lewis
A. C. Lyles
John Lee Mahin
Rouben Mamoulian
Daniel Mann
Tim Matheson
Michael Mazlansky
Joel McCrea
Elizabeth McDonald
Andrew McLaglen
Julian Meyers
Jason Miller
Walter Mirisch
Robert Mitchum
Elinor Moller
Roger Moore
Alice Thomas
  Moriarty
Don Morgan
Harry Morgan
Richard Mulligan
Miriam Nelson
Paul Newman
Florence Gaines
  Nichols
Jack Nicholson
Warren Oates
Carroll O'Connor

Nancy Olson
Ryan O'Neal
William T. Orr
Harriet Whitbeck
  Palmer
Jerry Pam
Jack Perkins
Robert Preston
Richard Quine
Helen Rackin
Irving Rapper
Ronald Reagan
Lee Remick
Gene Reynolds
Cliff Robertson
Mickey Rooney
Jane Russell
Art Sarno
Frank Schaap
Elliot Schick
Martha Scott
Vernon Scott
Phyllis Seaton
David Seltzer
William Sharmat
Alexis Smith
Sam Spiegel
Barbara Stanwyck
Ray Stark
Patricia Stauffer
Richard Steele
Caroline Steinberg
Herb Steinberg
Craig Stevens
James Stewart
Andrew Stone
Ezra Stone
Beatrice Straight
John Strong
John Sturges

Gloria Swanson
Loretta Swit
Dan Taradash
Don Taylor
Ted Taylor
Sherwin Tilton
Claire Trevor

Karl Tunberg
Robert Vaughn
Joseph Wambaugh
Richard Webb
Robert Webber
Frank Westmore
Richard Widmark

Billy Wilder
Richard Winters
Robert Wise
David Wolper
Loretta Young

1

"What a Lousy Fadeout"

JOE GILLIS

Yes, this is Sunset Boulevard, Los Angeles, California. It's about five o'clock in the morning. That's the Homicide Squad, complete with detectives and newspaper men. A murder has been reported from one of those great big houses in the ten-thousand block. You'll read all about it in the late editions, I'm sure. You'll get it over your radio and see it on television—because an oldtime star is involved, one of the biggest. But before you hear it all distorted and blown up out of proportion, before those Hollywood columnists get their hands on it, maybe you'd like to hear the facts, the real truth. . . .

—*Sunset Boulevard**

Monday morning, November 16, 1981. Police cars raced along Ocean Boulevard in Santa Monica, sirens shrilling, and converged on the Shoreham Tower, a thirteen-story apartment building overlooking the Pacific. An hour later, the news was released: William Holden, the movie star, had been found dead in his apartment. He had been alone for several days and had apparently been drinking. The manager of the building, which Holden partly owned, had unlocked the door and discovered the body.

The news of Holden's death was received with shock and incredulity in Hollywood, New York, London, Geneva, Hong Kong, Nairobi—cities where Holden's physical presence had been strongly felt. And elsewhere throughout the world, for William Holden had been a dominant image in the American film for forty years.

How could Bill Holden have died drunk and alone?

It was inconceivable. He had earned riches and honors beyond the dreams of most actors. He had been the lover of some of the most

---

*Copyright © 1939, renewed © 1967 by Columbia Pictures.

beautiful and talented women in the world. The adventure of his own life had matched the roles he had played on the screen. As news of his death flashed around the world, those who had known Bill Holden intimately—or had thought they did—tried to piece together the puzzle.

Blake Edwards was at the Dorchester Hotel in London when a reporter telephoned: "Could I have an interview with you?"

"What about?" Edwards asked.

"Bill Holden's death?"

Edwards froze. "I can't even talk with you," he said, and he hung up the telephone.

Julie Andrews entered the room and was startled to see the whiteness of her husband's face. "Blake, darling, what's wrong?" she asked.

"It's Bill Holden. He's dead."

"Oh, my God!" she gasped. "How? Where?"

"I don't know," he replied, slumping in a chair, unable to speak. His friendship with Holden transcended the usual director-actor relationship. Through two films together they had developed a solid comradeship. Edwards found rare delight in Holden's ebullience, his grace and style. As a director, Edwards knew exactly what conversational buttons to push in order to send Bill off on a flight of eloquence, and the surest button was marked Africa. Feeling his grief, as well as twinges of his own mortality, Edwards found it inconceivable and unacceptable that he would never again hear Bill's warm voice on the telephone: "Hi, buddy, when are we going to get together?"

Tony Adams, Edwards' assistant, telephoned from their London office. Gene Schwam, their publicist, had called from Hollywood to confirm the news. "What can we do?" Tony asked.

"Book us a flight to California," Edwards replied. "We must be there for the services."

Glenn Ford learned the news from a detective of the Santa Monica police department. A note containing Ford's telephone number had been found in Holden's apartment, and the detective, realizing the long friendship of the two actors, called for information. When Ford put down the telephone, he wept uncontrollably.

They had been like rival brothers in a family of achievers, endlessly competitive, sometimes at odds, but with an underlying affection because of their mutual history. They had started in films together barely out of their teens, contracted to the despotic Harry Cohn. Twice they had co-starred in western films, then their careers had parted. Only four weeks before, the two old friends had sat on the porch of Ford's home behind the Beverly Hills Hotel and talked about another movie that would reunite them.

Ford was still tearful when he told a reporter, "I've lost my best friend. He was my best man when I married. I'm trying to find out what happened. We were friends since 1938."

A White House aide saw the story on the news wires, and he carried it into the Oval Office, where Ronald Reagan was seated at his desk. The President sent for Larry Speakes, deputy press secretary.

When Speakes returned to his office, he glanced over the notes he had written: "Shocked, of course . . . great feeling of grief . . . close friends over great many years . . . Godfather . . . What do you say about a longtime friend? . . . great sense of personal loss . . . a fine man . . . friendship never wavered . . . best man at wedding."

Speakes prepared a statement from the notes and issued it to the press.

Billy Wilder had begun his Monday morning routine at the MGM studio, where he was preparing the release of his film *Buddy, Buddy*. More than anyone else, Wilder had caused Holden's emergence as an important film actor. Their relationship was more than that of actor and director. Despite his well-advertised cynicism, Wilder felt deep affection for Bill.

Wilder's fears were confirmed by the report of his friend's death. During the previous weeks, Holden had been urging Wilder and his wife Audrey to visit his showplace Palm Springs house, which they had never seen. Finally Wilder agreed to a weekend, and Bill said, "Fine, you come down on Saturday." Despite the cordial words, Wilder detected a disturbing tone in Holden's voice.

The Wilders were packed and ready to leave their Westwood apartment Saturday morning when he decided to telephone Bill of their departure. "Mr. Holden isn't here," the housekeeper replied. "Where is he?" Wilder asked. "I don't know," said the housekeeper. The Wilders unpacked amid grave concern for Bill.

Robert Preston was at his home in Connecticut when Robert Webber telephoned. The two actors had formed a fast friendship during the filming of *S.O.B.*

"A reporter just called me," Webber said. "Bill Holden has died. Cancer."

"Oh, my God!" Preston exclaimed. "Think of the agony he must have been in when we were all working together. No wonder he wasn't drinking."

Webber called again. The reporter had been in error. Webber had telephoned Holden's apartment and identified himself to a coroner's officer, who told him Holden had bled to death after a fall.

How cruel it was, thought Preston, to have a friendship of his youth taken away just as he and Bill were growing close once more. Both had gone from the Pasadena Playhouse to Paramount and had been members of the Golden Circle. But their careers diverged, and they had never worked together until Blake Edwards cast them in *S.O.B.* The experience had proved warm and satisfying, the years apart vanishing with a new, mature relationship between the two actors, survivors both.

The grieving Preston remembered his last conversation with Bill. It happened two days after they and other cast members of *S.O.B.* had completed their mad cross-country tour to publicize the film.

Holden telephoned from his Palm Springs home to Preston in New York. Said Holden: "We never said goodbye."

"Bill," Preston replied, "we had that conversation. Guys like us never say goodbye. We don't have to; it's silly. It's always 'See you when I see you.' "

"Yeah," said Holden, "but we had such fun, and we got so close for a change. I wanted to say goodbye."

Bob Hope was at his house in Palm Springs, a short distance from Bill Holden's. Hope's memories went back to when both were newly arrived at Paramount and when the Holdens and the Hopes were neighbors in Toluca Lake and dined at each other's houses. How often Bill would stop in at Hope's dressing room at Paramount and tell of his latest travels! And how Bob liked to kid about the suits Bill bought in Hong Kong at incredibly cheap prices: "All you have to do is sneeze, Bill, and the sleeve will fall off!" And what a good sport Bill had been to play a comedy skit on Bob's first television show for servicemen in Greenland, even though Bill was terrified at playing comedy before a big audience.

Hope had seen Bill just a year before, when Bill had come to a benefit at the Hopes' huge new house in Palm Springs. The two old friends hugged and tried to converse, but it proved impossible in a crowd of five hundred people.

Now Bill was gone. Their world travels and their active careers had kept them apart, even though their Palm Springs homes were within sight of each other.

"If only," Hope said, "I had stopped by the guard gate and asked if Bill was in the country and at his house, we could have had a visit—but I never did."

A friend called Barbara Stanwyck at her home in Trousdale Estates above Los Angeles. "N-n-no, it can't be!" Miss Stanwyck exclaimed. "Are you s-s-sure it's Bill?" She found herself stuttering, and she had never stuttered.

She could not reconcile herself to the news. Through years of glory and times of sorrow, she and Bill Holden had clung to their friendship. She had been there when his career had started, and he never missed an opportunity to proclaim that it would not have happened except for her. In public as well as face to face, he called her Queen, and her name for him was always Golden Boy.

Only two or three weeks before, they had been together at a small dinner party at the home of Nancy Sinatra. Bill had lacked his usual sunshiny optimism that night. He had been looking forward to a challenging role in *That Championship Season,* and now it appeared that filming would be postponed.

"You know as well as I, Queen," he said, "as we get older, the parts get harder to find. I don't know how much longer I can continue. A couple of years, I think. Then I'll go live in Africa. Oh, I'll keep the Palm Springs house; I'd never sell that. And I'll always come back to visit my sons and my mother. But I think Africa will be my real home."

He admitted that he had been depressed by the death of a close friend, the art dealer Charles Feingarten. He and Miss Stanwyck left the dinner party early so he could pay a visit to Feingarten's widow, Gail.

"Good night, Golden Boy," Miss Stanwyck said as he left her house. "Now take care of yourself."

Sterling Hayden heard the news on television at his home in Wilton, Connecticut. He was drunk, and the sadness of the passing of an old friend made him drink more. With the liquor came an onrush of memories, dating back to when he and Bill Holden were young, rebellious contract players at Paramount in 1940.

Hayden remembered when he owned the schooner *Quest,* and he and Bill and their wives spent Sundays, the only day off from filming, sailing out of Newport Harbor. Another memory: the night at the Luau restaurant in Beverly Hills, when the young Holden, bravado built upon mai tais, challenged: "In ten years, show me one better actor than Bill Holden!"

There was the time when Hayden testified of his communist past before the Washington Red hunters, and he feared that he had lost all his friends, both Left and Right. The first message he received was a telegram: "I've never been more proud of you in my life—Bill Holden."

After a lapse of twenty years, the two old friends had met again in 1981 when both appeared on The Merv Griffin Show. They went to a bar afterward, but Bill was drinking only mineral water. He had discovered that liquor did something chemically destructive to his body, he explained. Hayden felt no such constraint.

Hayden continued drinking in the wake of Bill Holden's death. In desperation, he sought the advice of Jason Robards, who had been appearing on television and radio with a message about alcoholism. Hayden entered a hospital for alcoholics and began a regimen of abstinence. To bolster his resolve, he kept two photographs in his wallet, one of his family, one of Bill Holden.

They tried to keep the news from Mary Ball Beedle, Holden's mother. She was eighty-six, and although she seemed in vigorous health, her memory played tricks. Her close friends feared that the circumstances of her son's death would be too much of a shock. She was told only that Bill had died.

"It must have been Bill's drinking," Mrs. Beedle said to a friend. "Something like that. They haven't let me see a newspaper for two days."

She lived in an apartment building for the elderly at Leisure World, in Orange County, seventy miles south of Los Angeles. Her rooms were on the ninth floor, with a sweeping view of the Laguna Hills. When she moved to the building a few years before, her apartment had been on a lower floor. "This won't do," Bill insisted. "We need to get you higher, where you can get fresh air and a view." Holden always caused a stir among the white-haired men and women in the lobby when he arrived to see his mother. They envied her, not only because she had such a famous son, but because he visited her so often.

Eventually Mary Beedle learned how her son had died. She had always been a strong woman, proud of her American roots, devoted to her family. Sometimes she still spoke of Bill as if he were alive. Then she remembered: "Bill's dead, isn't he? All of them gone now: my husband, my three dear sons. I'm the only one left. I never thought I would be the last to go."

Ardis Holden was in Palm Springs, Grace Kelly in Monaco, Audrey Hepburn in Paris, Capucine in Geneva, Pat Stauffer in Newport Beach, Stefanie Powers in Hollywood. All had played intimate roles in William Holden's life; each felt individual sorrow at his passing. None was prepared for what followed.

On November 18, two days after Holden's body had been discovered, Thomas T. Noguchi stepped before the floodlights for television cameras, a position he seemed to enjoy. As coroner of the County of Los Angeles, his impassive moon-shaped face had become familiar to television viewers when he reported his findings in the deaths of Robert F. Kennedy, Sharon Tate, and scores of other tragedy victims, famous and unknown. The model for the television series *Quincy,* he thrived on controversy, even when it concerned himself. In 1969, the county supervisors had almost fired him when an assistant reported the coroner was often high on amphetamines and once expressed his hope for the local crash of a jet airliner so his department could achieve more glory.

Noguchi addressed the assembled media on the matter of Coroner's Case No. 81-14582.

The coroner and the Santa Monica chief of homicide detectives had visited Holden's apartment that afternoon in an attempt to reconstruct the events leading to his death. They found no evidence of foul play. An empty quart vodka bottle was in the kitchen wastebasket, another quart bottle, still filled with vodka, was nearby. Holden had been found lying in a pool of blood beside his bed. The bedclothes were blood-soaked, and Noguchi theorized that Holden had slipped on a throw rug, hit his head on the sharp corner of the bedside table, and fallen on the bed. Eight or ten bloodied tissues were found nearby, indicating that Holden had tried to stop the bleeding from the two-and-a-half-inch cut on his right forehead. Within five or ten minutes he had lost consciousness, the coroner estimated; death came within half an hour. When the body was discovered, four or five days later, the television set in the bedroom was on, a movie script nearby.

"It may seem strange to us, but the telephone was never picked up," Noguchi told the press conference. "It seemed that Mr. Holden was not aware of the severe injury to himself. But then, he was a very private person and he was probably trying to handle it by himself, not even to call on the phone for help."

The coroner suggested that Holden couldn't respond to the emergency because he was too drunk. His blood contained .22 percent alcohol, and California law decrees .10 percent enough to arrest a drunk driver. Noguchi speculated that Holden either drank eight or ten shots of vodka all at once or a larger amount over a period of time.

Television viewers that night heard from the Los Angeles County coroner himself that Bill Holden had been too drunk to save his own life.

Bill Holden wanted no one weeping over his grave, and he was appalled at the thought that his might be a *Star Is Born* funeral, with fans clamoring for a sight of famous mourners. In 1979 he had paid the twenty-five-dollar membership fee to join the Neptune Society, a Burbank corporation that carried out members' wishes to be cremated after death, the ashes to be dispersed at the place of their choice. Holden's attorney, Deane Johnson, told reporters, "He asked me a hundred times to make certain there would be no funeral or memorial service, and that's the way it will be." After the coroner's office released the body, it was cremated, and the ashes were scattered in the Pacific.

His friends needed some kind of farewell, and Stefanie Powers provided the occasion: a Sunday gathering at her house in Benedict Canyon.

They came together out of the desire to talk about Bill, to express their outrage over the coroner's gratuitous remarks, to smile about crazy things Bill had done. They were careful to avoid sentiment, because they knew he would have hated that. Billy and Audrey Wilder were there, and Dick Quine, who had directed Holden in two films, one a triumph, the other at the time of Bill's crack-up. Don Hunt, Bill's partner in Africa, had just arrived from Australia, en route back to Kenya. Capucine had come from Switzerland for a television movie. And there were other Holden co-stars: Alexis Smith, Lee Remick, Nancy Kwan. Blake Edwards and Tony Adams, newly arrived from London. Natalie Wood and Robert Wagner, Stefanie's co-star in the television series *Hart to Hart.* Helen Rackin and Connie Wald, widows of producers; Jimmy Stewart, Richard Widmark, Craig Stevens, Irwin Allen, George Axelrod, Patti Davis. In one way or another, Bill Holden had enriched each of their lives, and it seemed unbelievable that they would never again see his grinning welcome or hear that leather-smooth voice full of boyish wonder.

Billy Wilder commented to Stephen Farber of *The New York Times:* "I really loved Bill, but it turned out I just didn't know him. If somebody had said to me, 'Holden's dead,' I would have assumed that he had been gored by a water buffalo in Kenya, that he had died in a plane crash approaching Hong Kong, that a crazed jealous woman had shot him and he drowned in a swimming pool. But to be killed by a bottle of vodka and a night table—what a lousy fadeout for a great guy."

2

The Boy from O'Fallon

O'Fallon, Illinois, was only twenty miles from St. Louis, Missouri, but its citizens had none of the big-city ways when William Franklin Beedle, Jr., was born there on April 17, 1918. The population of O'Fallon was 2,200, minus the young men who had gone off to fight the Great War.

A few of the residents commuted to East St. Louis or St. Louis itself for work, but most were farmers, railroaders, miners, and shopkeepers, sturdy Midwesterners who were proud of their town and aware of its heritage. The first settler, Captain Joseph Ogle, had built a cabin in 1802, and the promising farmland soon attracted others. The town grew more rapidly after 1854; that was the year the Ohio and Mississippi Railroad built a depot and water tank. The station was named after John O'Fallon, whose father had been a surgeon in George Washington's army. Young O'Fallon had been an Indian agent for his uncle, William Clark, partner in the Lewis and Clark expedition. A far-sighted and enterprising man, O'Fallon became the founding president of three railroads: the Missouri Pacific, the Wabash, and the Baltimore and Ohio.

Joseph Beedle, whose family had emigrated from England in the early colonial years, moved from Ohio to O'Falion in 1812 and settled on a farm on the old Vincennes and St. Louis road. The family remained there for four generations, and in 1892, William Franklin Beedle was born. He grew up on the farm and in O'Fallon, where his father had built a house at 319 North Cherry Street.

Everyone in O'Fallon considered Bill Beedle the town's most promising young man. He was handsome enough to make heads turn, and his physique matched a Greek statue. He starred in the decathlon, and for years afterward he held the O'Fallon High School records he set in 1910 for the fifty-yard dash (6.0 seconds), the hundred-yard dash (10.4 seconds), and the twelve-pound shot put (45 feet, 11 inches). Despite his achievements, Bill Beedle wasn't conceited. He was soft-spoken, perhaps a bit shy, a member of the Baptist church choir, an excellent student.

Bill Beedle went off to McKendree College to study chemistry. His fellow students considered the handsome athlete aloof, and many girls failed at efforts to win his friendship. Not so Mary Ball, a pretty and vivacious girl from Litchfield, Illinois. She was attracted to him, and she realized that his standoffish attitude was simply the shyness of a small-town boy amid the sophistication of a college campus. Soon they were studying in the library together and attending the school dances. They had much in common, although Mary's family were Methodists. The roots of both their families were deeply planted in the American soil, and Mary was proud to remark that she was related to George Washington.

After they graduated from McKendree College, Mary Ball and William Beedle decided to marry. The wedding took place in the parlor of his father's house on Cherry Street, and they took up residence there. Mary postponed the start of her teaching career to care for Bill's father, who was crippled with arthritis. Bill found work as a chemist for the Swift packing plant in East St. Louis. In 1918, young Bill was born. He was a cheerful and healthy baby, despite a siege of colic.

Mary Beedle called the boy Billy to differentiate him from her husband. Billy was lively and curious. By the age of two, he was wandering the neighborhood asking endless questions. A brother named Robert was born when Billy was three. When the baby was only a few days old, Billy insisted to his mother, "Put him on the floor; I want to play with him."

Arctic winds whipped through O'Fallon during the wintertime, chilling Bill Beedle on his daily drive to East St. Louis. Despite his strong physique, he suffered from recurrent colds, and doctors feared the young man's lungs would be damaged if he remained in Illinois.

"Let's move to California," Bill Beedle suggested to Mary. "I've been out there, and it's a beautiful place. It'll be a good place to raise the boys."

Mary Beedle agreed. She was concerned for her husband's health, and she, too, had felt the allure of California. Many of her Midwest friends had moved there, and they had sent her postcards of wide ocean beaches and orange groves with snowy mountains in the distance.

Los Angeles was too big and noisy for the Beedles. They settled twenty miles east in Monrovia, a small semi-rural hamlet that resembled O'Fallon. Bill and Mary moved with their two sons into a modest bungalow, and he found work as a chemist with Gooch Laboratories in

Pasadena. A year and a half after their arrival in California, Mary gave birth to another son, Richard.

Billy—he grew to hate the name and insisted on being called Bill —was five, and California seemed like heaven. He could ride his bicycle on the streets of Monrovia the year around, and there was no need to bundle into wool jackets and mittens in the wintertime. Nearby were the Sierra Madres, where he and his schoolmates could hike for hours and see no one. On summer Sundays, his father drove the family to Ocean Park, where he taught his sons gymnastics on the sand.

Mary Beedle recalls that her son Bill was outgoing and friendly, with a wide range of interests that provided little time for studying. Bob was the student of the family, sober-minded and conservative. Dick was a combination of his older brothers. The boys fought with each other, of course, and Bill defended Bob from Dick.

Their mother saw that they behaved. Mary Beedle was a strong-willed woman whose sense of rectitude dominated the family. Both she and her husband instilled their sons with the tried-and-true Midwestern values, but with William working long days at the lab, Mary assumed the major responsibility for keeping the boys in line. She dressed them in their best short-pants suits and sent them off to Sunday school at the Congregational church. One Sunday morning, she found Bill in his ragged blue jeans. "I'm not going to Sunday school; I'm going to ride my new bike," he announced. His mother viewed him calmly and said, "All right, Bill, but if you don't go to Sunday school today, you won't be able to go to the movies next Saturday." He changed his mind.

Such character-building lessons became part of the Beedle family legend. Like the time the ten-year-old Bill was invited to attend a practice session of the Chicago White Sox baseball team by Ray Schalk, star catcher and a family friend. Bill loved baseball and idolized Schalk and was eager to go. But his mother reminded him that he would have to miss school and he was making poor grades. He nearly cried, and Mary Beedle admitted later she would have relented if he had. With eyes glistening, he went to the telephone and called Schalk to say, "I'm sorry, Ray, I'd love to go, but I'm not doing so hot in school and I'd better not."

In 1930, the Beedle family faced a double crisis. The laboratory, like all other businesses, suffered hard times with the Depression. And the years of exposure to chemicals resulted in a severe case of pneumosilicosis for William Beedle. He was bedridden, and Mary Beedle taught school to help support the family. Young Bill assumed his responsibilities as eldest son. He forced Dick and Bob out of bed in the morning, made sure they washed their faces and brushed their teeth, fed them breakfast, and led them off to grammar school. When his mother returned home in the evening, Bill had dinner prepared, and he served her with a headwaiter's flourish.

Bill neglected his studies to devote his full enthusiasm to the Boy Scouts, school athletics, and something new he had discovered: acting. He first performed as Rip Van Winkle in a sixth-grade play. He thoroughly enjoyed standing before his fellow students and holding their attention with his voice, which was already beginning to lower in scale. Drama teachers were impressed by his voice, which seemed more mature than the boy himself, and they often chose him for leading roles. Bill met the challenge, learning the script faster than anyone.

The Beedle family moved from Monrovia, a place of orange growers, shopkeepers, and retired Iowans, to South Pasadena. The two towns were a few miles apart, but the differences were striking. South Pasadena had stucco bungalows and baronial estates, residences for the middle class and the very rich. South Pasadenans disliked the impermanence of Los Angeles and detested the gaudiness of Hollywood. Along with their neighbors in San Marino and Pasadena, they patterned their social affairs after the elite of Boston and Philadelphia, with cotillions, debutante parties, and charity balls. Only the children of the wealthy were invited. Although William Beedle's fortunes had improved—he had bought ownership of Gooch Laboratories—Bill did not qualify for young South Pasadena society. In the classrooms and on the athletic field, he was an equal with his rich friends. But he wasn't invited to their parties. It was not something he brooded over. But he was always aware of it.

When Bill was fourteen, he was placed in charge of his two brothers while his parents visited relatives in the Midwest. Upon Mary Beedle's return, she was presented with a report by her second son:

Bill has done the following while you was away. He:
1. Smoked (got sick inhaling)
2. Swore (used Lord name in vain)
3. Drove fast (wouldn't let anyone tell him)
4. Bossed (like only one in world)
5. Dishes (said for me to set, remove, stack, wash and put away)
Bible. Right hand.

Bob Beedle

Beneath the signature was a drawing of a Bible.

Two elements were at war within the character of the adolescent Bill Beedle: the desire to be a good citizen, the instincts of a daredevil.

He started with leaps from the garage roof, an umbrella for a parachute. Developing remarkable balance and leaping ability, he sought other challenges. He bet his playmates that he could jump over a four-and-a-half-foot spiked fence from a standing start; he won every time. One summer afternoon, Bill's mother heard sounds of a crowd in the street in front of her house. She went outside and found Bill, a balancing pole in his hands, walking along a telephone line twelve feet above the ground.

"If you fall, I'll send you to the hospital," Mrs. Beedle called, "and I won't come to visit you."

"This isn't dangerous," Bill said, teetering on the tight wire.

"Then why are all these people watching?" his mother asked.

His most famous feat took place on the Colorado Street bridge over the Arroyo Seco, nicknamed Suicide Bridge because of the many people who leaped from its 190-foot height during the Depression. Bill sometimes entertained friends and dates by walking on his hands along the outer railing. According to Ronald Reagan, the youthful Bill also rode his bicycle along the railing.

When he was sixteen, Bill Beedle pestered his parents for a motorcycle. His father finally said Bill could have one—provided he earned the money to buy it by working all summer for Gooch Laboratories. Bill readily agreed, even though it was smelly work, loading supplies of chemical fertilizer and climbing into railroad tank cars to secure samples. Long showers with laundry soap couldn't remove the odor, and he was embarrassed when girls asked, "What is that strange smell?"

The summer's labor provided a brand-new Harley-Davidson motorcycle, and Bill Beedle was never happier. He rode the Pasadena streets for hours, and after he had mastered the machine, he began to adventure. On nearby mountains he roared up the firebreaks, the cleared patches designed to halt brush fires. On city streets he was able to stand on the seat, arms outstretched, as the motorcycle continued on its course. Then he mastered the handstand on the handlebars. His great ambition was to join Victor McLaglen's corps of trick motorcyclists, who performed in the Tournament of Roses and other parades.

Bill found that the motorcycle held fascination for girls, and he thrilled them with high-speed rides. A school friend, Florence Gaines, retains a vivid memory of speeding along Orange Grove Avenue on Bill's handlebars and passing the Valley Hunt Club as her mother emerged from a society luncheon.

Despite his chance-taking, Bill avoided an accident until one day when a farmer's car swerved in front of him without a signal. The impact overturned the car and dented the motorcycle, but neither Bill nor the farmer was hurt. Bill was furious, and he insisted that the farmer go home with him and explain to his parents that the accident had not been Bill's fault.

Years later, Richard Beedle remarked of his brother, "Bill had few fears when he was young—in fact, he was almost born without fears. He did all the foolhardy things he did not so much to attract attention as to prove that he could do them, not to others but to himself. He accepted all challenges on a personal basis. He was a real competitor because he competed with himself."

Sex in South Pasadena was something boys talked about but didn't practice. They talked and talked, sharing the latest revelations, most of them spurious, exchanging racy jokes, comparing the breasts of the girls in their classes. Most of their knowledge of sex had come from each other. Their fathers, if they imparted any information at all, provided only the basic facts of life. It was out of the question for their mothers to discuss such things. The most a boy could hope for was heavy kissing with a girl after the third date. Only one or two girls in each class were reputed to allow boys to "cop a feel."

Frustration led to wet dreams and "going steady with Lady Five-fingers." The only other outlet was voyeurism: watching the strippers at the Follies and Burbank theaters on Main Street in downtown Los Angeles. There was always talk of pilgrimages to D Street in San Bernardino, the legendary red-light district. But the boys had been sufficiently scared by hygiene-class lectures about venereal disease, which, the instructor insisted, could make the male sex organ rot away. Also, in the hearts of many of the South Pasadena boys was the romantic notion that they were saving themselves for their wives, that they would remain virgins until their wedding nights.

Bill Beedle was no different from his South Pasadena fellows. He adored girls, but he was also respectful of them, and he would never insist that they "go all the way." He had no trouble getting dates; girls found him overwhelmingly attractive. He was almost six feet tall, with wide, muscular shoulders and slim hips. With thick brown hair, wide brow, clear blue eyes, straight thin nose, and dazzling smile, he presented an essentially masculine kind of handsomeness, as compared to the almost feminine beauty of the movie stars Robert Taylor and Tyrone Power. Bill Beedle treated his good looks with extreme casualness. To have been stuck-up about one's appearance would go against his upbringing; at any rate, his two younger brothers would have given him no peace if he had.

Girls were attracted to Bill not only because of his looks, but because he was always great fun. He had a talent for the romantic gesture, the outrageous prank. He liked entertainment, and he and his dates stood in line on Friday nights to enter the Paramount Theater in downtown Los Angeles. For forty cents apiece, they could see a brand-new Paramount movie like *Cleopatra* or *Anything Goes,* plus a Fanchon and Marco stage show with emcee Rube Wolf, the dancing Fanchonettes, and such stars as Bing Crosby, Ken Murray, or Eddie Cantor.

Bill had another favorite place for dates: the Palomar Ballroom on Vermont Avenue in Los Angeles. He was overwhelmed by the new swing music, and he listened every night to the bands that played on radio from places like the Palmer House in Chicago, the Palace Hotel in San Francisco, and the Cocoanut Grove in Los Angeles. His favorite radio show was the *Camel Caravan* with Benny Goodman's band. When the King of Swing played at the Palomar, Bill was in the front row before the bandstand, watching the musicians throughout the evening.

Bal Week was a tradition, the Easter vacation when the youth of Pasadena and South Pasadena gathered at Newport Harbor in Orange County. Many of their parents owned houses on Balboa Island, and at night the living rooms were jammed with boys in sleeping bags. During the day the vacationers boated on the bay or surfed in the ocean; Bill Beedle was one of the few who body-surfed in the huge waves at the Wedge, the pocket of turbulence next to the breakwater. Evenings were spent prowling the island for house parties, taking the joy rides at the fun zone on the peninsula, or dancing at the Rendezvous Ballroom.

Bill Beedle was one of the most popular members of the South Pasadena High School student body, which numbered eight hundred. The gymnastic training by his father helped make him a superior athlete; he could high-jump six feet, one inch, and do better than ten feet in the standing broad jump. He had so many skills that the gym department appointed him a student coach. Bill sang in the boys' glee club and for a time considered a musical career. He practiced for hours on the clarinet but could never make it sound remotely like Benny Goodman's. He became an enthusiastic drum player, but somehow couldn't maintain a consistent beat. His singing voice was strong, and he could be heard above all others during the school song (to the tune of "Constantinople"):

> South Pasadena—S-o-u-t-h P-a-s-a-d-e-n-a,
> South Pasadena—S-o-u-t-h P-a-s-a-d-e-n-a.
> We've got the rep,
> We've got the pep,
> We've got the spirit, too.
> If you don't think that we can fight,
> Just watch what we can do.
> South Pasadena—S-o-u-t-h P-a-s-a-d-e-n-a.

Although he sang with vigor, Bill fell somewhat short of being musical. (Years later, an expert Hollywood musician declared that Holden sang exactly a fifth away from the melody.) Surprisingly, in view of his physical agility, he was not a good dancer. Nevertheless, the girls of South Pasadena High were thrilled when he chose to dance with them at the junior-senior prom in the women's gym. Bill's only enduring musical talent was playing the "bones." Years later he enlivened Hollywood parties by breaking a wooden coathanger in half, placing the pieces between his fingers, and beating out an infectious rhythm.

Bill welcomed every opportunity to put on a show. Because of poor grades, he was forced to attend summer school in order to graduate from junior high school. Having missed the regular ceremony, he staged his own graduation for fellow students on the steps of the junior high school, delivering the valedictory and handing out the mock diplomas. He joined the dramatic society at South Pasadena High and was delighted when the school was chosen to perform plays on radio station KECA in Los Angeles. His mother and father listened proudly to the broadcast, but they considered Bill's acting simply another of the boy's hobbies. It was assumed that Bill would study chemistry in college and join his father's business.

Bill had many acquaintances in high school, but few close friends. The closest was Richard Steele. He and Bill became buddies, even though Dick was a year ahead in school and came from an old-line Pasadena family. Both were athletic and adventurous, both enjoyed planning elaborate pranks. They stuffed crumpled newspapers into old clothes and threw the dummies off Suicide Bridge, startling motorists who were driving past. One Halloween a friend borrowed a black Buick phaeton, and he and Bill and Dick bought dozens of eggs and tomatoes at a California street market. They loaded their purchases into the phaeton, which was parked in the alley behind the market. As the car emerged from the alley into the street, it was surrounded by three police cars and three police motorcycles.

"Jeez, let's get out of here!" shouted Bill, and he leaped over the side of the phaeton and started hurdling over backyard fences to make his getaway. The two other boys were caught, their eggs and tomatoes confiscated, and their parents were summoned to the police station.

Bill Beedle and Dick Steele became inseparable. During the summer they slept on the sand at Huntington Beach and rose to ride the early-morning surf, best of the day. They took dates to Pop's Willow Lake, a small resort in the heart of the San Fernando Valley. They spent weekends at Lake Arrowhead, where Dick's family owned a cabin. One day they struck up an acquaintance with a couple of girls from Van Nuys High School and took them for a ride in Dick's inboard motorboat, making sharp turns so the girls would be splashed with water. One of them was a full-chested brunette named Jane Russell.

On weekend nights, Bill and Dick joined the high school crowd at the C&L drive-in at Walnut and Lake, famous for its hamburgers and root beer. On Sundays, Dick picked up Bill at the Oneonta Congregational Church, where Bill sang in the choir, and they prowled the Pasadena streets in Dick's convertible, stopping for an occasional beer. Both smoked excessively, always Camels, out of allegiance to the *Camel Caravan* radio show, which provided the swing music of Benny Goodman.

The best times were on the desert.

Bill and Dick drove north of Barstow and then into the vast desolation of the Mojave Desert. They raced Dick's car along the pavement-hard expanse of Muroc Dry Lake, hurtling at ninety miles an hour. With pistols and .22 rifles and a muzzle-loading firing piece belonging to Dick's father, they hunted for rabbit, quail, and fox. They played like desperadoes, firing imaginary bullets at each other from behind rocks. As darkness fell, they collected mesquite for a campfire and drank beer under stars as big as dimes. As they lay in their sleeping bags in the overwhelming silence of the cooling desert, they talked of girls and swing music and college and settling down in South Pasadena. And then, numbed by the beer and exhausted from the day's adventures under the desert sun, they fell deeply asleep.

3

Joining the Golden Circle

In June of 1936, William Franklin Beedle, Jr., graduated from South Pasadena High School with a conspicuous lack of scholastic honors. His grades didn't qualify him for the University of California, so he would have to study for two years at Pasadena Junior College. "You must apply yourself, Bill," admonished his mother. "That's the only way you are going to get your chemistry degree and join your father's company." Bill agreed to do his best, though inwardly he realized that he hated chemistry.

During the summer of 1936, Bill worked for Gooch Laboratories, using his motorcycle to make deliveries and pick up supplies. It was a glorious time for Bill. He was free of school worries—at least until the fall semester—and he raced his motorcycle all over Los Angeles County, weaving through traffic with the skill of a professional cyclist. Forty years later, he remembered that summer as the happiest time of his life.

Before returning to school, Bill drove with a friend across the country to New York. It was Bill's first venture away from the insular world of South Pasadena, and he was fascinated by what he saw. Especially in New York City, where he experienced the excitement of the Broadway theater. He realized anew how much he had enjoyed acting in high school plays.

As in high school, Bill Beedle's principal interests at Pasadena Junior College were outside the classrooms. He excelled at gymnastics, following his father's advice to avoid the contact sports: "Why worry about someone else's body; learn to handle your own." Still convinced that he had a singing voice, Bill joined the a cappella choir. Robert Ben Ali, who was active in theater at the college, heard Bill sing and was impressed by the tone of his voice, though not by his way with a melody. Ali had written a play called *Manya*, which dramatized the discovery of radium by Madame Curie. He was planning to stage the play at the

Playbox Theater, a tiny experimental showcase at the residence of Gilmor Brown, impresario of the prestigious Pasadena Community Playhouse.

"I need someone to record a narration for the play," Ben Ali said. "Would you do it for me?"

"Hell, yes!" Bill replied.

During rehearsals for *Manya*, one of the actors dropped out. Ben Ali returned to Bill Beedle and asked if he would like to play a small role as Madame Curie's eighty-year-old father-in-law. "Why not?" said Bill.

Milt Lewis was a gnomish man who had become a fixture of the Los Angeles theater. At every opening night he could be seen breezing down the aisle to his customary seat, front-row center, where he would carefully study the list of players. As soon as every actor in the cast had appeared onstage, he would leave at the end of the act. By so doing, he could attend two or three plays in an evening. He visited not only the major theaters—the Biltmore, El Capitan, Hollywood Playhouse, Mayan, and Belasco—but also training schools like the Bliss-Hayden and outlying colleges and universities as well. Milt Lewis was talent scout for Paramount Pictures.

One night in 1938, Lewis attended the opening of *Manya* at the Pasadena Playbox. He was intrigued by the voice of the man playing Pierre Curie, Sr., his body bent, a white beard flowing almost to his shoes. Lewis went backstage after the final curtain and discovered who was behind the beard: a twenty-year-old boy.

"Who are you?" Lewis asked.

"Bill Beedle," the young man replied.

"Have you thought about going into pictures?"

Bill laughed. "Hell, I'm not an actor. I'm a student at Pasadena J.C."

"Look, kid, I think you have possibilities. Here's my card. Come see me at the Paramount studio tomorrow at ten o'clock."

"Sorry, can't do it."

"Why not?"

"I got a test tomorrow. Chemistry. I can't miss it."

"You better come to the studio, kid. Opportunity only knocks once."

"This time it'll have to knock twice," Bill replied.

Two days later, Bill Beedle rode his motorcycle from South Pasadena to the Paramount studio on Marathon Street. Milt Lewis studied the young man with a talent man's shrewd eyes. Beedle had the physical requirements for film acting: an athlete's physique with muscular shoulders and narrow hips, lively blue eyes and flawless face, though lacking in character—understandable at the age of twenty. But could he act? That wasn't a necessity in the movies, but it sometimes helped.

"Here's a script, kid," said Lewis. "Read it back to me."

He handed Beedle the script of a film, *The Bride Comes Home.* Bill studied the pages for a couple of minutes. Then he planted his feet apart, put his hands on his hips, and said, "Look at that sky! Boy, what a sky!"

Milt Lewis was electrified. The young man spoke not from his throat, the way most amateur actors did. It was the voice of a mature man, warm and resonant, rising from deep within him.

"Not bad, kid," muttered Lewis after Bill had finished his speech. The talent man had learned never to betray enthusiasm to a potential contract player; that could give an actor grandiose ideas about his salary.

"C'mon, I want Artie Jacobson to see you; he's head of the talent department," said Lewis. He led Beedle to the office of Jacobson, a brisk, fast-talking studio hand.

"Gimme a scene from a play you've done," Jacobson ordered.

Bill hunched over and started reciting the dialogue of the aged Curie.

"If we want Paul Muni, we'll buy Paul Muni," Jacobson snapped. "Gimme another play."

"That's the only one I've ever done," Bill replied.

"Okay, okay, tell me a funny story."

Bill tried, but he had never mastered the knack of telling a joke. Jacobson handed him a script and instructed, "Take this home and study it, then come back and we'll see if you're gonna be an actor."

Bill Beedle returned to Paramount to face the ordeal of the Fish Bowl, the test required of all candidates for acting contracts. They were directed to play scenes on a lighted stage behind a large glass screen. Hidden in the darkness on the other side were talent executives, producers, and directors. They sat in judgment like a revolutionary junta, decreeing contracts for a scant number, oblivion for the others. Bill Beedle passed the test of the Fish Bowl and was offered a contract for seven years, starting at fifty dollars a week. He would receive a salary during forty weeks of the year and spend twelve weeks on layoff. The studio had the option to sever his contract every six months. If he survived all the options, his salary at the end of seven years would be $750 a week.

Because he was not yet twenty-one, Bill's parents signed the contract for him. They were reluctant, but Bill assured them: "Don't worry, if I don't make it as an actor in a year, I'll go back to college and become a chemist."

When he reported to the studio on his first day as a contract player, Bill Beedle was refused entrance. "Your name isn't on the list," the guard said brusquely.

"Well, call Artie Jacobson's office; they'll tell you I work here," said Bill, barely controlling his anger.

He stormed into Jacobson's office and complained bitterly about what had happened. "All right, all right, don't get your balls in an uproar," said Jacobson. "We'll fix it so people will know who you are."

Jacobson led Bill into the office of Terry DeLapp, the idea-conscious, swift-talking head of the Paramount publicity department.

"Beedle, huh?" DeLapp ruminated. "That won't do. Sounds too much like an insect."

"Yeah, you're right," Bill said. "Kids used to call me Bugs in school."

"Wait a minute. I was just talking to an associate editor at the *Times*. Name is Bill Holden. Lemme give him a call."

DeLapp telephoned the newspaperman and explained, "I got a young kid in my office, wants to be an actor but he needs a new name. How about if I give him yours?"

"Does he look like the kind who'll get me in trouble?" Holden asked.

"He's from South Pasadena. Does that answer your question?"

DeLapp hung up the receiver and said, "How would you like to be William Holden?"

Bill shrugged. "I don't care."

"Okay, that does it," said the publicity chief. He assigned a publicist to write a release for the local newspapers. On February 22, 1939, the *Los Angeles Times* carried the item:

YOUTH SIGNED UNDER NEW NAME
Another juvenile find is registered. Paramount has signed one William Beedle (20 years of age) and changed his name to William Holden.

The new discovery, a student of Pasadena Junior College, is considered very promising and has been cast importantly in "What a Life," the Jackie Cooper feature.

Incidentally, it's his very first experience in the studios, although at the Pasadena Community Playbox, where he was observed by a scout, he acted the role of a 70-year-old man. Typical start for a juvenile.

Bill was excited when he read the item, and he thanked DeLapp. "I didn't know I was going to be in *What a Life,*" Bill said.

"You aren't," DeLapp replied. "That's just a gimmick we use to get a picture's title in print."

Although it wasn't required, William Holden reported to the Paramount studio every day, even on Saturday, when production offices were open until noon and filmmaking continued all day. He was curious to learn everything possible about the movie business. He wandered from the prop department to wardrobe to makeup, disarming the oldtime studio workers with his smile and his questions. Every day he visited the office of Phyllis Seaton, talent coach and director of tests.

"Got any tests I can do?" he inquired. He had learned that the cost-conscious studio never made individual tests; scenes were always shot with two actors, so both could be evaluated. Bill Holden volunteered to appear with any actress Phyllis Seaton was testing. She always gave him good camera coverage, not merely shots of the back of his head, and she coached him in how to get the best results from his scenes.

Bill became acquainted with other contract players, especially Robert Preston Meservey, with whom he had much in common. They were the same age, had gone to school in the Pasadena area, and had been discovered at the Pasadena Playhouse, though they had not known each other there. They arrived at Paramount days apart, and both were given new names; Meservey became Robert Preston.

One day Holden, Preston, and eleven other contract players were invited to a luncheon in the Paramount commissary. "Congratulations," said Terry DeLapp. "You are now the Golden Circle!"

"It was Paramount's publicity gimmick for that year," Robert Preston recalls. The young players were photographed playing volleyball on the beach, sailing on yachts, riding horses in the mountains. The Golden Circle attracted much press coverage, especially on a tour to publicize *Union Pacific.* All of their names were unknown in 1938, and a surprising number achieved prominence. Besides Holden and Preston, the Golden Circle included Susan Hayward, Betty Field, Ellen Drew, Evelyn Keyes, Patricia Morison, William Henry, Janice Logan, Judith Barrett, Joyce Mathews, Joseph Allen, and Louise Campbell.

Bill Holden enjoyed the publicity whirl, but he was impatient to prove himself as an actor in something more than screen tests. His first two screen roles were insignificant: as a member of a road gang in *Prison Farm*, a B picture starring Lloyd Nolan and Shirley Ross; and as a collegiate in *Million Dollar Legs*, a musical with Jackie Coogan and Betty Grable.

"I'm not getting anywhere!" Holden complained to Phyllis Seaton. "I'll get dropped when my first option comes up."

She urged him to continue studying and making tests with fledgling actresses. One of the assignments she found for him was a test with Margaret Young, who was being considered for a loanout to Columbia Pictures for *Golden Boy*.

4

Golden Boy

Harry Cohn, the indisputable suzerain of Columbia Pictures, wanted to star John Garfield in *Golden Boy*. Garfield had been electric in the Clifford Odets play as Joe Bonaparte, the gifted young man divided by careers as a prizefighter and violinist. But Garfield was under contract to Warner Brothers, and Jack Warner was in one of his periodic rages against Harry Cohn. Warner refused a loanout.

Cohn tried to borrow Tyrone Power from 20th Century–Fox, but Darryl Zanuck would not consider sharing his biggest star with a competitor.

Harry Cohn grumbled. He had a director for *Golden Boy*, Rouben Mamoulian. He had a script by two young New York writers, Daniel Taradash and Louis Meltzer. He had an impressive cast: Barbara Stanwyck, Adolphe Menjou, Lee J. Cobb, Joseph Calleia, Sam Levene. But Harry Cohn had no Golden Boy.

"Goddammit, what are we going to do about it?" he demanded of the film's producer, William Perlberg.

"How about going for an unknown, Harry?" Perlberg suggested. "We could have a Search for Golden Boy, like Selznick did for Scarlett O'Hara."

Cohn grudgingly agreed to the proposal, and the Columbia publicity department launched the campaign. Talent scouts interviewed actors and amateurs in New York, Chicago, and other cities; and the studio casting office held open auditions. Athletes, aesthetes, eager young men of all descriptions passed before the cynical eyes of casting agents. One of those who auditioned was an unknown actor named Alan Ladd. Learning that Golden Boy was Italian, he plastered his hair with mascara. He auditioned on a hot California day and was humiliated when black rivulets coursed down his face during the interview.

The role of Joe Bonaparte's sister also remained unfilled, and Columbia requested other studios to submit tests of young actresses. Paramount provided six tests, including one of Margaret Young.

As Perlberg and Mamoulian were watching the Paramount tests, the director was intrigued by the young man who played opposite Margaret Young. He had a compelling quality, even though only a third of his face was visible.

"Who is that boy?" the director asked.

"I don't know," said Perlberg. "I'll call Paramount and find out."

William Holden was summoned to Columbia for an interview with Rouben Mamoulian. Holden seemed inarticulate, shy, extremely young, but he had an engaging innocence that was vital for Golden Boy. He also had the handsomeness that bespoke a movie star and a physique that could match a prizefighter's. After a few days of dialogue work with Holden, Mamoulian was convinced he had found the right actor.

"Bullshit!" said Harry Cohn. "The kid's a nobody."

"That doesn't matter," Mamoulian argued. "I have a hunch he'll be good in the part."

It was a standard Cohnian tactic to test his filmmakers' decisions by rejecting them; if the men were strong enough in their conviction, Cohn might relent. "Send the kid to me, I wanna talk to him," the studio boss said.

The twenty-year-old Holden was understandably nervous as he sat in the waiting room outside Harry Cohn's office. He had been filled with lurid tales about the buccaneer ways of the Columbia boss, and they seemed to be confirmed by the white faces of producers and writers as they emerged from the office. After a half-hour, Cohn's secretary pushed a button that released the lock to the inner office. She told Holden he could enter.

Holden walked into a room that seemed wide and long enough for a half-dozen bowling alleys. At the far end sat Harry Cohn behind a huge upraised desk, at his back a display of Oscars won by Columbia movies. As Holden walked closer, he studied Cohn: square shoulders and thick chest, physique of a nightclub bouncer; large head, nearly bald; beefy face with fierce China-blue eyes.

Cohn offered no preliminaries. "Can you act?" he demanded.

"I'm not sure," Bill admitted.

"Can you box?"

"No."

"Can you play the violin?"

"No."

"Then what the hell are you doing here?"

"I'm here because you sent for me."

Holden's forthright reply changed Cohn's attitude. "In that case," he said, "we'd better make a test and find out why I sent for you."

The test was scheduled for five o'clock one evening. Cohn had ordered a full crew and assigned a contract actress, Joan Perry, for the role of Lorna Moon. She and Holden played the *Golden Boy* love scene, and he was pleased with how smooth it seemed. The test director asked for parts to be repeated, and Miss Perry was agreeable.

They were still filming at eight o'clock, and Bill said to her, "Gee, you've been so nice to me, I'd love to take you to dinner."

"Thanks," she replied with a smile, "but I have a date."

Harry Cohn and his chief aide, Samuel Briskin, arrived on the set and watched from behind the camera. Bill saw them over the actress's shoulder and whispered, "I'd sure like to know what those two sons of bitches are thinking."

"They're thinking," she replied, "that you are going to be Golden Boy."

When the scene was completed, Cohn walked into the set, and Bill was hoping for words of encouragement. Instead, Cohn addressed Joan: "I'm sorry, dear, but I won't be able to have dinner with you until ten-fifteen."

Holden stared at the pair in astonishment. Later he learned that Joan Perry was the future Mrs. Harry Cohn.

Her prediction proved correct. Cohn agreed to cast Holden in *Golden Boy,* warning Mamoulian: "This is on your head; if the kid can't handle the part, you're through."

Part of Cohn's willingness was his unfailing sense of a bargain. For a tiny investment, he could acquire a potential star. He telephoned Y. Frank Freeman, production chief at Paramount.

"This crazy Mamoulian wants to borrow one of your actors for *Golden Boy,*" said Cohn.

"Oh?" said Freeman, whose Georgia drawl seemed alien amid the New York accents of studio moguls. "Which one?"

"Some kid named Holden."

"Who?"

"William Holden, for crissake. Don't you know him?"

"Sure, sure. I'll have to see if he's available."

"He's available, all right. And I'll tell you something else: I want half his contract."

"I don't know about that, Harry. Paramount has never split a contract."

"Then it's time to start. If I'm gonna take your kid and make him a star, I want half the action."

Freeman quickly telephoned Artie Jacobson in the talent department: "Have we got somebody named Holden under contract?"

"Sure," said Jacobson. "He's that kid Milt Lewis found in Pasadena. Why?"

"Harry Cohn wants to borrow him for *Golden Boy*, and he wants half his contract. How much are we paying him?"

"Fifty bucks a week."

"Should we let him go?"

"What can we lose? For twenty-five bucks you might get half a star."

Bill Holden reported to the Columbia studio every day for a rigorous schedule. He boxed with an oldtime fighter, Cannonball Green. He studied how to finger and bow a violin with a concert artist, Julian Brodetsky. He spent long hours working over the *Golden Boy* script with the dialogue coach, Hugh McMullen. The worst ordeal for Holden was having his hair curled and dyed to make him look Italian.

Bill requested permission for a break in the routine so he could attend his first movie premiere. "Forget it," Harry Cohn decreed. "If you're any good in this picture, you'll have plenty of premieres to go to."

Studios customarily required actors in modern-dress films to supply their own wardrobe. When Bill learned that, he panicked. "I only own one suit," he told Mamoulian. The director went to Cohn's office and demanded a wardrobe allowance for the young actor.

During preparation for *Golden Boy*, Holden rose at 6 A.M. for his early-morning appointments at the studio and fell into bed after midnight. Mary Beedle became concerned, especially after a studio worker told her, "It's criminal the way they're working Bill; they're really taking advantage of him." One day he overslept, and an assistant called to say he was late for an appointment. Mrs. Beedle told the caller, "This boy needs his rest. I am going to let him wake up on his own."

Bill complained to Artie Jacobson that he was exhausted. Jacobson suggested that Bill could get more rest by sleeping at the Hollywood Athletic Club, where he was working out nightly. Columbia agreed, and Bill was saved the twice-daily drive to South Pasadena. When he received his next paycheck, he discovered that the studio had deducted sixty dollars for his room rent. Bill was furious.

"I'm living at the Athletic Club so I can take all these damn lessons!" he complained to Harry Cohn. "You're paying me fifty bucks a week and now you take out sixty bucks for rent. It's not right!"

Cohn was surprised by the young man's vehemence. "What do you want me to do about it?" he asked.

"I want you to pay my rent."

"Look, I'm making you a star. You oughta be grateful."

"Dammit, you pay my rent or I'll quit," said Holden, turning to leave Cohn's office.

Cohn waited until he reached the door. "All right, you hothead," Cohn said. "I'll pay your fucking rent. And if you can show some of that emotion in front of a camera, maybe I'll make an actor out of you after all."

Principal photography of *Golden Boy* began on April 1, 1939, sixteen days before William Holden would be eligible to vote or to buy liquor in the state of California. The weeks of boxing and fiddle lessons and drama coaching had been a kind of strenuous and exacting game to him. Now he was faced with playing the title role in a film with some of the most experienced actors of the stage and screen. Bill Holden was terrified.

On the first day of shooting, he met Barbara Stanwyck, and she helped calm him. He was overwhelmed by her vibrant good looks, the assurance stemming from ten years of starring in Hollywood, her immediate rapport with every member of the crew, who affectionately called her Missy. She tried to assuage his concern: "Look, Bill, we all had to start in this business sometime. You'll get through it. You're going to be terrific, I know you are. Just hold on, and if there's any way I can help, for God's sake let me know."

The atmosphere on the *Golden Boy* set was tense during the first three days of filming. The other actors scrutinized the boy from South Pasadena and wondered why Harry Cohn had picked him. "He's no Julie Garfield," they declared. Despite the constant support by Mamoulian and Miss Stanwyck, Holden seemed to have no real grasp of the character and little concept of film acting.

Holden failed to appear for the fourth day of filming. "Just nerves," diagnosed the studio doctor. Bill returned after two days, but his work didn't improve. Mamoulian was beginning to fear that he had chosen the wrong Golden Boy. Studio workers gossiped that Cohn was preparing to fire young Holden.

Barbara Stanwyck heard the rumor, and she confronted Cohn and Perlberg.

"Give the boy a chance," she argued. "My God, he's only had a week. He's developing. Leave him alone and he'll find himself. I don't know of any actor who could do it better. If you want youth, he's got it. If you want a good physique, he's got it. If you want a fairly good boxer, he's it. He can't be a champion, because that's not the story. He's a very sensitive, intelligent young man. I don't know what other qualities you want. None of us can walk on water."

Her persuasion worked, and Holden continued in the role of Joe Bonaparte. His work gradually improved, aided by Miss Stanwyck's coaching. Each night after filming, she and Holden remained in her dressing room to practice lines for the next day. Robert Taylor, whom she would soon marry, called for her every evening, and he waited outside until the coaching sessions were over.

As Bill Holden gained in confidence, fear transformed to arrogance. He became short-tempered, and the actors who once proclaimed that he was "no Julie Garfield" now muttered that he had a swollen head.

Mamoulian realized what was happening, and he told the dialogue coach, Hugh McMullen, to spend a day with Bill and try to straighten him out. Bill was delighted with the day off, which fell on his birthday.

McMullen was ten years Bill's senior and far more mature, a scholarly man with degrees from Williams College and Oxford University. He had taught music and art in Eastern schools, and his academic background made him seem out of place in the film world. But he was a sympathetic listener and a quiet, persuasive talker.

The two men lounged in their bathing trunks on the roof of the Hollywood Athletic Club, sharing a bottle of Scotch in the April sunshine. McMullen carefully led the conversation into the subject of acting.

"Do you really want to be an actor?" McMullen asked.

"I do now," Bill replied. "At first I thought it was a little silly, especially with that Golden Circle shit. Now I can see that acting can be serious work, something you can feel pride in."

"What actors do you admire most?"

Bill responded immediately: "Fredric March and Spencer Tracy. They're real *actors,* not just movie stars."

McMullen observed that both March and Tracy were at ease on the set and natural on the screen, but they were stage-trained actors who prepared conscientiously for their roles. They were modest men, unimpressed by their own positions, actors who considered everyone on a movie set their equals.

The day of sunshine and Scotch and friendly counsel helped transform Bill Holden into a level-headed, conscientious actor, and the patient advice from Mamoulian and Barbara Stanwyck helped him give a credible performance as Joe Bonaparte. Holden himself was amazed that he could portray emotions he had never felt or expressed before. And yet there were elements of Golden Boy that touched his spirit.

MR. BONAPARTE
You more better than them—some day you will be a big artist.
JOE
Some day! I want *today.* Poppa, I don't want to wait. I want to live now!
MR. BONAPARTE
It'sa worth to wait when later you can—
JOE
Everything moves too quickly—life passes by at two hundred miles an hour, and you want me to wait for the future! It may never come.
(then more soberly, almost pleading his cause)
Poppa, I want to *own* things and to give things. Everything you want from breakfast until you turn out the light—no sad faces. So laughing, smiling, even crying is a pleasure.

I want to be able to go to concerts every night. Downstairs. *Downstairs*, Poppa, with the ermines and the high hats. Downstairs so you won't have to bend your back and strain your eyes and ears. With money, even music is better. I—I want to take out a girl sometimes, I want to travel, Poppa—to go places it hurts even to talk about now, because I want to see them so badly. Money's the answer—and I can get it fighting—no other way. I won't get it playing a fiddle.*

---

*Grateful acknowledgment is made for permission to quote from the filmscript of *Golden Boy,* copyright © 1939, copyright renewed © 1967 by Columbia Pictures.

5

Enter Brenda Marshall

Golden Boy was scheduled to have its premiere at the Radio City Music Hall in New York on September 15, 1939. For weeks beforehand, the Columbia publicity department produced a drumbeat campaign to attract attention to Hollywood's newest star, William Holden, and hence to *Golden Boy.* Holden was interviewed by overbearing fan magazine writers and cynical newspaper reporters, and all were impressed by the likable, articulate young man, though his bland middle-class background gave them little to write about. Holden traveled in style to New York City for a round of interviews and appearances. He enjoyed the attention, and he learned to answer each interviewer's questions with spontaneity, even though he had heard them dozens of times before.

Golden Boy was not an overwhelming success, nor was William Holden.

New York critics, remembering the vital performance of John Garfield and the trenchant Odets play, found Holden inadequate and the story cheapened by Hollywood touches. They criticized the film's hopeful ending; in the play Joe Bonaparte had died. The two most important New York critics had misgivings about the new star.

Frank Nugent, *Times:* "William Holden, the newcomer in the title role, has been guilty, in scattered scenes, of the exaggerated recoils, lip-bitings and hand-clenchings one associates with the old-time melodramatic school. In sum, however, it has been a good interpretation of an unusual role."

Howard Barnes, *Herald Tribune:* "William Holden, in his first screen appearance, demonstrates unquestioned ability, but he is not felicitously cast as the twisted youth who is conned into giving up a musical career.... He rarely achieves the hysterical intensity which the high, emotional moments of the production demand."

The public reaction was equally restrained. *Golden Boy* was no flop, but it did not attract substantial business. Odets' Depression-era politics seemed dated at a time when war had started in Europe. Americans in 1939 had a feast of other, more appealing films: *Gone with the Wind, The Wizard of Oz, Wuthering Heights, Goodbye, Mr. Chips, Stagecoach, Dark Victory, Mr. Smith Goes to Washington, Drums Along the Mohawk, Dodge City, Ninotchka, The Women.*

Neither Paramount nor Columbia had plans for their new star. He was loaned out for his next two movies.

Warner Brothers considered Holden for the role of George Raft's brother in *Invisible Stripes,* even though the director, Lloyd Bacon, preferred Wayne Morris. Bacon didn't believe that the immature Holden could match the presence of Raft. To prove that he could, Holden accepted a tiny role with Raft in *Each Dawn I Die.* Bacon was convinced, and Holden played the role in *Invisible Stripes.* It was a humbling experience for an actor who had just starred in an important film.

Sol Lesser borrowed Holden for his independent production of *Our Town,* the much-acclaimed Thornton Wilder play. Holden was well cast as the earnest, innocent George Gibbs, the doctor's son. He and Martha Scott, who had created the role of Emily on Broadway, were especially convincing as the tragic couple.

Neither *Invisible Stripes* nor *Our Town* proved successful at the nation's theaters. After three films at other studios, Bill Holden returned to Paramount for less than a hero's welcome. He was cast in a low-budget comedy, *At Good Old Siwash* (released as *Those Were the Days*).

Holden played a campus prankster in a script based on the George Fitch stories of college life in the early 1900s. The film's main publicity gimmick was the kiss he gave Bonita Granville; it was the first screen kiss for the former child actress.

Ezra Stone, famed as Henry Aldrich on radio, co-starred as Bill's loyal roommate, and through him Bill learned the inequity of the studio system. Paramount was paying Stone $3,000 a week, as well as the expenses of bringing his radio show from New York to California. Bill Holden's salary was seventy-five dollars a week.

"There is an abyss between the moral standards of Hollywood and South Pasadena," Mary Beedle cautioned her son.

Bill assured his mother that he would not fall prey to the loose morality of the movie town. The common vision of Hollywood as a latter-day Sodom and Gomorrah was inaccurate, he added, arguing that most studio workers toiled long hours six days a week and had neither the inclination nor the energy for wanton pleasures.

Bill did not tell his mother about his delight in discovering that sex was far more available in Hollywood than in South Pasadena. Actresses, extras, and secretaries were attracted to the young actor with the strong physique and winning smile and required little persuasion to accompany him to bed. How different from the South Pasadena girls with their outrage at being touched on the breast by an amorous male.

Another thing that Bill didn't tell his mother—or anyone else— was how helpful alcohol could be in his new profession. Even after four starring roles, he experienced terror each time he walked on a movie set to face fifty near-strangers and express emotions that were foreign to his nature. The solution was easy. Before he reported to the set, he swallowed a shot of whisky, perhaps two. He brushed his teeth to eliminate the odor, then reported to the stage glowing with confidence.

Bill shared a small house in the Hollywood Hills with Hugh McMullen, who had become an adviser, confidant, and mentor for the young actor. McMullen counseled him on movie scenes, advised him how to dress on and off the screen, and recommended books to expand Bill's limited education.

Unlike other contract players in Hollywood, Bill Holden had two studios to determine the fate of his acting career. They were totally dissimilar. Paramount had the exuberant spirit of a college campus, presided over by an amiable but firm-minded dean, Y. Frank Freeman. Holden thought of Columbia as a penitentiary, with Harry Cohn as warden.

Even though he shared Holden's contract, Cohn considered the young man to be his own property, like every other employee of Columbia Pictures. Yet Cohn had respect for anyone who would stand up to him, as Holden had done over the Athletic Club rent. The studio boss took an almost paternal interest in Holden, even allowing him to remain present while company business was being conducted. "Pay attention, kid, you might learn something," Cohn instructed.

During one office session, Humphrey Bogart's name was mentioned. "Oh, yes," Holden said lightly, "he was in my picture at Warner Brothers."

Cohn glowered at him. "What did you say?"

"I said, he was in my picture at Warner Brothers."

Cohn slammed his fist on the desk. "Let me tell you something, kid. A lot of people work on a picture. It's no one man's picture. So you can say *'our* picture' or *'the* picture' or *'a* picture,' but don't ever let me hear you say *'my* picture' again. Understand?"

Holden soon learned the extent of the Cohn spy system, which was rumored to include hidden microphones in stars' dressing rooms. One day Cohn muttered, "I hear you've been running around with a dumb broad."

"What are you talking about?"

"I hear you've been going out with ———— ————."

Holden was taken by surprise. Cohn had mentioned the name of an actress he had secretly dated a couple of times.

"What about it?" Holden asked.

"You're making a mistake. She's a dumb blond broad, and she's six years older than you are."

"Dammit, I think you're invading my private life!" the actor said angrily. "What I do after I leave the studio is my own business."

"Listen to me. That dame is poison. She'll give you nothing but trouble if you hang around her."

Holden was incensed when he left the office. He had no romantic interest in the actress, but he thought Cohn had exceeded his authority. Later he discovered that she had lied about her age and the fact that she had been married. She had also been involved in a scandal that Cohn had been aware of but hadn't revealed to Holden.

Cohn discouraged camaraderie among his actors, or any of his other creative personnel, who by their alliance might conspire against him. He refused to install a studio commissary. The only studio eating place was the executive dining room, where Cohn could maintain close watch on his important employees. Knowing few people at Columbia and wary of the watchful eye of Harry Cohn, Bill Holden spent little time at the studio when he wasn't working on a movie.

Paramount was his home. He enjoyed the studio's easy atmosphere, a mood epitomized by Bing Crosby and Bob Hope; Bill spent hours watching the pair filming *The Road to Singapore* with Dorothy Lamour. Bill had a dressing room upstairs in the stars' building, but Paramount had no castes; he was welcome in any of the ground-floor suites occupied by Hope, Crosby, Brian Donlevy, Fred MacMurray, Ray Milland, Jack Benny, Charles Boyer.

Bill's special favorites were Joel McCrea and Gary Cooper. He idolized them, wondered at their naturalness on the screen, the way they seemed not to be acting at all. He visited their dressing rooms, sought their advice, poured out his frustrations. "Dammit, Joel," he said, "I'm too young to get good parts. I need lines in my face, like you and Coop."

"They'll come, Bill," McCrea said with a smile. "They'll come."

One of the friends Holden made at Paramount was A. C. Lyles, a young, enthusiastic Floridian who had started in the mail department and worked his way to publicity. Lyles had helped Bill move into the Hollywood Athletic Club, and Bill often invited Lyles to the Beedle house for home cooking on the weekend.

One night the pair had dinner at the Brown Derby on Vine Street and then took a drive down Hollywood Boulevard. *Invisible Stripes* was playing at the Warners Hollywood Theater, and "William Holden" appeared in lights on the marquee. "That must make you feel very proud," Lyles suggested.

"It doesn't mean a thing to me," Bill replied. "That's another fellow up there on that theater. I'm Bill Beedle, who is somebody entirely different. I'm grateful that they changed my name. I want to keep myself separated from that other guy."

"There's a girl out at Warners you ought to meet," Hugh McMullen told Bill Holden. "Her movie name is Brenda Marshall, but I knew her as Ardis Ankerson when she was acting in New York. Nice girl. You'd like her."

"No, thanks," Holden replied. "I read about her. Married and with a kid."

"Separated," McMullen corrected.

"She's not divorced, so that means she's married. No, thanks."

Holden gave Brenda Marshall no further thought until one day when he was filming *Invisible Stripes*. She came on the set to visit Jane Bryan, who introduced her to Bill. Working in the world of motion pictures, Holden had grown accustomed to beautiful women. But he had seen no one like the slender brunette with porcelain skin and almost too-perfect features. They chatted for a few minutes, then she left to return to her own stage. For three months, Bill convinced himself he would be unwise to become involved with a woman who was still married and had a young daughter. For three months he couldn't erase the vision of that flawless face.

Ardis Ankerson had been born in 1917 on the Philippine island of Negros, where her father, Otto Peter Ankerson, was overseer of a large sugar plantation. Her mother died when the girl was young, and Ardis and an older sister were sent to San Antonio, Texas, to complete their high school education. Ardis appeared in plays at Texas State College, then went to New York to study dramatics with Maria Ouspenskaya. After playing summer stock in New Hampshire, she found work in the Federal Theater Project. In 1936, she married a Federal Theater actor, Richard Houston Gaines; and a daughter, Virginia, was born in 1938.

As Ardis Gaines, she appeared in *Allison's House, The Guardsman, One Sunday Afternoon, She Stoops to Conquer,* and other plays, attracting interest from studio scouts. She made screen tests in New York, but no contracts resulted. During one of his periodic talent-hunting trips to New York for Paramount, Artie Jacobson was introduced to Ardis Gaines by an agent. Jacobson gave her a screen test and was so pleased with the results that he carried the film back to California in his suitcase. Paramount executives were equally impressed until they learned of her demand for a starting salary of $250 a week. "Forget it," Jacobson was told.

Jacobson bootlegged the test to other studios after the thirty-day option period ended, and Warner Brothers quickly responded. Within forty-eight hours, Ardis Ankerson Gaines was headed to California with a contract, a new name, and the leading role opposite Joel McCrea in *Espionage Agent.*

Co-starring with Errol Flynn in *The Sea Hawk* established her as one of Warners' leading ladies. Gaines remained in New York, where he replaced Raymond Massey in *Abe Lincoln in Illinois.*

"A distance of only 3000 miles keeps Brenda Marshall and husband Dick Gaines from being the two happiest people in the world," burbled Hedda Hopper in her syndicated column. But in truth, the marriage was over.

Bill Holden finally telephoned Ardis—throughout his lifetime he never called her Brenda—one late afternoon he asked if she was busy that evening. She admitted she wasn't.

"Then I'll come around right away," he said. "They're shooting some night battle scenes for *Fighting 69th.* I thought you'd be interested in watching. We'll pick up something to eat on the way."

It was the start of an unorthodox courtship. Bill was delighted to discover that Ardis was not as fragile as she looked. She had learned to enjoy the outdoor life in the Philippines and Texas. On their Sundays off from the studios Bill and Ardis drove to the desert and the mountains. They swam at Malibu, rode horses in Griffith Park, played badminton at Artie Jacobson's house. Everyone who saw them realized the two extraordinarily handsome young people were in love.

To Bill Holden, still rooted in the traditional values of South Pasadena, a love such as that he felt for Ardis meant marriage. He pressed her to find a legal solution to the estrangement with Gaines. It took time to work out the arrangements between New York and California. Finally Ardis engaged a high-powered Hollywood lawyer, Gregson Bautzer, who made a settlement. On June 9, 1940, she was granted a divorce in Los Angeles Superior Court on grounds of desertion. She waived alimony and was given custody of Virginia.

Still, Ardis balked at a quick marriage to Bill. Both were deeply involved in their ascendant careers, as well as with each other. They worked at different studios and often on locations. Would they be able to devote enough time to each other to make a marriage work? Ardis wasn't sure, and she didn't want to risk the shattering experience of another broken marriage. They would wait.

6

Marriage and War

Like other important films of his career, *Arizona* befell William Holden by default. The producer-director, Wesley Ruggles, wanted Gary Cooper for the role of the gunslinger Peter Muncie. Cooper declined. Harry Cohn decided to cast his bargain actor William Holden. Ruggles argued that the twenty-two-year-old Holden was too immature to appear opposite Jean Arthur, ten years his senior. As always, Harry Cohn's will prevailed.

Holden could sense Ruggles' resentment during the Tucson location shooting. That didn't spoil Bill's enjoyment of horse chases and shootouts, enactments of the games he and Dick Steele had played in the Mojave Desert a few years before.

Back to Paramount for *I Wanted Wings*.

As America began mobilizing against the threat of war, Hollywood started making films glamorizing the armed services. *I Wanted Wings* was Paramount's salute to the Army Air Corps. It was filmed at Randolph Field in Texas, where the director, Ted Weeks, treated the officers and enlisted men like extras. When a squadron spoiled a scene by flying overhead, he shouted to a general, "Get those planes out of the air!" Two days later, Weeks was replaced by Mitchell Leisen.

The film company was housed on a floor of the St. Anthony Hotel in San Antonio, and it was the scene of partying each night. One of the stars entertained a Texas ranch girl in his room, and he later recounted to Bill Holden the girl's amazing proportions and unbelievable passion.

As Holden passed through the lobby on his way to the location the next morning, he noticed three rough-looking Texans, all bearing shotguns. They asked at the front desk for the whereabouts of the amorous star. Holden rushed up the stairs and spirited the star out of his room and to the back elevator. For the remainder of the location, the star slept at the YMCA.

Holden was next assigned to another western at Columbia, *Texas*. To the astonishment of both his studios, he balked.

"I have no complaint about the role or the script," he told a columnist. "They're just not paying me enough money."

To his well-ordered sense of right and wrong, the complaint seemed reasonable. Co-starring with actors who were paid $2,000 to $3,000 a week, he was drawing $125. How could he possibly support Ardis and her daughter on such a salary? It wasn't fair.

"A contract is a contract, young man," huffed Y. Frank Freeman, the Paramount chief. "Nobody put a gun to your head to make you sign it. You will abide by it."

Bill Holden didn't think so, and he was supported by his agent, Charles Feldman, whom Rouben Mamoulian had recommended to him during *Golden Boy*. Paramount placed Holden on suspension, an embittering experience for the young actor. He had performed uncomplainingly, even on loanouts for which Paramount and Columbia sold his services at a handsome profit. Suddenly his salary was stopped, and he was even barred from entering the studio. He had saved nothing during his film career, and he could not hold out for long. Even a powerful agent like Charlie Feldman couldn't dissuade Freeman from his vow to hold the line against demanding actors. Bill Holden agreed to report for work on *Texas*, enlightened in the paternalism of big studios.

William Holden and Glenn Ford had been introduced to each other in the hallway of the Columbia Pictures executive building. During their casual meetings afterward, they eyed each other assessingly, like two light heavyweights in a boxing gym. Both were contenders. Ford, from Quebec by way of Santa Monica High School, had arrived at Columbia shortly after Holden; but he had made a slower start in B pictures like *Convicted Woman* and *Blondie Plays Cupid*. Cohn had plans for Ford, whose first name had been changed from Gwyllyn, and he delighted in pitting him against Holden.

"You'd better watch out for this Ford guy," Cohn told Holden. "He's going to be getting your pictures."

"You're never gonna catch up with Holden," Cohn warned Ford. "He's too far ahead of you."

The rivalry honed, Harry Cohn cast William Holden and Glenn Ford in *Texas*, a western about Confederate army buddies who fought on opposite sides of the law out west.

The director was George Marshall, a hardened veteran of silent westerns. Like Cohn, he realized that actors sometimes produced their best work through competition. Marshall urged actors to perform their own stunts whenever possible. When a difficult scene approached, he said to Ford, "Bill says he'll do this stunt, how about you?" When Ford agreed, the director said to Holden, "Glenn is willing to take this fall; I don't suppose you would." Holden quickly assented.

Marshall worked the technique on both actors for a scene to be filmed at Lake Sherwood in the Malibu Mountains. He wanted them to herd two hundred head of cattle into the lake, then swim their horses across the water to the other side. Ford and Holden agreed separately, then conferred with each other.

"Did you ever swim a horse?" Bill asked.

"Never," said Glenn. "How about you?"

"Nope. George says it's easy, but I wonder."

They consulted a stunt man who told them, "You guys are crazy to do something like that. If your horses fall over in the water, they'll kick you to death."

The two young actors had agreed to the stunt and neither could back down. The stunt man gave them instructions: Don't try to lead the horse, just let it swim; lean back, hold on to the mane and the pommel; hope to God your horse is a good swimmer.

Ford and Holden followed the cattle into the lake, shouting encouragement to their horses and to each other. After several anxious minutes they reached the opposite shore, and George Marshall happily shouted, "Cut! Print!"

The experience of making *Texas* solidified a friendship that would be long-lasting but never without the element of rivalry. Whether at poker, horsemanship, cars, houses, movie roles, or women, William Holden and Glenn Ford would always compete against each other.

In July of 1941, Bill Holden was making another Paramount movie, *The Remarkable Andrew,* with Brian Donlevy. The schedule included a location in Carson City, Nevada, and Bill couldn't face a lengthy separation from Ardis.

"Let's get married in Las Vegas this weekend," he said eagerly. Ardis agreed.

With great excitement, Bill made his plans. He chartered a plane, which would be standing ready as soon as he finished work on Saturday. He scheduled a midnight wedding at the Congregational church in Las

Vegas. He reserved the honeymoon suite at El Rancho Vegas. To avoid a leak to Hedda Hopper or Louella Parsons, Bill told no one about the plan except his friend Donlevy. "Marjorie and I will go along and stand up for you," Donlevy volunteered.

The adventure began poorly. The director, Stuart Heisler, continued filming two extra hours, and neither Holden nor Donlevy dared divulge their urgency to leave. Still in makeup, they dashed to the airport with Mrs. Donlevy and the future Mrs. Holden. They celebrated on board the chartered plane with champagne, and Bill predicted they would arrive at the church with time to spare.

"Sorry, folks," the pilot told them. "Las Vegas airport is closed because of a storm. But I've got permission to land at a new army airstrip not too far away."

The pilot didn't know that the landing strip had not been paved. The plane was able to land, but it couldn't taxi on the muddy runway. Bill, Ardis, and the Donlevys carried their luggage through the mud to the makeshift terminal a mile away. Bill telephoned for a taxi, which came an hour later.

The wedding party arrived at the Congregational church at 4 A.M. and found it deserted. At El Rancho Vegas Bill was told the honeymoon suite had been released to another couple. He signed the register for two rooms and telephoned the Congregational minister, pleading with him to come to the hotel and perform the ceremony.

"We were married," Ardis later told an interviewer, "in a hotel bedroom, standing at the foot of a double bed, by a one-armed man who held the book with his hand and turned the pages with his chin."

The Holdens and the Donlevys were celebrating with a champagne breakfast in the El Rancho lounge when their pilot approached. "Sorry, folks," he said. "The fog's rolling in. If you want to get back to Los Angeles today, we'd better leave now." Holden and Donlevy had no choice; they would be in grave trouble if they did not report to the studio Monday morning.

Bill and Ardis returned to the apartment Bill had rented in the San Fernando Valley. He reported his wedding to the studio, and the publicity department released the news, enraging both Louella and Hedda because they hadn't been given the story exclusively. Newspapers featured the wedding story, largely because of the bride's prominence. Many carried headlines like BRENDA MARSHALL MARRIES ACTOR.

Three days after the wedding, Warner Brothers informed Ardis she would be replacing another actress in *Captain of the Clouds*, opposite

James Cagney, and would have to leave immediately for locations in Ottawa, Canada.

She returned a month later to find that Bill had departed for *his* location in Carson City. He came back in an ambulance—acute appendicitis. He was taken to Hollywood Hospital for an operation, and his bride visited him daily.

"Funny thing," she said one day. "My side hurts, too."

"Sympathetic pain," Bill remarked.

The pain persisted, and she mentioned it to Bill's surgeon. He took her to the next room for an examination and ordered an immediate operation. Bill vacated his bed for Ardis, who remained in the hospital three weeks. Two and a half months after the wedding, Bill and Ardis Holden were able to begin their married life.

For a few brief happy weeks, Bill Holden enjoyed his new life as husband and father. He adored young Virginia and made plans to adopt her. He and Ardis shopped for furniture, and Bill closely eyed the price tags. Although Ardis was earning $750 a week from Warner Brothers, he insisted on keeping their expenses within his own salary, $175 a week.

Despite their happiness, Bill and Ardis felt an impermanence about their marriage, and not merely because of the demands of three studios. With war raging in the Pacific, Bill announced his intention to volunteer for the service. His brother Bob had joined the naval air corps, and Bill felt equally patriotic.

Holden's studios managed to employ him in three more films. First was Paramount's *The Fleet's In,* a wartime entertainment with an inane plot interspersed with specialty acts. Next, *Meet the Stewarts,* with Holden and Frances Dee as newlyweds in a routine script at Columbia.

The wife of Joel McCrea, Miss Dee had been absent from films to become a mother. During the early filming, she seemed unsure of herself, and the director, Al Green, wanted to replace her. Holden interceded with Harry Cohn.

"Are you trying to tell me how to run my studio?" Cohn demanded.

"No," said Holden, "I'm just saying that Frances is a good actress and a real beauty, and I think it would be a mistake to take her out of the picture."

"All right, all right," Cohn said impatiently. "You're wasting my money by being away from the set. Get back there. And tell Al Green to go fuck himself."

For Bill Holden, *Meet the Stewarts* was unmemorable except for a single brief moment he never forgot. He and Frances Dee were filming a scene in a car, the passing highway appearing behind them on a rear-projection screen. Suddenly the light on her hair, the sparkle of her eyes, the perfect contour of her face combined for a heart-stopping glimpse of pure beauty. He said nothing, did nothing, but the moment remained distinct in his consciousness to the end of his life. It would not be the only time he fell in love with his leading lady.

One more film for Paramount: *Young and Willing.* Overstocked with product, Paramount sold it and other movies to United Artists for release. Ever afterward, when Holden was asked which was his worst film, he replied, *"Young and Willing."*

In April of 1942, William Holden was notified by the army that his enlistment would be processed within two weeks. He made the rounds of the departments and dressing rooms at Paramount to bid farewell to his fellow workers, then drove up Gower Street to do the same at Columbia. After visiting the stages and departments, he went to see Harry Cohn.

"So you're going in the service, huh?" said Cohn.

"That's right, Mr. Cohn," Bill replied. "I leave tomorrow."

"Well, it's a good thing."

"What do you mean?"

"I mean the army can do you a lot of good. Make a man out of you. Remember how Wes Ruggles wanted to fire you on that western because you looked too young."

"Sure. I remember."

"Well, I wouldn't let him have his way, but he was right. You *were* too young. The army'll toughen you up, put some character in that pretty face. When you come back to Columbia, you might be able to carry a picture by yourself, like Gable or Cooper."

Holden left the office with another insight into the byzantine mind of Harry Cohn. Holden was shipping off to war, perhaps to lose his life, and Cohn's only concern was how the experience would affect a property owned by Columbia Pictures.

7

A Son Born, a Brother Lost

WILLIAM HOLDEN, "GOLDEN BOY,"
FIRST MARRIED STAR TO ENLIST
William Holden, 24-year-old film actor and husband of actress
Brenda Marshall, who sprang to prominence in 1938 when he
was selected for the leading role in "Golden Boy," embarked on
a new way of life yesterday by joining the United States Army.

The first married star to enlist in the service, the smiling,
clean-cut young actor enlisted under his real name, William F.
Beedle, Jr., and was sworn into service at the Army Recruiting
Station, 406 S. Main St.

He was allowed until tomorrow to wind up his business and
then will report to the Ft. MacArthur Reception Center.
—Los Angeles Times, April 21, 1942

Holden was assigned to Tarrant Field Air Base near Fort Worth, Texas.
He was miserable. The base was surrounded by unplowed fields, and
the ever-blowing dust stung his eyes and choked his throat. Sergeants
badgered him because he was a movie star. He missed Ardis so much
that he sometimes cried in his bed at night. The communal life and
constant discipline of an army barracks were stifling. He had not yet
been assigned to basic training, and he began to feel that his patriotic
gesture of enlisting had been wasted.

He was delighted when a familiar face turned up on the base. A
rising young director at RKO, Garson Kanin had been drafted before
Pearl Harbor. Bill had met him on the set of *Golden Boy* when Kanin
was visiting his friend Sam Levene. Holden had found in Kanin someone who talked his own language, who wasn't awed or intimidated by
his fame, who could give him tips on how to deal with army life.

"Is there any place on the base where I can go to the bathroom by
myself?" Holden asked.

"Not that I know of," said Kanin. "Why?"

"I haven't been able to take a crap for two days. I just can't do it with a bunch of guys staring at me."

"Follow me and I'll show you," said Kanin, leading him to the latrine.

They took seats side by side along the row of open toilets. "Now close your eyes," Kanin instructed. "Put everything else out of your mind. Just concentrate on what you're doing."

They remained seated in silence for several minutes until Holden said, "Hey, I think it's working." He felt a tap on the shoulder and looked up to see a fuzz-faced young soldier standing over him. "Mr. Holden, could I have your autograph for my mother back home?" the boy asked.

Private Beedle was sent to Fort Monmouth, New Jersey, for basic training with the signal corps. Shortly after arriving, Bill encountered Richard Webb, who had been a fellow contract player at Paramount.

"God, am I glad to see you!" said Bill. He failed to notice a passing second lieutenant, whom Webb, a regular army man before the war, saluted smartly.

"Soldier!" the officer commanded. He began circling the offending private, barking out reprimands. When he noticed the soldier was a movie star, the attack became more vituperative. "And don't you forget it!" he concluded.

As the deflated Holden walked away with Webb, he sighed, "Remember when we were making *I Wanted Wings* at Randolph Field? We had brigadier generals carrying our bags."

The two actors learned that *I Wanted Wings* was opening at the Paramount Theater in New York, and they were determined to see it, despite the fact that Holden was confined to camp while in basic training. Webb borrowed a car from another sergeant, and Holden hid under a blanket in the back seat as they passed through the guard gate. As they stood in line for tickets at the Paramount on Broadway, the assistant manager recognized them.

"Come right in, gentlemen," he said. "We're honored to have you as our guests." After the anonymity of the army, Holden and Webb enjoyed being ushered to reserved seats on the main floor. They sat through the movie laughing and chattering about incidents during the filming.

"Let's stay for the stage show," Holden urged. "I haven't seen any real entertainment in months." Webb agreed, and they watched eagerly as the huge curtain rose to reveal a popular swing band. After the band's theme song, the leader stepped to the microphone and said, "Ladies and gentlemen, we have very special guests today—two of the stars of the movie you just enjoyed. They're both now serving our great nation in our fight against the Japs and the Huns. Let's show them how much we appreciate their sacrifice. Stand up, please, Richard Webb and William Holden!"

The two soldiers tried to slump in their seats, but a spotlight shone down on them. They stood sheepishly and nodded to the wild applause. Holden whispered to Webb, "If this gets back to Monmouth, I'm dead." Fortunately, no one at the base heard about their unscheduled personal appearance.

Private Beedle qualified for officer training, and he was sent to school at Miami Beach. He graduated a second lieutenant on January 20, 1943, and flew home for a joyous reunion with Ardis. Warner Brothers had kept her working in films like *Background to Danger* and *The Constant Nymph*, and she had been unable to join him during his training.

After his leave, Bill reported to duty with the First Motion Picture Unit Training Command at Fort Worth. In May, Bill was back in California for a legal proceeding. He and Ardis appeared in Superior Court to change their names to William Franklin Holden and Ardis Ankerson Holden.

An officer's life at Fort Worth was far different from what Bill had experienced as an enlisted man. He found himself in officers' quarters with a roommate as famous as he was—Hank Greenberg, the baseball star. Because of robberies on the base, Bill had started the practice of sleeping with a .45 pistol under his pillow. One night Greenberg returned to the quarters late, and Bill was awakened by footsteps on the stairs. He slipped the gun from under his pillow and fixed its aim at the door. "Are you awake?" Greenberg whispered in time to prevent Bill from pulling the trigger. "Yeah, I'm awake," Bill replied, returning the gun under the pillow.

Lieutenant Holden was assigned to public relations duty, appearing on radio programs and in training films, acting as master of ceremonies at talent programs, lending his presence to war bond rallies. He hated the work and repeatedly asked for combat duty. But the air force considered him more valuable in building service and civilian morale.

Bob Beedle was also in Texas, training as a naval flier for combat duty. They exchanged letters and made a date for a rendezvous when both were on leave. But when the weekend arrived, Bill was assigned to a radio show to promote war bonds. He was devastated. Bill and Bob had been rivals throughout their young years, but as adults they had developed a deep respect and unspoken affection. Bob was openly proud of Bill's success as an actor, and Bill was in awe of Bob's achievements as a pilot.

In mid-November of 1943, Bill Holden received news that Ardis was about to give birth to their first child. He managed to get a ride on a bomber to California, arriving in time for the birth of a son at Hollywood Hospital on November 17. The boy was named Peter Westfield Holden. Westfield was Bob Beedle's middle name.

Bob wrote a letter of congratulations to his brother. "You must send me a picture of all of you—the proud papa and Ardis and Virginia and young Peter Westfield," said Bob. Before Bill could send the photograph, Bob had been shipped overseas.

On New Year's Day 1944, Bill Holden awakened early in his quarters at Fort Worth. He felt strange. It wasn't just a hangover, though he had had many drinks at the celebration for New Year's Eve. He was perfectly sober, but extremely disquieted. He felt the need to telephone Ardis.

"Hi, honey, just called to wish you a Happy New Year," he said. "Is everything all right? Baby okay?"

Reassured, he telephoned his parents in South Pasadena. They were well. For days he couldn't shake the oppressive feeling. On January 4, Bill's mother called with the terrible news: Bob had been shot down by enemy fire during the New Year's Day raid on Kavieng, New Ireland, in the South Pacific.

Ensign Beedle, who had already destroyed two Japanese Zeros, had been part of a carrier-based squadron of Hellcats escorting dive bombers on the raid. The Hellcats were attacked by half a dozen Zeros, and Beedle's plane was apparently hit as he turned to intercept a pair of Japanese planes that concentrated on him. Said his section leader: "His Hellcat swept upward in a lazy loop, pulled out just above the water, flew level for a few seconds, then plunged into the whitecaps. His guns were still blasting."

Bill shared his sorrow with no one, locking himself in his room to weep and blame himself. Why didn't I meet Bob on leave in Texas? he asked. Why didn't I send that photograph Bob wanted?

"Did I say that I failed him?" he said cryptically to an interviewer a few years later. "I didn't fail him. I failed myself."

Once more Holden sought overseas duty, but the air force turned him down. He was assigned to an endless series of war bond rallies, talent shows, radio programs, training films. In 1945 he joined the First Motion Picture Unit at the Hal Roach Studios, which the government had commandeered for instruction and morale films.

Holden reported to Fort Roach with Richard Webb, his friend from Paramount and Fort Monmouth. Both went to the adjutant's office to present their credentials. They were required to stand at attention for twenty-five minutes while the adjutant recited the regulations.

"That son of a bitch," muttered Bill Holden as he and Webb left the office of the adjutant, Captain Ronald Reagan.

Holden served the last nine months of his air force duty at Fort Roach, spending weekends at home with Ardis and the children. That contributed to his guilt over not fighting in the war as his brother Bob had. Holden was discharged in September of 1945, and he was eager to resume his career with the two studios that still held him under contract. He didn't work for eleven months.

8

The Curse of Smiling Jim

On his first day back at Paramount after three years and five months in the service of his country, William Holden was barred from entering the studio. The gateman didn't know who he was.

"Just like old times," said Holden, less angry than amused by the irony. The executives and producers of Paramount gave him a more cordial welcome, with promises of important films for the returning veteran. As Holden walked around the lot, he sensed the changes that had occurred in his absence. Many of his buddies in the publicity, makeup, prop, and other departments remained; but there were new faces as well. He found new names on the doors along the row of stars' dressing rooms: Alan Ladd, who had played a bit part when Bill starred in *Those Were the Days;* Sonny Tufts; John Lund.

Holden felt a similar strangeness when he made his return to Columbia. Like Paramount, it had boomed during the war years. Columbia was almost unrecognizable as the studio Harry Cohn had built from Poverty Row. Ramshackle buildings had been replaced by huge concrete stages. And there were new stars like Cornel Wilde and Larry Parks.

Harry Cohn greeted Holden warmly. "I told you the army would do you good," Cohn said. "Now you look like a man, not just some snotty-nosed kid outa Eagle Rock."

"South Pasadena, Harry," Holden corrected.

"Same thing. I'm gonna have some work for you, but you're only half Columbia's, you know. I gotta take care of my own people. Like Glenn Ford. He's been back from the marines, and he looks terrific. I'm lending him to Jack Warner for a picture with Bette Davis. That ain't bad. You keep an eye on that Ford kid. He's gonna be terrific."

"Yes, you've told me that before, Harry."

Paramount announced that William Holden would make his return to the screen in *Dear Ruth,* a comedy based on Norman Krasna's popular wartime play. But start of production was postponed repeatedly, and Holden remained idle. The fan magazines published the obligatory "Johnny Comes Marching Home" stories about Bill Holden and Brenda Marshall, but there was little else to write about. Holden tried to occupy his time by reading scripts and looking at movies.

Ardis was pregnant again, and Bill asked her not to return to Warner Brothers after the baby was born. He wanted no more of the absences that had been so punishing during the war, and he had seen too many failures of actor-actress marriages. His conservative upbringing dictated that he alone should be the breadwinner of the family. Ardis was agreeable. She had found little pleasure in her movie career; Warner Brothers had used her as little more than decoration for the male stars. After the birth of Scott Porter Holden on May 2, 1946, Brenda Marshall announced her retirement from the screen.

As the idle months continued, Holden became nervous and irritable. Now he had a wife and three children to support, and his name hadn't been on the screen in four years, an eternity by Hollywood standards. New actors were being hired by Paramount and Columbia, yet neither studio assigned him to a film.

"You can always come to work for me," said Bill's father, and Holden briefly considered giving up his career for Gooch Laboratories. That had been William Beedle's longtime hope. But Bill couldn't reconcile himself to such a humiliating defeat.

He began avoiding friends, unable to face more questions of "When are you going to work?" He said later, "For eleven months, I was a fugitive from a psychoanalyst, short-tempered, moody, depressed."

His first postwar film was inauspicious: *Blaze of Noon.* An Ernest K. Gann story about barnstorming pilots, it seemed designed to provide employment for Paramount's contract actors. *Dear Ruth* enjoyed more success. A likable comedy, it helped establish Holden's postwar image as an affable, handsome WASP who could grin his way through any situation.

Holden was loaned to RKO for *Rachel and the Stranger,* in which he co-starred with Loretta Young and Robert Mitchum. Both had been in the news, Miss Young for winning an Academy Award, Mitchum for being busted on a marijuana rap. Holden was amused by the contrast between the ethereal Loretta and the roughneck Mitchum. She had a tradition on her movie sets of a collection cup to which company members contributed if they uttered swear words—twenty-five cents for "hell," fifty cents for "God damn," etc. The money was contributed to a home for unwed mothers. Exasperated during a scene, Mitchum jammed a five-dollar bill into the cup and loosed a string of expletives.

When *Rachel and the Stranger* moved to Oregon for locations, Miss Young noticed that Bill Holden seemed totally at ease until Mitchum arrived. Then he appeared nervous and insecure because of the presence of the flamboyant actor.

"Relax, Bill," Loretta said to Holden. "You're the lead in this picture. You get the girl at the end."

"What do you mean?" he demanded.

"You're nervous as a cat. You're worried about the competition of Bob Mitchum."

"That's absolutely not true," Bill contended, but his nervousness continued.

To relieve the boredom of the Oregon location, Loretta Young entertained members of the company at her rented house for Sunday dinners. One day on the set she said to her two co-stars, "You know something? Last Sunday you two fellows drank a bottle and a half of whisky at my house. Now I'm not complaining about the liquor; I can afford it. What I'm concerned about is you two. Both of you are going to have big careers in our business. But you won't have the stomachs to enjoy them if you continue drinking like that."

Holden nodded thoughtfully. "I think you're right, Loretta. I'm going to cut down."

Mitchum gave her a stony stare. "Well, are you finished, Mother Superior?" he said.

Apartment for Peggy marked the beginning of a fruitful relationship between William Holden and George Seaton.

They had become acquainted through George's wife, Phyllis Seaton, who had coached Bill in his earliest days at Paramount. A tall, thoughtful man with unexpected flashes of droll humor, George Seaton had played the Lone Ranger on radio, had written scripts for the Marx Brothers, and had become a writer-director. With William Perlberg as producer, Seaton had made several films at 20th Century–Fox, including *Miracle on 34th Street*.

Bill Holden stopped at Seaton's house in Beverly Hills one afternoon and complained that Paramount and Columbia had forgotten him. Seaton suggested a script he was planning to film at Fox; he had written it as a tribute to his brother, a longtime college professor.

Edmund Gwenn and Jeanne Crain had already been cast in the film, *Apartment for Peggy*.

"Can I read it?" Bill asked.

"Sure," Seaton replied.

"How about now?" Holden retired to Seaton's den, emerged a half-hour later, and said, "If you want me, I'd love to do it."

Apartment for Peggy was followed by Holden's initial postwar film for Columbia, *The Dark Past,* his first major challenge as an actor. He was cast as a ruthless killer.

Holden was reunited with his father from *Golden Boy,* Lee J. Cobb, who played a psychiatrist trying to cure the escaped convict's murderous instincts. Cobb was a self-dedicated actor who was not noted for helping his fellow players. Each morning he arrived on the set in a black mood, grumbling at his script, "How can we make anything out of this shit? Impossible!" He continued his tirade, picking each line apart. Gradually he found his own method to play the scene. By that time, Bill Holden's confidence was destroyed.

Nina Foch, who was cast as Holden's moll, observed what was happening. She invited Bill to come to the set fifteen minutes early, and she served him coffee and doughnuts in her dressing room.

"Bill, don't let Lee get you down," the actress argued. "In ten years, what will Lee Cobb be? A character actor. A very good character actor, but still a character actor. In ten years you'll be a really big star. Not just a personality, but an important star."

"Tell me again, Nina," he said with a grin. She did. Every morning they observed the same ritual, and Bill's confidence was restored.

Reviewers remarked that William Holden displayed in *The Dark Past* an unsuspected depth of character. Harry Cohn was less impressed. He next cast Holden in a routine western, *The Man from Colorado.* The dominant role was played by Holden's friendly rival Glenn Ford.

During the filming of *The Man from Colorado,* Holden decided it was time to move to a bigger house. He had been saving money so he could afford to take suspensions when Paramount or Columbia offered him bad pictures. But he and Ardis, the three children, and two housekeepers were crowded into a house that once held three. After Charlie Feldman negotiated a more favorable contract with Paramount, Bill agreed to look for larger quarters.

Ardis wanted to move to Beverly Hills or Bel Air. Bill refused. He didn't want to enter the competitive social world of the major stars and producers. He preferred the country life of the San Fernando Valley, with its crisp winters and hot summers, its casual outdoor atmosphere. He wanted his sons to grow up in a normal community such as he had known in South Pasadena, not on the west side, where governesses took stars' children to birthday parties complete with clowns and carousels.

A real estate agent tried to interest Bill in a Toluca Lake house owned by the comedian Leon Errol. It was a two-story Georgian style with flagstone front, four bedrooms, four baths. It sounded too expensive to Bill. For days the agent showed Bill and Ardis house after house —ranch style, Spanish stucco with tile roof, Cape Cod, English cottage.

One afternoon, the agent drove the Holdens along Sancola Avenue, a quiet tree-lined street in Toluca Lake. Bill noticed a for sale sign on one of the houses and said, "Now why couldn't you find us a house like that?"

"That," said the realtor, "is the Leon Errol house I've been trying to interest you in for five days."

The house was exactly what Bill and Ardis wanted, but Bill balked at the price: $100,000. The mortgage payments would be too great for his salary. As Ardis was trying to persuade him, the telephone rang and she answered it.

"That was Leslie Fenton," she said when she returned. "He's directing *Whispering Smith* with Alan Ladd. It has a good woman's part, and Leslie wants me to play it."

"And?" Bill said.

"I told him I would. Now we can buy the house."

Ardis' salary contributed to the down payment, and the Holdens moved into the Sancola Avenue house. The $50,000 mortgage continued worrying Bill. He told friends, "Every night I sleep three feet over the bed, worrying about how much I owe."

Like other valley residents, entertainment for the Holdens consisted of informal dinners at home or at their friends' homes. Ardis gave the housekeepers the night off, and she prepared the dinner while Bill presided over the barbecue. Their guests were mostly from the studios: Jane Wyman and Ronald Reagan, Dinah Shore and George Montgomery, Eleanor Powell and Glenn Ford, the Arthur Kennedys, the Richard Carlsons, Paul Clemens, the portrait painter, and his wife Ruth.

The guests arrived early and swam in the pool on warm evenings. Bill was an attentive bartender, making sure that no glass was empty, especially his own. Conversation ranged from the latest Hollywood gossip to the usual suburban topics of children, schools, diets, and household help. Bill prided himself on his newfound knowledge of wines, and he offered his latest discovery at dinner. Brandy and coffee followed, and on mellow evenings the guests took turns performing. Bill's specialty was the bones, which he played to the accompaniment of his favorite record, "How High the Moon."

On a stifling August Sunday, Paul Clemens arrived in the early evening at the Holden house, accompanied by his wife Ruth, Ava Gardner, and Maddy Comfort, a stunning black model whose nude portrait Clemens had been painting. Bill invited them into the backyard, where he was preparing the barbecue.

"My God, it's hot out here in the valley," said Ava as she stepped into the furnace heat outdoors. She cast her eyes at the cobalt cool of the swimming pool.

"Hey, let's skinny-dip!" she exclaimed.

"Why not?" agreed Clemens.

Bill watched with amusement from behind the barbecue as the four guests stripped off their clothes and dived into the pool. As they were splashing and exulting over the coolness, the Reagans arrived at the front door. Ronald strolled into the backyard and was startled to see the four nude figures in the swimming pool. He looked closer and said smilingly, "Gee, Paul, you've got your glasses on."

"I'm no fool," Clemens replied. "I'm as nearsighted as you are."

"Well, you'd better get out," Bill said, "Ardis says it's time for dinner."

Relations between Jane Wyman and Ronald Reagan concerned their friends. Jane had been working in one film after another, and the strain was beginning to show, especially after the demanding deaf-mute role in *Johnny Belinda*. Ronnie was drawing good parts at Warners, notably *Voice of the Turtle* and *The Hasty Heart*, but his career was not flourishing like Jane's, especially after her Academy Award. He seemed more interested in Screen Actors Guild and national politics. While he was a good storyteller and a congenial guest, Ronnie sometimes monopolized dinner conversations with speeches. Jane's boredom was clearly visible to the other guests.

Both Ardis, who had worked with Jane and Ronnie at Warner Brothers, and Bill grew alarmed by the growing tension between the Reagans. One day Louella Parsons printed the news: Jane Wyman and Ronald Reagan announced a trial separation.

A few weeks later, Arthur Kennedy received a call from Bill

Holden, who said, "Ardis and I are having a dinner party Saturday night. Can you come?"

"Sure," Kennedy replied. "You sound excited. What's the occasion?"

"I'm going to get Jane and Ronnie together again," Bill said.

Holden staged the entire evening with great care, hiring caterers to serve an elegant meal. He poured a French red wine that everyone agreed was superb. Bill strove to keep the conversation on a level of gaiety, not an easy feat because of the coolness between Jane and Ronnie.

At the end of dinner, Bill stage-managed Jane and Ronnie into the den and closed the door behind them. The other dinner guests waited in the living room with brandy and subdued anticipation.

After a half-hour, the den door swung open and Jane strode out unpacified. "It's the same old Ronnie," she announced.

Bill and Ardis were invited to a birthday party for Arthur Kennedy at his house on Mulholland Drive, along with the George Montgomerys, the Wayne Morrises, the Burl Iveses, and a few others. By midnight only the Kennedys, the Holdens, and the Iveses remained; and Bill resisted Ardis' suggestions that it was time to go. Ives had brought his guitar and was singing folk songs. Bill was enthralled with the music and enjoying the drinks, as were Kennedy and Ives.

"Now here's one that —— sings, very badly," said Ives, mentioning the name of a rival singer.

When he finished the song to Bill's wild applause, Ives announced another song: "—— made a recording of this one, and it's rotten."

Kennedy was sitting woozily on a low stool. When Ives finished the song, Kennedy said, "What's the matter, Burl? Are you afraid of ——?"

Suddenly Kennedy found himself turning a back somersault on his living-room carpet. "By God, he hit me!" Kennedy exclaimed. He charged toward Ives, who had put down his guitar and was facing him defiantly. Kennedy recalls what happened next: "I threw a left at his stomach as hard as I could. When my fist bounced back, I knew I was in trouble."

Ives grabbed his host by the hair and started pounding his face, while the women screamed and Bill said calmly, "Now look, fellows, there's no need to resort to violence."

Kennedy managed to break loose and, concerned for his furniture, challenged Ives to go outside. The fight resumed on the patio, and Ives picked up a redwood lounge and hurled it at Kennedy, who ducked. The lounge crashed through a sliding glass door.

"Burl, this has gone too far," said Holden in a conciliatory voice. "Let's sit down, have another drink, and talk this over."

The battle had moved to the front of the house, where a long flight of brick steps led to Mulholland Drive. As Bill tried to reason with Ives, Kennedy rushed into the house for a fireplace poker to defend himself. When he returned, he said, "Bill, I think Ardis has fainted."

"Why, you son of a bitch," Bill shouted, and he landed a fist in Ives's face, sending him hurtling down the steps.

"I don't think you should have done that, Bill," said Kennedy.

"Why not?" Bill replied. "Look what he did to you—two shiners and a bloody nose."

"Yes, but he's a guest in my house."

As they argued, Ives struggled back to the top of the stairs. Bill slugged him again, and Ives made the return trip to the bottom. A red light shone out of the darkness, and two uniformed men stepped out of a black-and-white car: police summoned by alarmed neighbors. The officers recognized the participants in the disturbance, delivered a lecture, and departed.

Kennedy and Ives met the following day, and they laughed over the events of the evening. Ives's advice: "The next time you have guests like us over at your house, you'd better drink from glasses with glass bottoms. Then you can see who's coming at you."

Bill Holden enjoyed entertaining at the new house and was proud of the way Ardis had decorated it, but he still worried about paying for it.

For Ardis' first birthday in the new house, Bill wanted to buy her a special present. He decided on a poodle of a rare and expensive pedigree. He was making a film, but got permission to leave early for the special celebration. The assistant director telephoned the house to report: "Mr. Holden will be there in fifteen minutes."

With the poodle in a box on the front seat, Holden drove expectantly over the Cahuenga Pass and down Dark Canyon to Toluca Lake. When he arrived at his house, they were all out in front: Ardis, the three children, two housekeepers, a nurse, the gardener. At the studio the next day, he told Nina Foch what happened: "I said to myself, Shit, I'm supporting all these people! I can't afford this dog! So I turned around and took the dog back to the kennel."

His misgivings were real. His postwar movies had done nothing to fulfill the promise of *Golden Boy*. Alan Ladd was the first choice for good scripts at Paramount, Glenn Ford at Columbia. Holden was offered what was left over.

Bill stopped at the Toluca Lake market one weekend to buy steaks for the Sunday barbecue. As he stood at the meat counter, he felt the discomforting stare of a woman shopper nearby. She walked over to him, and he sighed, "Here it comes."

"For a minute there you gave me a thrill," she told him. "I was almost positive you were—Alan Ladd. You know, you ought to try for a job in the studios. You could double for Alan anytime."

Holden's new films fell short of success. *Streets of Laredo* was a well-produced western, but the plot was a rehash of two earlier Paramount scripts. *Miss Grant Takes Richmond*, at Columbia, was an amusing comedy with Lucille Ball. But her film career was sliding, and the movie was little noticed.

Holden detested the next two movies: *Dear Wife*, a dreary sequel to *Dear Ruth*; and *Father Is a Bachelor*, a treacly story with Holden miscast as a carnival performer. Holden found himself repeating the same character, whom he labeled Smiling Jim.

He offered this analysis to an interviewer:

"Smiling Jim does not have a powerful personality. On the other hand, he isn't the killer type. If he gets into a tough spot, he smiles his way out of it. If a stranger gets mad at him in traffic and yells and curses, ole Smiling Jim just keeps smiling and before long the stranger isn't mad anymore. He's smiling, too.

"Good ole Smiling Jim. I hate his guts."

9

Sunset Boulevard

Montgomery Clift reneged.

He had signed a contract with Paramount to star opposite Gloria Swanson in *Sunset Boulevard*. The cast had been hired, the sets built. Two weeks before the start of production, Montgomery Clift changed his mind. "I don't think I could be convincing making love to a woman twice my age," he announced.

"Bullshit!" raged Billy Wilder, director and co-writer of *Sunset Boulevard*. "If he's any kind of an actor, he could be convincing making love to *any* woman."

Montgomery Clift had another reason. With *The Search* and *Red River*, he had become the most sensational new star in postwar Hollywood, praised by serious critics and adored by teenaged girls. His advisers convinced him that he would alienate his young fans by playing gigolo to a faded movie queen.

Wilder and Charles Brackett, his producer and co-writer, needed a leading man immediately. Fred MacMurray? They had provided his best acting role in *Double Indemnity*. MacMurray read the partially completed script and replied that he didn't want to play a kept man. Marlon Brando? He was a Broadway sensation in *A Streetcar Named Desire* but untested in films. Gene Kelly? MGM wouldn't lend him.

Brackett and Wilder turned to the Paramount contract list. William Holden was a possibility, even though he seemed too blandly wholesome to play Joe Gillis, the luckless screenwriter willing to accept the ex-star's love and money.

Wilder remembered his casting problem with *The Lost Weekend*. He had wanted the alcoholic Don Birnam to be played by José Ferrer, then a dynamic Broadway star. The studio boss, Buddy DaSylva, insisted on Ray Milland, arguing, "The public won't give a damn about your drunk unless he is an attractive man, a life worth saving."

William Holden was certainly attractive, Wilder realized, although he had been unimpressed by the actor's work. And, unlike most actors, Holden *looked* as if he could be a writer.

Wilder, who had known Holden casually on the Paramount lot, invited him for drinks. As they talked, Wilder realized there was more depth to the young man than what he had displayed on the screen. Holden took a copy of the *Sunset Boulevard* script home and read it. He telephoned Wilder: "I like it. I'll do it. Let's go!"

Bill Holden was immediately plagued with self-doubt. "Jesus, I'm scared," he admitted to Ardis. "I've agreed to do this picture, and I'm not sure I can deliver."

Sunset Boulevard was the final and the most inspired collaboration of Charles Brackett and Billy Wilder. They were a curious match: Brackett the benign, urbane graduate of the New York literary world; Wilder the acerbic, cynical refugee from Nazi Germany. They began their partnership as writers, then Brackett produced and Wilder directed their scripts. Together they created an astonishing number of literate and popular films. After a dozen years of close association, the strain of diverse egos began to wear, and they argued throughout the preparation and filming of *Sunset Boulevard*.

The idea for the film started with Brackett. He suggested a different kind of movie about Hollywood, viewed through the eyes of a faded movie queen eager for a comeback. It would be a comedy depicting her adventures in the New Hollywood and ending in triumph over her old enemies. Wilder liked the notion, and he and Brackett worked with a third writer, D. M. Marshman, Jr., a former *Life* magazine film critic, perhaps as referee.

Wilder sparked to the idea of a relationship between the actress and a younger man: "She lives in the past and refuses to believe her days as a star are gone. She has sealed herself in one of those immense old rundown mansions on Sunset Boulevard amid a clutter of mementos, like a Grand Rapids Louis Quinze commode and a huge swan-shaped bed. We see the young man as a screenwriter. He's a nice guy, from the Middle West maybe. But he can't make the grade in Hollywood, and he's really down on his luck."

The trio continued mulling the plot with little inspiration until Wilder suddenly borrowed a note from Balzac's *Le Père Goriot:* "Suppose the old dame shoots the boy."

The writing progressed in a conspiratorial atmosphere, Brackett and Wilder fearing Paramount would veto their jaundiced view of

Hollywood. They reported fictitious plots for the script they were writing, which bore the official title *A Can of Beans*. Only when they were ready to start production did Brackett and Wilder disclose their subject to the startled executives. They had only forty pages of completed script.

Wilder wanted Mae West to play Norma Desmond, but she recoiled at the idea of being cast as a passé star. Pola Negri also declined to play a has-been. Mary Pickford liked the script but wanted it rewritten to make her more of the central figure. Brackett and Wilder declined.

Wilder told his casting troubles to George Cukor, who said the choice was obvious: Gloria Swanson.

After Swanson, everything fell in place. The casting of Max von Mayerling, Norma's chauffeur and former husband, was inspired: Erich von Stroheim, who had directed Miss Swanson in the uncompleted *Queen Kelly*. With the substitution of Holden for Clift, shooting began on April 11, 1949.

Miss Swanson was fifty, but her dedication to health and fitness made her appear ten years younger. Holden was thirty-one and looked it, but Joe Gillis was supposed to be twenty-five. He worried that the difference between the ages of Joe and Norma would not be dramatically apparent. Brackett gingerly suggested to Miss Swanson that she would need to wear makeup that would age her. She objected, arguing, "Can't you put the makeup on Mr. Holden instead, to make him look younger?" Her suggestion was accepted.

Miss Swanson and Holden formed an immediate rapport. She recalls that Holden, having joined the film so late, seemed uncertain of how to play his role. He admitted to Wilder, "I'm having trouble getting a bead on Joe Gillis."

"That's easy," the director replied. "Do you know Bill Holden?"

"Of course."

"Then you know Joe Gillis."

The real truth, suggested Wilder biographer Maurice Zolotow, was that Joe Gillis was not William Holden but a replica of Billy Wilder. As an impoverished young man in Berlin, Wilder had been a gigolo in a dance hall. While preparing *Sunset Boulevard*, he was engaged in a May-December romance, with himself as December and a beauty named Audrey Young as May. The character of Joe's real sweetheart, played by Nancy Olson, contained traits that friends recognized in Audrey Young.

Despite Miss Swanson's long absence from the screen, the filming of *Sunset Boulevard* progressed smoothly. Holden was amused with the byplay between Wilder and von Stroheim, who protested that his role was limited to opening limousine doors and saying, "Yes, madam." Once the feared autocrat of movie sets, von Stroheim arrived in the morning with script pages suggesting scenes such as Max's washing Norma's underwear. Wilder ignored them.

Nancy Olson, recently a UCLA student and an actress with only one previous film, was awed in such company. She found Bill Holden to be supportive and helpful, even mildly flirtatious, which contributed to their portrayals of the young lovers. She was the victim of one of Wilder's pranks.

The director was filming a love scene between Holden and Miss Olson at night on the balcony of the Paramount writers' building. Realizing the embarrassment of a girl in a kissing scene before a film crew and numerous visitors, Wilder made the rehearsal brief. He called for a take, which the actress performed ideally, despite her nerves.

"Cut! Print!" Wilder called. "Let's do it one more time, just for protection."

Holden and Miss Olson repeated their lines and began the embrace. This time the kiss didn't end with Wilder's call of "Cut!" Bill continued kissing Nancy as the crew members stifled their laughter.

"Cut!" The voice came from behind the camera. It was Ardis, who was among the visitors.

Sunset Boulevard was previewed in Evanston, Illinois, with catastrophic results. Over Brackett's strong protest, Wilder had opened the movie in the county morgue, with Joe Gillis conversing with other cadavers. The Illinois audience found the scene hilarious, and laughter continued throughout the movie. Wilder sought a more sophisticated audience on Long Island, New York. The response was worse. Paramount postponed release of *Sunset Boulevard* for six months amid rumors that the film might be shelved permanently.

Wilder realized the morgue opening had to be scrapped. He wrote a new scene with Gillis narrating the events leading to his death as his lifeless body floated in the swimming pool. It worked.

Paramount scheduled an August 1950 release for *Sunset Boulevard,* but the executives realized the film would be hard to sell. Miss Swanson was sent on a cross-country tour to call attention to her film return. The studio scheduled special screenings for the Hollywood press and film luminaries, hoping to spread a favorable word of mouth within the industry and thence to the nation. In one instance, the strategy failed.

Louis B. Mayer, still a powerful figure and guardian of Hollywood morality, emerged from a screening of *Sunset Boulevard* in a rage. "You bastard!" he ranted at Wilder. "You have disgraced the industry that made you and fed you. You should be tarred and feathered and run out of Hollywood."

Ordinarily master of the riposte, Wilder merely replied, "Fuck you."

Sunset Boulevard was Holden's first postwar film to play the Radio City Music Hall in New York, and the critical reaction was almost unanimously favorable. Thomas M. Pryor in *The New York Times* said Holden was doing the finest acting of his career—"his range and control of emotion never falter." While praising his work in the film, Pauline Kael added a personal note: "When in a mixture of piety and guilt, he makes love to the crazy, demanding old woman, he expresses a nausea so acute that we can almost forgive Holden his career during the past decade: this man knows the full self-disgust of prostitution."

Despite the favorable reviews, *Sunset Boulevard* was not a box-office hit. Its baleful view of Hollywood and its tragic ending *and* beginning failed to appeal to American audiences, especially in the sticks. Many persons were offended by the spectacle of a fifty-year-old woman seducing a man half her age.

For William Holden, *Sunset Boulevard* was a watershed film, signaling the unlamented death of Smiling Jim. A dozen years afterward, the *Golden Boy* promise had been realized. Hollywood's creative community could no longer dismiss him as a vapid pretty boy.

Sunset Boulevard provided the beginning of a long and productive relationship with Billy Wilder, extending beyond the normal interplay between filmmaker and star. Holden found Wilder a brilliant conversationalist, a brittle observer of the human comedy, both on and off the screen. The wry Viennese made Holden realize there was a world beyond the barbecue pits of the San Fernando Valley, a world of impressionist paintings and complicated music, of Escoffier food and far-off places. Holden was dazzled by Wilder's quicksilver wit and restless mind.

Holden intrigued Wilder, not merely as a manly Galatea, but as a talented actor and a complicated human being. Wilder says in retrospect, "This man, who was torn by many things, was an absolute, total professional. He was never late, he never came unprepared. I did find out on the second picture I did with him that he was an extremely shy, retiring, non-showoff actor who felt totally embarrassed. In my opinion, that drove him to the straight glass of gin before even breakfast. When he showed up on the set, he had taken measures of overcoming this kind of paralysis, of shyness, of what-am-I-doing-in-this-business? He was not a partygoer, you know. If you shot on location with him in Paris or Greece, he would go to the smallest hotel with the crew. He was not a showoff; he was the exact opposite. He was about the shyest actor I ever worked with, with the exception of Gary Cooper. Having been at it so long, Cooper took other measures to be able to face the makeup, the whir of the camera, the eyes fixed on him. Holden at lunchtime would need to have two or three martinis. But he was young, he was strong, and it didn't seem to matter. He was not the kind of actor who suddenly disappears and you find him in a hotel in Des Moines. Absolutely not. Going into the safari business, the endangered species reserves later on—that was what Holden was born for, not to be an actor."

Wilder, who had spent a lifetime dealing with actors of varying temperaments, found Holden refreshing. He enjoyed watching the young man's curiosity roam into country he had never explored. The interests of the two men merged, and their reactions grew similar. As always, Wilder could joke about it. One day Holden was seeking advice on the purchase of a painting. Wilder began, "If I were you—and I am . . ."

Another subtle change began in Bill Holden's life, and it concerned his marriage to Ardis. Friends believed that as long as Bill remained a journeyman actor the marriage retained a degree of stability. But after he became an unquestioned star, tensions began to appear. Ardis always claimed she hated her life as Brenda Marshall. Yet ambition had propelled her into the acting world in New York, and determination had kept her striving for success. She had achieved stardom in films, and for a time she was more famous than Bill. Now she had withdrawn from the alluring spotlight to become someone called Mrs. William Holden. No one called her Brenda anymore.

Ardis found ways to deflate Bill's ego. During an at-home interview, a reporter gushed, "Mrs. Holden, what's it like to be married to such a handsome man?" Ardis stared at her husband blankly and answered, "Oh, do you think that he's handsome?"

Confirmation of Bill Holden's new status in the film industry came with his Academy nomination for best performance by an actor in 1950. On March 29, 1951, he and Ardis arrived at the Pantages Theater and smiled through the blinding flash of news photographers. The Holdens took seats beside Billy Wilder and his bride, Audrey. Wilder himself was a nominee for his direction and co-writing of *Sunset Boulevard*.

For Holden, the ceremonies were disappointing. *Sunset Boulevard* had been nominated in eleven categories, and all were losing, including Nancy Olson, Erich von Stroheim, and Gloria Swanson. Wilder won an Oscar for co-writing the script but not as director. *All About Eve* was named best picture, and for best actor: José Ferrer in *Cyrano de Bergerac*.

Paramount had planned a celebration after the awards at the Mocambo on the Sunset Strip, and the Holdens and the Wilders dutifully attended. Holden managed a loser's smile for the photographers, but Wilder understood his crushing disappointment. With a mixture of caustic wit and helpful encouragement, Wilder tried to brighten the glum evening.

"It was a miscarriage of justice, Bill," Wilder commented over the nightclub din. "You really should have won tonight."

"Oh, I don't think so," Ardis remarked. "José Ferrer was much better than Bill."

Holden stared at her icily and poured himself another drink.

10

Solid Citizen

William Holden resolved to use *Sunset Boulevard* and the Academy nomination as leverage to exact better contracts from his two studios. For a dozen years, minus his time in the service, he had been working at terms he considered servitude, forced into inferior films, paid ludicrously low salaries. His contracts had been improved because of Charlie Feldman's intervention, but his pay was far from that of longer-established stars. Through embittering experience, he had grown to distrust all studio authority, and he insisted that his working conditions be detailed in his contracts. He became a tough fighter in the studio arena.

Francisco (Chico) Day, a veteran assistant director at Paramount, had known Bill Holden as the most professional of actors. If he saw Chico approach, Bill would put aside what he was doing and inquire, "What is it, Chico? Do you need me on the set?" Chico noticed a change in Bill during the studio filming of *The Streets of Laredo*.

One afternoon at four-thirty, Leslie Fenton, the director, ordered lighting for a complicated scene he wanted to film before the end of the day's shooting. At five fifty-five, Chico Day went to Holden's dressing room and asked him to report to the set.

"You see what time it is?" Holden snapped. "I don't work after six o'clock. It's in my contract."

Day relayed the information to Fenton, who burst into Holden's room and declared, "These people—electricians, grips, cameramen—have been working for an hour and a half to get this shot so we can finish with the set, and now you say you're not going to stay here and finish! Well, you are!"

Holden sulkily reported to the set and remained for three takes, then walked away. He accused Day of betraying him. "You know that I have a six-o'clock closing time," Holden said.

"I didn't know that," Day protested. "The front office has to tell me those things. I just follow directions around here."

After brooding over a couple of drinks in his dressing room, Holden climbed the stairs to Day's office. His apology was so moving that Chico wept. At the end of filming, Holden apologized again and presented the assistant director with a silver tray.

Holden had become a more worthy adversary of Harry Cohn. No longer would the actor accept assignments from Columbia unquestioningly. Holden once told me of an incident when Cohn had proposed a project that sounded like a B picture. Holden expressed his unhappiness to Cohn, neither accepting nor rejecting the film.

Four days later, Holden was summoned to Cohn's office, where he found the studio boss flanked by his chief assistant, Ben Kahane. "You're going to start the picture next week," Cohn declared.

"Wait a minute," Holden protested. "I haven't said I was going to do it."

"I sent you a script, you said you would do it," Cohn insisted. "I have witnesses."

Holden exploded: "You dirty cocksucker! Why don't you call all your flunkies in here to lie for you!" He raged out of the office, slamming the door behind him. He was overcome with remorse afterward. When he arrived home, he told Ardis, "Well, I did it today. I lost my head and screamed and raged at Harry Cohn. I'll probably be run out of the business."

At eight in the evening, Holden decided to call Cohn and apologize. Before he could reach for the telephone, it rang. Harry Cohn was on the other end. "I want to apologize," Cohn said. "I didn't treat you right today."

Holden laughed. "Another minute, Harry, and I would have called you to apologize."

"Look, Bill, you don't have to do that picture."

"Okay, Harry. I'm sorry I lost my temper. It taught me a lesson. I'll try never to do it again."

"Next time you're at the studio, drop into my office. We'll have a chat. Good night."

Holden's distrust of his employers and his concern that the profession of film acting lacked dignity led him to activism in the Screen Actors Guild. His close friend Ronald Reagan was president of the Guild, and he appointed Holden to the board. Holden served faithfully, maintaining regular attendance at meetings. He enjoyed the offstage camaraderie with his fellow actors, the bull sessions about grievances against the producers. He traveled to labor conventions, observed the inner workings of the Guild, took part in contract negotiations. He was elected first vice-president under Reagan and seemed the heir apparent.

Glenn Ford was a member of the SAG board at the same time, and Holden kidded his old rival without mercy. Most of the other members used normal expletives to express themselves; with Ford it was always "jeepers creepers!" Holden adopted that to refer to Ford. "Let's ask Jeepers Creepers about that," he'd say.

Contract negotiators sometimes spent long hours waiting in committee rooms for producers to respond to proposals. At such times Reagan drew from his large supply of show-business stories to relieve the boredom. One of them concerned Eddie Cantor and Joan Davis, who were conducting a brief romance while making a film together. One day Cantor was scheduled to perform a relatively easy stunt. The assistant director decided that Cantor, for safety's sake, should wear a protective jockstrap. "Bring Mr. Cantor's cup," the assistant called. From Joan Davis' dressing room came her unmistakable voice: "Make it a demitasse."

Inevitably, the talk at the midnight sessions turned to sex. One night the men exchanged myths about which race has the greatest sexual prowess. One of the actors suggested blacks, another Italians. Said another: "You're all wrong; the greatest lovers are Arabs." Bill Holden commented, "Gee, I hope I never have to follow Turhan Bey."

After late-night sessions at the Guild headquarters on Hollywood Boulevard, some of the board members went across the street to eat and drink and discuss Guild business at the Gotham, a delicatessen and bar.

Dana Andrews remembers a significant occasion: "After a meeting, Bill, Ronnie, and I went to the Gotham to continue our discussion. All three of us ordered drinks, and after we had talked for a while, the waiter came to the table, and Bill and I ordered another round. Ronnie said with surprise, 'Why do you want another drink? You just had one.'

"See what happened: Bill and I became alcoholics, and Ronnie became President of the United States."

In his autobiography *Where's the Rest of Me?* Ronald Reagan wrote of how he and Bill Holden conspired to fend off radical influences in the Screen Actors Guild. Hollywood was a battleground of opposing ideologies during the late 1940s, with many far-left figures trying to control guilds and unions. The struggle came to a bloody climax with a jurisdictional strike between the ultraliberal Conference of Studio Unions (CSU) and the conservative International Alliance of Theatrical Stage Employees (IATSE). John Howard Lawson, Dalton Trumbo, Sterling Hayden, and other leftists tried to organize support for the CSU.

Reagan told in his book of a telephone call from Bill Holden, who said excitedly, "I've found out there is a meeting at Ida Lupino's."

"But Ida isn't one of *them*," Reagan replied.

"I know. They're just borrowing her patio." Holden explained that Ida Lupino was one of a few innocents whose support of the CSU was being sought. "Let's go!" Bill said eagerly.

Holden drove Reagan to Miss Lupino's house, where they drew a chilly reception from the seventy-five guests. Sterling Hayden was chairman of the meeting, and the speakers heatedly denounced the IATSE and lauded the CSU, with slurs at the Screen Actors Guild for not joining the struggle.

As Reagan related: "I writhed in my seat but Bill held me back, like a jockey going into the stretch. At last, as the denunciations—in pretty familiar language by this time—had run down, Bill patted me. He said, 'Now!'

"I bounced to my feet and asked for the floor. Hayden gave it to me. I confronted one of the most hostile audiences I could ever hope to address. 'The SAG has been investigating this thing,' I said cheerfully, 'and we're happy to see groups like this so interested. But I thought there might be some facts you didn't know.' "

Amid the angry questions and jeering that followed the speech, John Garfield spoke up: "Why don't you listen to him?" Reagan noticed a well-known character actor push Garfield against a tree and jab a finger at his chest. Afterward Reagan and Holden discussed the incident, and they considered seeking out Garfield for a talk. They didn't, and Reagan later wondered how Garfield's life might have changed if they had. Blacklisted from films, he admitted to federal authorities shortly before his death in 1952 that he had been controlled by the Communist Party, though he was never a member. Once he had tried and failed to speak for himself—on Ida Lupino's patio.

Ronald Reagan appointed Bill Holden to serve with him as the Screen Actors Guild representatives on the Motion Picture Industry Council. Hollywood had suffered an attack of bad publicity, ranging from congressional exposés of Communists to the Ingrid Bergman–Roberto Rossellini scandal. Producers, guilds, and unions formed the Council in an attempt to win a better press by mutual constructive actions.

One evening Reagan and Holden took their places at a large round table at the producers association office where the Industry Council held its meetings. Reagan was uncharacteristically inattentive as the industry leaders discussed current problems. He wrote on a notepad and passed it to Holden. The message: "To hell with this, how would you like to be best man when I marry Nancy?"

"It's about time!" Holden exclaimed, and the Council members watched with concern as the two actors strode out of the room.

Bill was delighted with Reagan's decision. After Jane Wyman divorced him, Ronnie had seemed wounded and lost. Then he began dating Nancy Davis, the MGM actress, and he became the same buoyant Ronnie again. Both Bill and Ardis tried to help the romance along, inviting Nancy and Ronnie to dinner almost every weekend. The pair became engaged, but film commitments kept postponing a wedding. Bill worried that it might never happen.

Ardis made all the arrangements. The wedding was to be held March 4, 1952, at the Little Brown Church in the Valley, a tiny nondenominational church on Coldwater Canyon Boulevard. Ardis would be matron of honor, Bill best man. No one else was invited.

On the day of the wedding, Ardis was furious at Bill about something he had done and refused to talk to him or sit on the same side of the church. Neither the bride nor the bridegroom noticed. The bridal party went to the Holdens' house, where Ardis had arranged for a cake, a photographer, and a reception for a few friends. It was a joyful event, and Ardis smiled at everyone, except Bill.

William Holden's participation in film industry affairs prompted Norris Poulson, mayor of Los Angeles, to offer him an appointment as one of the five members of the Parks and Recreation Commission. Holden protested that he was already overloaded with activities and that shooting schedules and lengthy locations would hamper service as commissioner. Poulson persisted, citing the city's need for places where young people could play—young people like Holden's three children. He was persuaded. Holden began the routine of monthly meetings at City Hall, as well as periodic trips throughout the city to inspect future locations for parks and playgrounds. Included in the Commission's jurisdiction was Griffith Park, largest municipal park in the nation.

As Holden's career continued to build after *Sunset Boulevard*, he became the subject of national magazine articles, and writers stressed his qualities as a sound, normal, public-spirited citizen who was active not only in industry and city affairs but attended PTA meetings at his children's schools as well. Holden himself contributed to this impression in interviews.

Ezra Goodman of *Time* magazine interviewed Holden at a time when Humphrey Bogart and his chums were attracting notoriety as the free-spirited and hard-drinking Holmby Hills Rat Pack.

Said Holden: "It's terribly important for people to realize that their conduct reflects the way a nation is represented in the eyes of the world. That's why the rat-pack idea makes our job so tough. If you were to go to Japan or India or France and represent an industry which has made an artistic contribution to the entire world and were faced then with the problem of someone asking, 'Do they really have a rat pack in Holmby Hills?' what would you say? It makes your job doubly tough.

"In every barrel there's bound to be a rotten apple. Not all actors are bad. It may sound stuffy and dull, but it is quite possible for people to have social intercourse without resorting to a rat pack. . . ."

Holden's normalcy was depicted in the magazine stories by anecdotes of the minor catastrophes that plagued him. During an interview in Los Angeles in December 1981, Ronald Reagan related some of the stories. He remarked that he and Holden had been simpatico because each considered himself "the original guy who would be caught with a fork if it was raining soup."

The President cited an incident when Holden and Leon Ames, as board members of the Screen Actors Guild, were flying to New York on guild business:

"They got on one of those Constellations—that was the plane of the day then—and the only seats available were those two against the bulkhead facing backward. You couldn't sit back; you had to sit up straight all the way to New York—and you didn't get there as fast as you do now.

"Leon was bellyaching about this, and Bill said, 'Leon, why? I expect this sort of thing. It always happens to me.' He looked down the aisle, and a stewardess was coming with a tray full of coffee cups. He said, 'You see that girl with the coffee?' Leon said, 'Yeah, what about her?' Bill said, 'When she gets here, she'll spill that on me.' Leon said, 'You're out of your mind.'

"She was right opposite him when the whole damn tray dropped in Bill's lap. The girl was just frantic, and Bill said, 'I expected it.' "

Reagan cited another incident when he and Nancy Davis were

courting at the home of Bill and Ardis Holden in Toluca Lake. Ronald and Nancy arrived on a late summer afternoon.

"We pulled up in front of his house and the sprinklers were on, and they did come across the walk. Well, we honked and we yelled, and we couldn't get any attention. Finally we just ducked and ran through the water up to the door. And when Bill came to the door, I said, 'Fine thing, you know, how unwelcome can we be?'

"And he looked and said, 'Oh! I turned them on this morning. They've been on all day!' We looked, and the gutters were full of water flowing both ways down the street."

The President continued the story of what happened after dinner, when the two couples were conversing in the den. Reagan remarked, "Bill, what's a motorboat doing on your lawn?"

"Funny joke," Holden replied. "I didn't turn off the sprinklers."

"Bill, there's a motorboat on your lawn!" Reagan insisted.

All four gazed out the window and saw a Chris-Craft speedboat mounted on a trailer, attached to a Cadillac convertible. The trailer had sunk up to its hub in Holden's lawn. Holden stormed out to meet the interlopers, and his wife pleaded with Reagan: "You've got to go out there with him; he'll get in trouble."

"I wouldn't go out there for anything in the world," Reagan replied.

On his back lawn Holden encountered four drunks whose car and trailer had gone out of control during a U-turn. Holden blasted them: "You know, a guy tries to have a beautiful lawn and guys like you come along—"

"You're right," said one of the drunks contritely. "Most beautiful lawn we ever saw. We're sure sorry." Holden ended up helping them push the car and trailer out of his yard.

Reagan remembered a formal dinner at the Hollywood Palladium in honor of William Green, president of the AFL-CIO. Among the three thousand guests was Bill Holden, dazzlingly handsome in a white dinner jacket. As president of the Screen Actors Guild, Reagan went to the platform to add his words of praise for the labor patriarch. When he returned, he noticed a cluster of waiters at Holden's table. Reagan asked Nancy what had happened.

"A waiter spilled a tray of dessert," she said.

"Who on?"

"Who else? Bill—right down the back of his white dinner jacket."

One of the magazine articles told of the night Bill took Ardis to a neighborhood movie house. He was shocked to see ushers being rude to customers waiting in line. "They're ruining our industry," he ranted. "I'm going to complain to the manager."

"Calm down, Bill," Ardis urged.

"Who's the manager?" Bill demanded of a theater attendant.

"Mr. McConnell."

Bill tramped into the manager's office and began, "Mr. Holden, my name's Mr. McConnell, and I want to tell you—"

"No, no," the manager corrected. "*My* name's Mr. McConnell, and *your* name is Holden."

"Aw, the hell with it," Bill said, retreating to the lobby.

Holden's hypochondria was another subject for the article writers. One story concerned the time Holden and his old friend Hugh McMullen were starting to leave the Holden house when Bill was summoned to the telephone. As he was talking, he suddenly grabbed his chest. "My God, Hugh, I'm having a heart attack!" he gasped.

"Bill, we just had an earthquake," said McMullen.

Bill was repeatedly obsessed by the belief that his heart had stopped. He broke into Glenn Ford's dressing room at Columbia one day and exclaimed, "Glenn, my heart isn't beating!"

"That's ridiculous, Bill," Ford replied. "You wouldn't be standing here if your heart had stopped."

"I'm serious, Glenn! I can't feel it beating!"

"Bill, do me a favor. Run around the stage once. You'll find out your heart is beating." Only after he had raced around the stage was Bill satisfied that his heart was indeed functioning.

The magazine articles were titled "Bill Holden: I.Q. at the Box Office"; "Everything Happens to Him"; "The Guy with the Grin"; "Hollywood's Most Improbable Star." All proclaimed the theme of William Holden the good, solid, normal, all-American guy.

11

Waiting for Billy

"Don't worry, Bill," Billy Wilder assured his new friend. "I'll find another picture for you."

Meanwhile, William Holden was an actor under contract to two studios, and he was required to fulfill commitments. His first Paramount film after *Sunset Boulevard* was *Union Station,* a routine melodrama. To Bill Holden, it seemed like a retreat to the potboilers of his earlier career.

Holden told Harry Cohn he didn't want to make *Born Yesterday.*

"What the hell do you mean?" Cohn demanded. "It's a goddam hit play!"

"I know it's a hit play, Harry. I've seen it. There are two great parts: Harry Brock and Billie Dawn. The reporter is nothing."

"We can fix that. We'll build the part up."

"You know as well as I, Harry, that every time you build up a part you destroy the balance that made the story work."

Harry Cohn would not accept Holden's refusal. He realized that he had to make *Born Yesterday* succeed. Over the protests of his brother and ever-critical partner, Jack Cohn, Harry had bought the play for $1 million, a record in the film industry. If the movie did not prove a hit, Jack could accuse his brother of squandering Columbia's treasury. *Born Yesterday* held a special attraction for Harry Cohn: he could identify with Harry Brock. No wonder. Garson Kanin had named the character after his longtime adversary and had borrowed Cohn's personality traits.

"That goddam Holden won't do your play," Cohn complained to Kanin. "Tell the stupid bastard that he's got to do it."

"I'm not going to tell him anything," Kanin replied. "An actor has to come to a role with a certain enthusiasm. He can't perform if you force him."

74

"Bullshit! I do it all the time. Talk to Holden. He's your friend."

"Not really. I knew Bill for a while in the army, that's about it. But I'll talk to him."

Kanin met with Holden and reasoned: "Why don't you do the picture. It's pretty sure to be a hit."

"I know that," Holden replied. "It's a terrific comedy. But the reporter is the third part. I'd rather do the lead in a less important picture."

"Look, Bill, I conceived *Born Yesterday* with three equal parts. Paul is just as important as Harry and Billie. Paul is the guy who gets the girl. He's the intellectual who scores the points. What happened with the play was that I had great luck in finding Judy Holliday to play Billie, and I had great luck in finding Paul Douglas to play Harry. But I couldn't find an actor who could stand up to them. Gary Merrill is a good actor, but he just couldn't match Judy and Paul. But you've got the experience and the presence to make the difference."

"Not if the words aren't there."

"That can be fixed."

"So Harry Cohn said. But how can you believe Harry Cohn?"

Holden told Cohn he would appear in *Born Yesterday*. Paul Douglas declined to repeat his role as Harry Brock, claiming the movie script had been written to favor the Billie Dawn role. Cohn chose Broderick Crawford, who had won an Oscar for another Cohn-like role, Willie Stark in *All the King's Men*. George Cukor was assigned to direct; and he, Kanin, and others persuaded Cohn to hire the original Billie Dawn, Judy Holliday.

Cohn did not announce the casting of Miss Holliday, hoping to collect publicity with a Search for Billie Dawn, as he had done with *Golden Boy*. Cohn ordered Holden and Crawford to perform in screen tests with several well-known actresses, including Paul Douglas' wife, Jan Sterling.

"This is embarrassing," Holden confided to Crawford. "What do we say to them? That the part is already filled? That'll break their hearts."

"I agree," said Crawford. "I'll tell you what we'll do. You and I will overact so much in the tests that those girls will look good."

George Cukor needed ensemble playing from three actors who had never worked together. He persuaded Cohn to let him rehearse *Born Yesterday* for two weeks, then perform it for six nights in a makeshift theater on the lot. Although he hadn't been on a stage since he played Papa Curie, Holden was pleased with the plan. Both Crawford and Miss Holliday had played *Born Yesterday* in the theater. Appearing before an audience would give him a chance to match their knowledge of how audiences responded to the play.

Holden embarked on the play with enthusiasm, learning the entire script in three days. He worked intensely with Brod and Judy, and they cued him where the laughs occurred. Cukor directed the rehearsals. One day he was called to a meeting in Cohn's office, and the stage manager from the New York production substituted. He repeatedly chided Holden: "That's not the way Gary Merrill did it."

Bill seethed under the corrections, finally snapped, "I'm not Gary Merrill, I'm Bill Holden, and this is the way *I* think it should be played."

The staging of *Born Yesterday* at Columbia became a Hollywood event, with stars and producers from other studios invited to the performances. The audiences cheered at the final curtain, and Bill felt an added confidence, having maintained pace with the stage-trained actors. He was especially proud the night his father and mother attended, and he took them backstage to meet his co-stars.

The filming of *Born Yesterday* created an intimacy among the three stars that transcended the customary closeness of a movie set. Both men adored Judy, and she was grateful for their encouragement and support for her once-in-a-career opportunity. Bill and Brod had known each other casually as Columbia contract players; now they became friends. Bill delighted in Brod's irreverence toward authority and was enthralled by stories of Crawford's theatrical family.

"My grandfather, William E. Broderick, was a comic opera singer and a great character," said Crawford. "He gave me some advice which I still observe to this day."

"What was that?" Holden asked.

"He said, 'Always stand in back of the man who fires a gun and in front of the man who shits. Then you won't be shot at or shit on.'"

Crawford and Holden became eager co-conspirators in the needling of Harry Cohn. Their proudest achievement started one noon in the executive dining room, where Cohn held court each day over lunch. Crawford and Holden were among the few actors allowed in the dining room, and they delighted in taunting Cohn by ordering large glasses of Scotch. "You guys are going to be too drunk to work this afternoon," Cohn thundered.

One day Holden glanced at a racing form on the table. "Let's take a look at that," he suggested to Crawford.

Both had been to the racetrack with James Cagney to watch his pacers and trotters, but they knew nothing about regular thoroughbred racing. They studied the day's entries.

"That seems like an interesting name for a horse," said Crawford.

"I like this one, too," said Holden.

"Let's bet yours to win and mine to place," Crawford suggested.

Cohn, who was such an avid horseplayer that he had a private telephone line to his bookmaker, listened to their selections with derisive amusement. "Dumb actors," he grumbled.

In five races, the actors picked two winners and three places. On the following day, they bet six races and no horse finished less than second. The dining-room busboy conveyed the news to Harry Cohn.

Holden was called to the telephone on the *Born Yesterday* set. "Where did you get your information?" Cohn demanded. He would not accept Holden's answer that he and Crawford had made their choices solely on hunches. Holden put down the telephone and told Crawford, "You're next." Then Crawford received Cohn's call and denied access to track information. Cohn was unrelenting. He assigned his legal counsel, Lester Roth, a former appellate court judge, to discover the identity of the two actors' bookie or tout. Roth failed in his search, and Cohn decreed that neither Holden nor Crawford would be allowed outside telephone calls.

Born Yesterday completed filming of interiors at the studio, and the company shifted to Washington, D.C., for location scenes. Judy Holliday traveled by train, since she wouldn't fly. Bill Holden and Brod Crawford went by plane, spending most of the flight in the lounge. As they were drinking, Bill glanced at the stewardess advancing toward them with another round of drinks.

"I'll bet you a hundred dollars that when she gets here she spills the tray on me," said Bill.

"You're on," said Brod. When the stewardess reached them, the plane shook, and the drinks landed in Holden's lap.

"Don't worry, I won't even charge the airline to clean my suit," said Holden, pointing to Crawford. *"He'll* pay for it."

The film company was lodged at the Hilton Hotel, where Holden and Crawford regularly ordered beluga caviar and Dom Pérignon champagne and charged them to Columbia Pictures. "Wait till Harry Cohn sees that!" they chortled.

Born Yesterday proved to be a huge success, making a star of Judy Holliday and vindicating Harry Cohn's million-dollar investment in the play. As Bill Holden had expected, the major attention went to Judy, then to Brod Crawford. Only a few perceptive critics cited William Holden's contribution to the comedy.

Force of Arms, a Warner Brothers war film with an obvious resemblance to *A Farewell to Arms,* reunited Bill Holden and Nancy Olson. She was miserable, being pregnant in a failing marriage to Alan Jay Lerner and subjected to the verbal abuse of the director, Michael Curtiz. Bill seemed unaware of her problems. He was having his own with Ardis.

Submarine Command was the fourth Holden-Olson film, and reviewers predicted an enduring team. It was their last movie together.

Co-starring in *Submarine Command* was Don Taylor, an easygoing, affable actor who became Holden's partner in drinking and pranks. Dressed in naval uniforms, they left their set one afternoon to visit a nearby stage where Ronald Reagan was acting in a South Seas movie. They surprised Reagan by turning up in a crowd scene. The assistant director told Holden his appearance required an extra's check, adding, "Shall I sent it to charity?"

"Yes," said Bill, "my favorite charity: Bill Holden."

Boots Malone at Columbia and *The Turning Point* at Paramount continued the string of routine films that Bill Holden feared would dissipate the advance he had made in *Sunset Boulevard.*

"Where's that picture you said you'd find for me?" Bill kept asking Billy Wilder. Finally Wilder found it.

12

Triumph: *Stalag 17*

Billy Wilder was hungry for a hit. After the breakup with Charles Brackett on *Sunset Boulevard,* he had become his own producer. His first film was *Ace in the Hole,* a bitter tale disliked by reviewers and audiences. Paramount reasoned the title was at fault and rereleased the film as *The Big Carnival.* Same result.

Wilder was impressed by a Broadway play, *Stalag 17,* a comedy-drama about American prisoners in a German camp. Although the play was a hit, no studio was interested in an all-male story centered in a prisoners' barracks. Wilder himself bought *Stalag 17* for $50,000.

He took the play to Paramount and began writing a script with Edwin Blum. The central figure was Sefton, a cynical survivor with a well-hidden heroic streak. At first Wilder designed the script for Charlton Heston. But as Sefton became more cynical and less heroic in the writing, Wilder began thinking of Bill Holden.

When Holden was leaving on a publicity trip to New York, Wilder advised him to see *Stalag 17.* On Holden's return, the director asked his opinion.

"I walked out after the first act," Holden admitted. "I just didn't find it very exciting. And I thought Sefton was just a con man without any motivation for the deals he's pulling."

"I've changed that, Bill," said Wilder. "You'll see when you read the script. I want you to play Sefton."

"But I thought you were writing it for Charlton Heston."

"I can't get him. So you're my boy."

"Second choice again, huh?"

"Well, you didn't do so badly the last time, Bill."

When Holden read the *Stalag 17* script, he was both thrilled and apprehensive. Sefton was the best role he had ever been offered, better than Joe Gillis, who was subject to the looming shadow of Norma Desmond. Sefton was always center stage, whether visible or not, reviled, suspected, assaulted, and, finally, applauded. Bill had played pleasant young men for so long that he worried whether he would be convincing as an anti-hero.

"Couldn't I have a line or two that would show Sefton really hates the Germans?" Holden asked.

Wilder allowed no tampering with his scripts. He emphasized that on the first day of filming when he announced to the assembled cast that not one syllable of the dialogue would be changed during production. The edict was meant for all the actors, but especially Holden and Otto Preminger, the director who took the role of the sadistic camp commander.

Holden, his hair crew-cut and his face unshaved to mask his handsomeness, approached the role with intensity. Normally an affable figure on a movie set, he seemed withdrawn and introspective. Members of the cast had worked together in the play, and some were comedians. The *Stalag 17* set was often noisy with wisecracks and horseplay. One day the noise level reached a peak and Holden yelled: "Goddammit, can't you guys shut up for a minute! Some of us are trying to get some work done!"

Everyone on the set was startled and embarrassed, especially Bill Holden. Wilder quickly started the scene, and nothing was said about the outburst.

Don Taylor, cast as a heroic prisoner, noticed a change in Holden. During *Submarine Command,* Holden had complained, "Dammit, I was so negative in that scene. I wish I could play it like you; you're always all-out, wide open all the time." As Sefton, Taylor observed, Holden himself was playing wide open, holding nothing back.

As his confidence in the performance grew, Holden became more at ease on the set, even frivolous. One day he invited a beautiful actress to his dressing room for romance in the afternoon. He and Taylor were called for a scene atop the water tower. When they completed a take, Holden looked down in horror. Ardis was standing at the bottom of the tower, white-faced.

"Oh, my God, there goes my whole life!" he gasped. "I'll lose everything—the children, the house, my savings. She's caught me with a girl in my dressing room!"

Bill climbed slowly down the ladder, and he was shaking when he faced the distraught Ardis.

"Something terrible has happened!" she exclaimed.

"What?"
"I smashed up the car."
"Marvelous!" he exclaimed.

Having played the scrounger and suspected collaborator, Holden re-
lished the scene of Sefton's vindication when he accuses Price (Peter
Graves) as the spy who had betrayed the Americans to their captors.

> SEFTON
> *(confronting Price)*

Sprechen sie deutsch?

> PRICE

No. I don't sprechen sie deutsch.

> SEFTON

Maybe just one word? Kaput? Because you're kaput, Price.

> PRICE

Will you get this guy out of my hair so I can go?

> SEFTON

Go where? To the Kommandant's office and tell him where
Dunbar is?

> PRICE
> *(starting for him)*

I'll kill you for that!

> SEFTON

Shut up!

> *(slaps his face)*

Security office, eh? Screening everybody, only who screened
you? Great American hero! From Cleveland, Ohio! Enlisted
right after Pearl Harbor! When was Pearl Harbor, Price? Or
don't you know?

> PRICE

December seventh, forty-one.

> SEFTON

What time?

> PRICE

Six o'clock. I was having dinner.

> SEFTON

Six o'clock in *Berlin*. They were having lunch in Cleveland.

> *(to the others)*

Am I boring you, boys?

> HOFFY

Go on.

SEFTON

He's a Nazi, Price is. For all I know, his name is Preismaier or Preissinger. Sure, he lived in Cleveland, but when the war broke out he came back to the Fatherland like a good little Bundist. He spoke our lingo, so they put him through spy school, gave him phony dogtags . . .

The other prisoners recognize Price's perfidy and pounce on him. Lest he be considered soft, Sefton has a final word for his comrades before the concluding escape: "If I ever run into any of you bums on a street corner, just let's pretend we never met before. Understand?"

Stalag 17 was released in the summer of 1953 and became an enormous hit, amassing $10 million at the nation's theaters. Holden was nominated for an Academy Award, along with Marlon Brando for *Julius Caesar*, Richard Burton for *The Robe,* and Montgomery Clift and Burt Lancaster for *From Here to Eternity.*

"I really thought Burt would win," Holden told me at the time. "After I saw *From Here to Eternity,* I was so overwhelmed that I sent wires to everyone concerned with it. I honestly believed that Burt did the best acting of the year, and I told him so when I saw him one night in Chasen's. I felt adequate in *Stalag 17,* but I was never really simpatico with Sefton."

Holden escorted Ardis to the Pantages Theater on March 25, 1954, with the expectation that he would lose the Oscar again. But this time he won. He hurried to the stage, ready to thank his parents, his wife, Billy Wilder, and all those connected with *Stalag 17.* He was told that the telecast was running overtime, so he said only, "Thank you." At the party afterward in Chasen's, Bill lifted his champagne glass to Wilder, the man who had remembered to find him another part.

Bill didn't want the evening to end, and he and Ardis drove to the home of Paul Clemens and his wife. The two couples sat in the comfortable den, drank brandy, and relived the evening's events.

"I still can't believe it," said Bill, gazing wonderingly at the golden statuette on the coffee table.

"Well, you know, Bill," Ardis said in a matter-of-fact tone, "you really didn't get the award for *Stalag.* They gave it to you for *Sunset Boulevard.*"

Bill lowered his eyes and ground his teeth, as he always did in moments of stifled anger. He was still seething when he arrived home.

He missed the driveway, hit the brick post, and tore a fender off his Cadillac. When Bill awoke the next morning, he was sitting in his favorite leather chair in the den, still wearing his tuxedo, the Oscar in his lap.

With the Oscar, William Holden was acknowledged as an accomplished film actor. It helped establish his financial independence as well. Despite improvements in his contracts, Bill had been unable to acquire any savings. If he took a suspension rather than accept a film he disliked, he could hold out for eight months before his resources would be exhausted. He devised another method to avoid unwanted films, telling his bosses, "Lend me out to another studio, pay my salary, and you can keep whatever's left over."

After *Stalag 17*, Paramount realized it could no longer hold on to its underpaid star. Charlie Feldman negotiated a new contract, which tied Holden to Paramount for only three months a year at $250,000. He was required to make only two more films at the previous salary, one for Paramount and one for Columbia.

Holden's first movie as an independent star proved a bonanza.

Otto Preminger had become friendly with Holden on *Stalag 17*, and he proposed a partnership to produce *The Moon Is Blue*, based on a mildly risqué Broadway comedy by F. Hugh Herbert. The film created sensational publicity in 1953 when Preminger defied the Production Code, refusing to excise such banned words as "virgin," "mistress," and "seduction." It was the first challenge to the industry's self-censorship, and Preminger fueled the controversy with skill. Public curiosity was aroused, and *The Moon Is Blue* provided Bill Holden with his first big profit in fifteen years as an actor. His income from a one-third interest amounted to $600,000.

Holden returned to Paramount for the final film under his old contract, *Forever Female*. He hated it and resented working for a fraction of his value. He found a drinking companion in Paul Douglas, and they remained drunk through most of the production.

Escape from Fort Bravo was a happier experience. It was an MGM western with Eleanor Parker, who had recently married Bill's friend Paul Clemens. Others complained about the 120-degree heat on the Death Valley location; Bill delighted in it.

Holden was second choice for the lead in *Executive Suite* at MGM. The producer, John Houseman, had sought Henry Fonda, but Fonda dropped out to train for a Broadway musical that was never produced.

Holden joined a multi-star cast that included his two favorites, Fredric March and Barbara Stanwyck.

Directing on a tight budget with dialogue-heavy scenes, Robert Wise rehearsed the actors before the start of filming. Bill Holden, realizing he would be working with stage-trained actors, memorized his entire dialogue before the first rehearsal. June Allyson did not.

Miss Allyson was cast in her familiar role as the loyal wife. She arrived late to the first rehearsal and read her lines with script in hand. During an embrace, Holden glanced over her shoulder to Wise with an expression of "What the hell is this?"

Miss Allyson's agent telephoned Houseman that evening to report that the actress was in hysterics, claiming that the rest of the cast was persecuting her. The matter was smoothed over, and Miss Allyson was neither late nor unprepared thereafter.

Bogie was in a snit.

Every evening as he passed Bill Holden's dressing room, he could hear the rattle of ice cubes and the tinkle of Audrey Hepburn's laughter and Holden's hearty guffaw as they listened to Billy Wilder's witticisms.

"Those Paramount bastards didn't invite me," he muttered as he drove to his home in Holmby Hills. "Well, fuck 'em."

Humphrey Bogart knew that he hadn't been Wilder's first choice to play the hardworking brother of a rich Long Island family in *Sabrina*. Wilder—along with Samuel Taylor, author of the play *Sabrina Fair*, and young Ernest Lehman—had designed Linus Larrabee with Cary Grant in mind. But Grant had declined the script, and Bogart was chosen. Wilder had planned to cast a young actor as the wastrel David Larrabee, but Bogart's weathered face required a brother closer to his age. As always, Bill Holden was a willing substitute.

The title role of the chauffeur's daughter who enchants both brothers had already been decided: Audrey Hepburn, Paramount's number-one leading lady after her Academy Award debut in *Roman Holiday*.

Sabrina was troubled from the start. Because of commitments for the three stars, Wilder was forced to begin production without a completed script, and he and Lehman could barely supply pages in time for each day's shooting. One day Lehman finished new dialogue and delivered his only copies to Wilder and Holden. Bogart, who felt like an outsider among the Paramount regulars, became incensed and stalked off the set. He refused to report for work the following day, and Wilder was forced to shut down production.

Above: The Beedle home, 319 North Cherry Street, O'Fallon, Illinois (photo: Barbara Hertenstein). *Left:* One-year-old Bill with his father. *Below:* With his mother in O'Fallon.

Left: Bill on horseback in the Illinois farmland. *Below:* His first bicycle in California.

Left: Bill at fourteen in South Pasadena. *Below:* Showing his strength during workouts for *Golden Boy* (1939). © Columbia Pictures

Holden hated the hair curling and dyeing for
Golden Boy. Movie Star News

Joe Bonaparte's father (Lee J. Cobb) confronts him as
trainer (Don Beddoe) looks on. © Columbia Pictures

Those Were the Days (1940), a letdown for the new star (with Bonita Granville, Ezra Stone, Judith Barrett). © Paramount Pictures

Right: Holden and Glenn Ford with Badman Addison Richards, *Texas,* 1941 (photo: © Columbia Pictures). *Below:* With Jean Arthur in *Arizona,* 1941 (photo: © Columbia Pictures).

On the set of *Texas*. © Columbia Pictures

With Claire Trevor, *Texas*. © Columbia Pictures

Conventional studio portrait, about 1947.
Movie Star News

Landlady harasses Richard
Webb, Holden, and Ellen
Drew, *The Remarkable
Andrew* (1942).
© Paramount Pictures

Young and Willing (1943),
Bill's last film before army
service (with Mabel Paige,
James Brown, Susan
Hayward, Eddie Bracken).
United Artists

The Holdens at the Oscar
ceremonies during the war

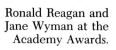

Ronald Reagan and
Jane Wyman at the
Academy Awards.

bove: With Jeanne Crain, *Apartment for Peggy* (1948). 20th Century-Fox

Right: Glenn Ford, Ellen Drew, Holden, *The Man from Colorado* (1949). © Columbia Pictures

Below: Brian Donlevy (as Andrew Jackson for *The Remarkable Andrew*) admires wedding ring. © Paramount Pictures

Paul Clemens' portrait of Ardis and the children

New stepfather plays cards with Virginia.
© Columbia Pictures

Scott, six years old, Bill, and West, nine, on diving board at Toluca Lake.
© Paramount Pictures

Left: Director George Marshall teaches Lucille Ball and Holden to roll cigarettes, *Miss Grant Takes Richmond,* 1949 (photo: © Columbia Pictures). *Below:* A publicity shot for the American Cancer Society (photo: Pictorial Parade).

The film that changed Holden's career: *Sunset Boulevard* with Gloria Swanson (1950).
© Paramount Pictures

Judy Holliday, Broderick Crawford, Holden, *Born Yesterday* (1950).
© Columbia Pictures

Teaching Billie Dawn to read the newspaper in *Born Yesterday.*
© Columbia Pictures

Another setback, *Boots Malone*
(1952) with Johnny Stewart.
© Columbia Pictures

Brod Crawford, restrained by
Howard St. John, tries to throttle
Holden, *Born Yesterday*.
© Columbia Pictures

Brother Richard Beedle played a
small role in *Stalag 17* (1953).
© Paramount Pictures

Above: Holden's first big moneymaker, *The Moon Is Blue* (1953) with Maggie McNamara (photo: United Artists). *Left:* Presenting the Oscar to Grace Kelly for *The Country Girl,* 1954 (photo: Wide World Photos). *Below:* Stanwyck and Holden in a tense scene from *Executive Suite,* 1954 (photo: MGM).

Top: Han Suyin (Jennifer Jones) asks her family's permission to marry Mark Elliott (Holden) in *Love Is a Many-Splendored Thing,* 1955 (photo: 20th Century-Fox). *Middle:* The Reagan wedding (photo: Wide World Photos). *Bottom:* As a playboy in *Sabrina,* 1954 (photo: Pictorial Parade).

1954 portrait by Philippe Halsman in his studio in New York
City. Copyright by Philippe Halsman

When Bogart received new pages of dialogue, he made snide comments to Wilder. He asked if the director had any children. Yes, Wilder replied, a young daughter. "Did she write this?" Bogart cracked.

Wilder refused to defer to Bogart, and the bitterness intensified. Bogart dismissed *Sabrina* as a "crock of crap" and complained to *Time*'s Ezra Goodman that "Wilder is the kind of Prussian German with a riding crop. He's the type of director I don't like to work with. He works with the writer and excludes the actor. I didn't even know what the end of the picture would be, as to who gets Sabrina."

Wilder, the Austrian Jew, explained: "Of course Bogart gets the girl. That's because he is getting three hundred thousand for the picture, and Holden is getting a hundred and a quarter."

Bogart sometimes directed his anger at Miss Hepburn. When she had trouble with dialogue, he snapped, "Maybe you should stay home and study your lines instead of going out every night."

Holden made no complaint about losing the girl or even the bleaching of his hair, which Wilder suggested for a Jay Gatsby look. Bill enjoyed the locations at Glen Cove, Long Island, and many times repeated an incident that happened there.

The *Sabrina* principals had been invited to several parties by the Long Island wealthy but had resisted, pleading the press of work. One invitation could not be avoided. They were bidden to the mansion of an enormously rich family who had helped enlist their rich friends to work as extras in party scenes. Holden, Bogart, and Audrey Hepburn dutifully agreed to attend.

The dinner was unbelievably lavish, with butlers standing behind the chairs of each guest. At the end of the feast, the host tapped his wineglass with a fork and announced that his daughter, an accomplished pianist, would play for the guests. The guests moved on to the gilded music room to prepare for the concert. They were joined by the matriarch of the family, a Victorian lady in a wheelchair.

The room quieted, and the daughter began playing a Chopin sonata. Suddenly the Great Dane that had been sleeping under the piano leaped up and raced out the open doors and down the wide sweeping lawn toward Long Island Sound. The concert continued, and afterward Holden asked his host what had happened. "Oh," the man replied, "we always beat the dog when Grandma farts." This story was later used in Blake Edward's film *10*.

Holden was eager to please his mentor. One scene called for him to vault over a fence as he approached Audrey. He performed the leap with total ease on the first take. "That was good, Bill," said Wilder, "but a little too fast. Could you do it a little slower, please." To the astonishment of the director and everyone else, Holden repeated the leap and seemed almost to pause in the air before landing.

A climactic scene called for Bogart to land a haymaker on Holden's chin, sending him the length of a corporate board table. "It's very simple," Wilder instructed Holden. "You just take the blow, do a back flip, then roll down the length of the table."

"I know, Billy." Holden nodded. "It's just the usual roll-down-the-board-table shot."

As the camera turned, Holden took Bogart's fake blow, reeled back to the table, did a reverse somersault and landed in a sitting position, continuing his dialogue.

Offstage, Holden had no quarrel with Bogart and tried to maintain an atmosphere of congeniality. He hadn't slighted Bogart on his dressing-room cocktail gatherings; he presumed Bogart would hurry home to his wife and children. In any case, Bill's mind was on other matters besides a paranoiac co-star.

Ernie Lehman recognized what was happening when he dropped into Bill's dressing room one day. Lehman had been working so hard on rewrites of the *Sabrina* script that he had broken down in a weeping fit in a corner of the stage. "Go home and get some rest; you deserve it," Wilder said. Before leaving, Lehman wanted to say goodbye to Bill Holden.

He walked into Holden's dressing room unannounced. He found Bill and Audrey standing a foot apart facing each other, their eyes meeting. Lehman said his farewell and departed, realizing something profound was happening between Bill Holden and Audrey Hepburn.

13

"Warm Up the Ice Cubes"

"I have to pull out all the stops when I talk about Holden," Ronald Reagan told me in 1955.

"Bill can be pretty excitable. Sometimes he gets all wrought up from worry and overwork, and I have to take him aside and say, 'Bill, the sun will still come up on schedule tomorrow. There's no sense in making a federal case out of everything.'"

Reagan added prophetically, "Every once in a while Bill goes flying off on a tangent. I've wet-nursed him through the sports-car stage and many another. He's just as liable to read a book on Africa and announce he's leaving on safari."

After the Oscar for *Stalag 17*, Holden managed to sublimate the wildness of his nature. He liked to think of himself as a businessman, as if acting in movies equated to selling bonds or managing real estate. His base of operations at the Paramount studio was designed not as a dressing room for a star but as an office. It was across the street from dressing-room row, where the other Paramount stars were located. Holden was assigned his own studio secretary, whereas other stars shared the services of Alice Moriarty, known in publicity releases as the Secretary to the Stars.

Y. Frank Freeman approved Holden's special status because of the actor's service in public relations. Holden acted as Paramount spokesman for such promotions as VistaVision, the studio's wide-screen answer to 20th Century–Fox's CinemaScope. Visiting royalty and political dignitaries were taken first to Holden's office before tours of the studio.

Elinor Moller, a petite, quiet-spoken, intelligent blonde, was assigned to be William Holden's secretary. He gave her three instructions: never hurry back to the office from anything; never worry about missing a phone call—if it's important, they'll call back; everything in the office is yours, food, drink, etc. She quickly learned his daily routine when he was not filming. He telephoned from home at eleven with the instructions "Warm up the ice cubes." He arrived ten minutes later for the first of his two drinks before lunch. He dictated answers to mail from business associates, exhibitors, and servicemen he had met on his travels, and for matters concerning the Parks and Recreation Commission, Screen Actors Guild, and the Academy of Motion Picture Arts and Sciences, of which he was a governor. He chided Elinor for answering fan letters, but she insisted some of them were worthy of answer and his attention.

The office was decorated with artworks Holden had collected during his travels, and he enjoyed rearranging them for visual impact. Often he took a feather duster to the paintings and sculptures. Elinor made regular orders of liquor, which Holden paid for, from the studio commissary. Only the best: Johnnie Walker Black Label Scotch, Jack Daniel's bourbon, Beefeater gin, Smirnoff vodka. The abundance of good booze and genial company made Bill Holden's office a mecca for other stars on the lot. Fredric March, who didn't like to eat in the commissary because of a nervous condition, lunched in Holden's office and liked to spend part of the hour dancing with Elinor to phonograph records. Dean Martin was a steady customer, and Bill delighted in his humor. As he was stirring martinis, Martin stared up at three Javanese puppets spotlighted in a wall niche. "I always wondered what happened to the Andrews Sisters," he said.

After several drinks, George Gobel admired a small Japanese sculpture, and Bill insisted that the comedian take it with him. The next day Gobel returned and remarked, "I'm a collector, too." He presented Holden with an airplane spanner wrench. Holden had the wrench mounted, and it became one of the wall decorations.

Bill found the decoration he needed for over the bar. Paul Clemens loaned his painting of Maddy Comfort, the black model who had skinny-dipped in the Holden pool. The portrait showed her nude and languorous on a flowered chaise, sunning herself amid geraniums. Bill was enchanted with the painting, but Ardis wouldn't allow him to hang it in the house. He moved it to the office, anxious for the approval of his art adviser, Billy Wilder.

Wilder came to the office one evening and sipped a drink while discussing industry affairs with Holden. Wilder said nothing about the Clemens painting, seemed not even to notice it. When the conversation was over, Wilder rose, kissed the nude figure on the crotch, and walked out the door.*

Holden was sometimes not amused by Jerry Lewis, especially when the comedian during his tie-cutting period snipped off Bill's tie with scissors. When Lewis heard that Holden's office was being redecorated, he insisted that his dressing room be redecorated first. Bill and Elinor occupied a small one-room office until the work was completed.

When Jerry Lewis was going through his Al Jolson period, he played his records of "Mammy" and "Rockabye My Baby" full blast in his dressing room across the street. Holden found it difficult to conduct business, and he asked Lewis to reduce the volume. The sound was turned louder. Holden went to the prop department and borrowed an elephant gun. He crashed into Lewis's dressing room and ordered, "Turn that fucking record down or I'll blast you all the way to Vine Street." The record was silenced.

Not only stars and directors visited the Holden office. He had friends in every department: Rufus Blair from publicity, Wayne Warga of security, Bud Fraker the still photographer, Victor Honig the barber. Bill remembered those who had helped him in the early years. When he won the Academy Award, he sent an Oscar medallion to Milt Lewis, the man who picked him out of the Pasadena Playbox. Lewis had bet him at five-to-one odds that he would beat out the other four contenders. The inscription: "M.L. The odds were always 5 to 1. B.H."

Holden sent another medallion to Artie Jacobson. Bill had often told the talent chief that if his acting career failed, "I can always go back to selling horseshit in the family business." The inscription on the medallion: "A.J.—instead of a pack of shit—B.H."

An important member of the Holden team was Sugar.

He was the subject of legends: that his high, soft voice and feminine manner were the result of a World War I wound; that he had been a championship boxer; that he had saved Brian Donlevy's life in a movie-set accident; that Holden had won Sugar from Donlevy in a poker game.

Little was known about Sugar, and few knew his real name, Byron Fitzpatrick. He arrived in Hollywood in the 1930s, became Donlevy's

---

*When he moved overseas, Holden returned the Maddy Comfort painting to Clemens. Blake Edwards owned it for many years, then presented it to Holden, who kept the painting in the bedroom of his Palm Springs house during his final years.

stand-in, dresser, and gofer. When Donlevy moved to Universal after the war, Sugar stayed at Paramount, which was close to where he lived. He shifted his allegiance to Bill Holden.

While Bill was at the studio, Sugar was ever present. He laid out Bill's wardrobe, made sure the dressing room was warm enough, chided Bill for taking an extra drink. Bill was tolerant of Sugar's attentiveness and amused by his manner, which was as effusive as a schoolgirl's. Bill would allow no derision of Sugar in his presence.

Not that Sugar needed defense. When Holden moved to MGM for *Executive Suite*, Sugar encountered crew members who were unfamiliar with his peculiar ways. Mutterings of "fairy" and "faggot" were heard until Sugar decked an electrician with a single blow to the chin. The mutterings ceased.

Sugar was fearless in his service to Bill. During a violent studio strike, Paramount asked some of its stars and directors to remain on the lot overnight to avoid disruption of filming. One morning, Sugar passed through a line of surly pickets to fetch breakfast for Bill at Oblath's, the restaurant across the street from the studio. When Sugar tried to return to the studio with the tray, his passage was blocked by tough-looking protesters.

"Pardon me, I have Mr. Holden's breakfast here," Sugar explained quietly. A picket told him what he could do with Mr. Holden's breakfast, and others barred Sugar's way. He handed the tray to a studio cop and started to challenge the pickets until other Paramount workers dissuaded him.

"Why, dear me, Bill," he said when he delivered the breakfast, "those men out there were going to stop me! Why, it was simply awful! Four or five of us would have ended in the hospital."

Sugar continued as a stand-in for years, even though he bore little resemblance to Holden, being stocky and bald. In his early sixties, Sugar was hospitalized for eye surgery. Every day Holden sent Elinor Moller to the hospital to pay Sugar's bill in currency. The money was taken from the office petty cash and later replaced by Holden, who didn't want his business manager to know he was paying Sugar's hospital bills.

Lucey's became a favorite hangout for Bill Holden. Built like a Spanish monastery, it was a former speakeasy located across Melrose Avenue, equidistant from Paramount and RKO. The owners were Steve Crane and Al Mathes, who served ample drinks and hearty Italian-style food. They had a liking and a tolerance for movie people. Crane, a former husband of Lana Turner, was also discreet, and he provided hideaway booths for stars and directors who lunched or dined with women who were not their wives. Originally the booths had curtains, but Crane removed them because of wives' suspicions.

Holden used Lucey's for quiet meetings with Gail Russell, Diana Lynn, Audrey Hepburn, and others. He also enjoyed the male camaraderie of the bar, which attracted such RKO figures as John Wayne, Robert Mitchum, Dick Powell, and Robert Ryan, as well as the Paramount crowd: George Marshall, Ray Milland, John Farrow, William Demarest, William Bendix. His drinking companions enjoyed Holden's company but sometimes wondered why a star reputed to have such an ideal family life didn't go home. Some nights he went pub-crawling down La Cienega Boulevard's Restaurant Row with Don Taylor. Ardis grew accustomed to the after-work calls from Bill telling her not to wait dinner for him.

He tried to be a good father. When a trip to New York coincided with the Fathers and Sons Banquet at West's school, he postponed his departure and sat up all night on a late flight. When the boys' grades were declining, he took the whole family to Hawaii for a summer and enrolled West and Scott at Punahou School.

Bill tried to invoke the same kind of stern but loving discipline he had known from his own parents. The boys were spanked if they misbehaved. When they were watching Hopalong Cassidy during a chase on television, West and Scott became so excited they threw their toy pistols at the screen. Their father paddled them, but admitted later to Brod Crawford, "If I had been watching, I might have done the same thing."

Bill tried to avoid a Hollywood-style upbringing for his children, and he was glad to be away from the Bel Air–Beverly Hills–Brentwood society, where parents treated their children like young royalty. Like many postwar parents he sometimes couldn't resist buying things he had been denied in the Depression.

One Christmas he presented Scott and West with ninety-dollar bicycles decorated with leather fringe, cowboy style. The boys were thrilled, neighboring parents were not. One of them complained to Bill, "You son of a bitch, you made me a heel in the eyes of my own son." Holden told Brod Crawford, "Every Christmas since then, I check the neighborhood to see what the other parents can afford."

As his career blossomed, Bill found Ardis less and less supportive, more and more critical of him. He once told Mike Connors that he bought scuba gear and spent a half-hour daily on the bottom of his swimming pool to avoid domestic squabbles. He accepted more far-off locations and promotional tours, and with the absences his guilt grew. Guilt was always present in the Holden psyche, stemming from his Midwest, Protestant upbringing. Guilt that Bob had died in the war while his famous brother had safe, easy duty. Guilt that he had achieved success so easily while his brother Dick had to work hard for a living. Guilt that he was engaged in the undignified, unmanly profession of acting. Guilt that he was a poor father and an inconstant husband.

Booze helped assuage the pain of guilt, converting Bill's world into a place of gaiety and romance. His friends remarked that Holden carried his liquor well, and he did. Perhaps he carried it too well; he always felt the need for one more drink to reach his high.

14

Days of Change

Bill Holden and Brod Crawford sat on stools at the bar of the Bantam Cock restaurant on La Cienega Boulevard staring glumly at their drinks. They had attended a three-hour evening meeting of the board of the Screen Actors Guild, listening to a succession of stupefyingly dull speeches. Crawford gulped his drink and announced, "I'm resigning from the board."

Holden was surprised. "Why?"

"Because the people running the Guild are not working actors."

Holden was pensive for a moment. "I'm quitting, too."

"Same reason?"

"Yeah. What a waste of time, listening to actors who haven't worked in five years. I became active in the Guild because I thought actors needed to balance the power of the studio bosses. But the Guild isn't interested in that anymore."

Holden also resigned from the Los Angeles Parks and Recreation Commission. He had been appalled by the amount of politics and graft he had seen. "Even the milk concession at the parks involves a payoff," he complained. He also resented how politicians tried to exploit his fame and position. A county supervisor often sent visitors for tours of the Paramount lot, claiming he was "a high school buddy of Bill Holden's." Bill commented, "Sure, I knew him in high school, but he was from the right side of the tracks and didn't speak to me."

Holden turned more to personal pleasures. With his new wealth he could indulge himself in things he had been denied as a struggling actor.

His first extravagance was a Thunderbird. To help popularize its sporty new car, the Ford Motor Company sold early models to Fred Astaire, Randolph Scott, William Holden, and other movie stars. When Ford asked Holden to appear in a Thunderbird advertisement, he said, "Why should I? I paid for the car." He changed his mind when Ford offered to supercharge the motor at no cost.

Bill decided he had to own the hot new racer, the Le Mans Ferrari. He ordered one from Italy, waited impatiently as it was shipped to California. Finally the fire engine–red car arrived, and he claimed it at the dock in San Pedro. With immense pride, he drove the car northward on the freeway, urging it to as much speed as he dared.

Leaving the freeway on Sunset Boulevard, he found himself at a signal next to a teenager in a stripped-down hot rod. Bill made the gesture for a drag race, and the other driver nodded. As soon as the signal changed, the hot rod charged forward with a screech of rubber. Bill was frantically trying to urge the Ferrari into gear.

Nothing about the car seemed to work, and he feared his friends would have another Bill Holden Story to tell. One day as he was taking the Ferrari to the garage for another repair, both exhaust pipes dropped to the pavement, creating a cascade of sparks. Bill stopped at a service station, but the attendants couldn't help him. He borrowed a couple of wire coathangers to fasten the exhaust pipes until he could reach the garage.

With the Ferrari at last in working order, Bill delighted in showing it off to his friends. He insisted on taking Billy Wilder for a ride during the director's lunch break at Warner Brothers studio. Holden drove off the lot and headed for a little-driven road alongside the Hollywood Hills. Within a minute the Ferrari was racing at a hundred miles per hour, and Wilder was screaming for Bill to slow down.

"Sweet car, huh?" Bill said proudly.

"Yeah," said the terrified Wilder. "And you're driving on the right street." He pointed to the sign: Forest Lawn Drive, leading to Hollywood's most famous cemetery.

Bill Holden was thirty-four years old before he left the United States. He was among the celebrities the Defense Department sent to Korea to improve troop morale during the stalemated war. Not being a stand-up entertainer, Holden talked to soldiers in small groups, always insisting that no officers be present. He spent two weeks in Korea, traveling by jeep and helicopter, sometimes hitchhiking to the front lines, where soldiers interrupted conversations to fire artillery at enemy lines.

The Korean trip in late summer of 1952 marked the beginning of a change in direction for Bill Holden's life. The journey also took him to Tokyo and Hong Kong, and his senses were overwhelmed by the serenity of the art, the starkness of the landscapes, the pungency of the food, the beauty of the women, and their gracious, uncomplicated approach to sex.

A few months later, Bill Holden continued his education in the art of travel. His tutor: Billy Wilder.

"It's time you saw Europe," Wilder announced. "And I'm going to show it to you."

Bill and Ardis embarked on the Grand Tour with Billy and Audrey Wilder, and Billy was almost demonic in his campaign to show Bill how civilized the Old World was. No major museum went unvisited, no significant work of art overlooked. Billy took special delight in taking Bill to the haunts he had known as a young film writer in Paris and as a boy in Vienna. Of Berlin, Wilder recognized little.

Holden eagerly followed Wilder until the party reached Bad Ischl, Austria. After a day of visiting two churches and a museum and climbing a mountain, Holden collapsed in his hotel room and told Wilder he was going to sleep all night and through the next day.

The ring of a telephone awakened Holden from a deep sleep. He looked at his watch: six o'clock. It was dark outside, so he presumed it was morning. "Hello," he said groggily.

"Where are you?" demanded the martinet voice of Billy Wilder.

"In bed, for crissake. Where do you think I would be at six in the morning?"

"We're waiting for you in the lobby," said Wilder.

"Billy, I told you last night I was too beat. I can't make it."

"You must come down here and go with us!" Wilder said sternly. "If you do not come, I will never forgive you!"

Holden struggled into his clothes and joined Wilder and the others in the hotel lobby. Billy fed him bread, cheese, ham, brandy, and coffee and rhapsodized on the sights they would view that day. It was a memorable lesson. As Holden later noted: "We made four important stops that day, and it was one of the most wonderful days of my life." Never again would he decline a potential adventure.

The tour ended at Bad Gastein in the Austrian mountains near Salzburg, where Wilder conducted his final lesson: the ritual of the European spa. Holden reveled in the soothing, sensual pleasure of the mineral-heavy waters. He returned to Hollywood with new intensity, ready to continue his astonishing succession of box-office hits.

The Bridges at Toko-Ri had been a popular novel by James A. Michener, a sentimental tale of navy fliers in the Korean War. William Perlberg and George Seaton, who had shifted their company from Fox to Paramount, offered the film to Holden. He agreed on one condition: no happy ending; the pilot must be killed, as in the novel. Perlberg, Seaton, and the director, Mark Robson, consented.

Holden left Los Angeles on a Tuesday morning. He arrived in Tokyo in the evening, rose at 2 A.M. to drive three and a half hours, then board a navy plane to the west coast of Japan. A carrier plane flew him three hundred miles into the Yellow Sea, where a nineteen-ship task force was cruising south of Korea. Holden's plane made a rough landing on one of the two carriers. Wrong carrier. A helicopter carried Holden to the one where the film company was stationed.

When Holden finally ended his journey by stepping onto the carrier deck, the first person he saw was Artie Jacobson, who was production manager on *Toko-Ri*.

"You son of a bitch!" Holden shouted over the aircraft noise. "You put me in this goddam business! I could be happy selling horseshit!"

Jacobson introduced Holden to the ship's admiral and asked, "Will you be nice to him?"

"Yes," Holden replied, "if he'll give me a drink."

Holden enjoyed the carrier life and learned to taxi a plane on the deck for close-up shots. He found amusement in the company of Mickey Rooney, who staged shows during his off hours to entertain the navy personnel. Rooney was surprised to walk in Holden's cabin one morning before work and find him mixing martinis. "Want one?" Holden asked cheerfully.

"God, no," Rooney replied. "Why don't you knock that off? You don't need that."

"Just something to open my eyes," Holden replied and swallowed his drink.

After nine days at sea, the company moved to Tokyo for six weeks of shooting there and in Yokosuka. Jacobson and Robson were having drinks one evening in the director's penthouse suite when they heard someone call, "Artie." Jacobson went into the next room and saw no one. Again: "Artie." Jacobson looked to the open window and saw eight fingers on the ledge. He stepped closer and saw Bill Holden dangling ten stories above downtown Tokyo. The terrified Jacobson couldn't speak.

"Don't you think I ought to get off here?" Holden asked.

"Y-yes, I do," Jacobson said. Holden climbed back into the room and poured himself a drink.

The story of Holden's feat quickly circulated among his co-workers in the *Toko-Ri* company, and they carried it back to Hollywood, where it was widely disbelieved. Such a stunt was inconceivable for a star who was one of the pillars of the film community, a respected citizen, even slightly square. Bill Holden? Impossible!

Bill Holden looked forward to the Hollywood filming of *Toko-Ri* for two reasons: he would be working again with Fredric March; he would be acting for the first time with Grace Kelly. He had never met the Philadelphia beauty who had become Hollywood's most in-demand leading lady, and he wondered if she would prove as cool and distant as the press had indicated. To Bill's delight, he found her skill-ful and sympathetic as an actress, and soft and affectionate as a woman.

Perlberg and Seaton planned to follow *Toko-Ri* immediately with *The Country Girl,* with George Seaton directing his own script based on the Clifford Odets play. Bing Crosby and Jennifer Jones had been cast as the alcoholic stage star and his persevering wife, and Seaton wanted Bill Holden to play the director who formed the other side of the triangle. Even though he would have only a Palm Springs weekend between the two pictures, he agreed to *The Country Girl.* Having seen the play in London, he realized that his was the third role. But he had learned with *Born Yesterday* and *Sabrina* that the third role in a hit was better than the lead in a flop.

Jennifer Jones dropped out of the film because of pregnancy, and her place was taken by Grace Kelly. Holden, who had enjoyed a brief but satisfactory romance with Miss Kelly, was delighted. Even though his contract called for his name to appear second, he volunteered to let Miss Kelly's appear before his. George Seaton was astounded: "You're the first actor in Hollywood history to lower his own billing."

Crosby seemed uncomfortable and distant during the early filming of *The Country Girl.* Frank Elgin was the first unsympathetic role he had played after twenty-five years in films, and Seaton had persuaded him to appear without his hairpiece. Under Seaton's sensitive direction, Crosby responded to the challenge, realizing that the role could add a new dimension to his career.

Early in the filming of *The Country Girl,* Crosby invited Holden into his dressing room. This surprised Holden, because Bing seldom fraternized at the studio. After small talk about the day's work, Crosby came to the point.

"This Kelly girl, she's a knockout, isn't she?" he said.

"She sure is," Holden agreed. "I've never known a young actress with so much know-how."

"I'm talking about her as a person. I don't mind telling you, Bill, I'm smitten with Grace. Daffy about her. And I was wondering if—"

"If I felt the same way?" Bill grinned. "What man wouldn't be overwhelmed by her? But look, Bing, I won't interfere."

Crosby had been embarrassed by the conversation, and he seemed greatly relieved. "Thanks, Bill, I appreciate it," he said.

At considerable sacrifice, Holden withdrew from his pursuit of Grace Kelly. He did so out of respect for Crosby, whom everyone at Paramount viewed with admiration and a degree of awe. As Holden expected, Bing was not successful in his courtship of Grace. She, too, admired him, but the twenty-seven-year difference in their ages proved too much of a barrier.

With Bing out of the picture, Bill Holden resumed the romance with Grace. For the first time in his career, his name was attached to scandal. *Confidential* magazine printed an article alleging he and Grace were meeting secretly for trysts. The purported evidence: Holden's white Cadillac convertible had been parked all night outside Miss Kelly's apartment.

Holden was outraged. He directed his attorney, Robert Lerner, to demand a retraction from the magazine. The retraction was printed, but the damage had been done. Holden tried to repair it by telling Hedda Hopper, "I picked Grace up at her apartment, but *Confidential* didn't bother to find out why. I took her to our home for dinner. She dined with Ardis and me about four times. I don't understand all this publicity about Grace. I like her, but I don't think she's the femme fatale she's built up to be. She's pretty femme. But she's not fatale."

To his secretary, Elinor Moller, Bill said, "It's ridiculous. That white Caddie is Ardis's car. Does anybody think I'm so dumb as to park my wife's car outside an actress's apartment all night?"

Bill's meetings with Grace Kelly were far more discreet. They managed a weekend in Palm Springs together, but Bill was disappointed when a friend of the Kelly family came along as chaperone. Bill solved the problem by taking Grace on moonlight horseback rides into the desert.

They were entranced with each other and even talked of marriage. There was one huge problem: the unswerving Catholicism of the Kelly family. Grace consulted the family priest and was told that if Holden would embrace the Catholic Church, his previous marriage would be considered invalid.

"I couldn't do it," Bill later told Brod Crawford. "I loved Grace and wanted to marry her. But I'd be damned if I'd let any church dictate what I could do with my life."

Holden accepted *Love Is a Many-Splendored Thing* from 20th Century–Fox largely because it entailed a location in Hong Kong. He had no illusions about the script, an old-fashioned romance between a Eurasian doctor and an American correspondent, but he felt he was in safe hands with Henry King as director.

The love scenes between Holden and Jennifer Jones evoked tears from millions of American women, but the film was a rare instance when he lacked affection for his leading lady. Miss Jones complained about her makeup, her costumes, the dialogue; and when Holden failed to sympathize, she complained about him. "I'm going to tell David about this," she said repeatedly; and her husband, David O. Selznick, sent a stream of memos to Fox about her complaints.

The acrimony reached the point where the two stars were scarcely speaking to each other except during their love scenes. Holden decided to seek a truce, and he presented Miss Jones with a bouquet of white roses. She threw them in his face.

15

Close-ups

William Holden in his late thirties stood six feet, and his weight seldom varied from 165 pounds. He remained in superb physical condition though he did no regular exercise. He swam in his home pool and played excellent badminton. He showed promise of being a superb golf player, but he found it boring to practice strokes. He dressed conservatively in business suits and tweed sports jackets; he chose the fabrics for his suits and had them tailored by a traditional Los Angeles haberdashery. He ate lightly, especially when he was drinking.

He was obsessed by speed and delighted in taking his sons to stock-car and motorcycle races. Regretfully, he sold his Ferrari. He loved to race it, and once in the desert pushed the car to 140 miles per hour. When he drove it in the city, he found himself under constant surveillance by traffic cops. He bought a Bentley; cost: $22,000.

Unlike his friend Ronald Reagan, Holden displayed little interest in politics. He never endorsed a political candidate. Some of his friends thought he was a Roosevelt Democrat, some believed him to be a conservative. Influenced by his South Pasadena upbringing, he considered himself a Republican; but except for human rights, he had no strong opinions about political matters. He was against Communism, but he refused to join the frenzied Red hunting in early 1950s Hollywood.

Holden had an uncanny control over animals. Brod Crawford came to the Columbia studio with his boxer Duchess, a gift from James Cagney. Crawford held the dog back from Holden, explaining that she had a bad habit of jumping on people. "She won't jump, let her go," Holden said. Duchess leaped at Holden, but he laid a hand on her back and she calmed immediately. He explained to the astonished Crawford: "Stray cats even answer my call on the street."

His favorite place was the desert. He loved the sun and was always planning to go somewhere to "bake out."

Music was a great enthusiasm. He often pulled friends into his office, urging, "You gotta hear this new record." He was ecstatic when he discovered "The Pines of Rome," conducted by Toscanini.

He had little interest in business matters. Ever since *Golden Boy,* his business manager had been Andrew Hickox, who had handled Ardis' financial affairs. Hickox maintained the Holdens on tight allowances, even after Bill started earning large salaries. Each Tuesday night, the business manager came to the Toluca Lake house with checks to be signed, and he issued money to maintain the house and for spending by Bill and Ardis. Holden made no sizable purchase, even on a store charge account, without notifying Hickox.

Holden rarely used obscene language—never in the presence of women—and he seldom told bawdy jokes.

He remained a cigarette smoker all his life. He always held the cigarette between his index finger and thumb "because I hate tobacco stains on my fingers."

He despised makeup and used as little as possible. Often he could be seen sitting in the sunshine outside a movie stage with a reflector around his neck. He also installed a sun lamp over his office toilet, explaining to visitors: "We don't like to waste a minute around here."

Holden was a stickler for cleanliness, often taking four showers a day. Throughout his career he retained the same hairstyle. At Paramount studio and later in Palm Springs, he had a weekly haircut by Victor Honig, a Hungarian immigrant who was barber for Ronald Reagan, James Cagney, and other stars. Holden wanted his hair neatly trimmed, never touching the ears. Honig says, "He never wanted to look as if he had just come from the barbershop."

Although his diction seemed perfect, Nina Foch noted that Holden had trouble delivering lines with T's and L's. His speech was unaccented, though he did say "warshing machine" and "George Warshington," perhaps a Midwest peculiarity.

He was devoted to his mother and father, and the Holden family always had Thanksgiving and Christmas dinners at the Beedle house in South Pasadena. Bill wished he could spend more time with his brother Dick, who had married and was working for his father. Bill often invited Dick to come by the studio, and the office bar was always stocked with San Miguel beer, which was Dick's favorite.

Holden hated large Hollywood parties, and he attended them only when he considered it his duty. The same with premieres. New Year's Eve at the Holdens' house became a ritual. The guests were usually Nancy and Ronald Reagan, Jan and Bob Lerner, Eleanor and Paul

Clemens. At midnight, Bill put on a 78-rpm Victor record of the Old-timers singing "Auld Lang Syne," and husbands and wives kissed.

Despite his seeming self-assurance, he was extraordinarily shy. During a visit to New York, he was invited to a reception for Pearl Bailey at Sardi's. He entered the restaurant gloomily, then brightened when he saw a familiar face, Caroline Steinberg, wife of Paramount publicist Herb Steinberg. "Ah, good, Carrie!" he exclaimed. "Come on upstairs to the party with me." She protested that she was with friends, but he took her by the arm and led her up the stairs, explaining, "I want you to walk in with me." He was afraid to enter the gathering alone.

Once inside a party, he demonstrated the Holden charm, as well as a memory for names and faces. He always paid attention to wives, not merely to flirt with them, but to make them seem attractive and important. Whenever he entered an office at a studio or at his lawyer's or agency offices, he always spoke to all of the secretaries, not conde-scendingly like a movie star, but as a man who was interested in their lives and remembered their names.

When he lunched in the Paramount commissary, he never ate in the separate dining room with other stars and directors. He always sat in the main room, often joining the legal department table. The com-missary manager, Pauline Kessinger, maintained a tradition of naming menu items after stars: Turkey and Eggs Country-style à la Crosby; Dorothy Lamour Salad; Strawberries à la Heston; Hope Cocktail. When she asked if she could name a dish after Holden, he replied, "Don't you dare! I don't want my name on a menu!" Nor would he allow his portrait to appear on the commissary wall along with those of other Paramount stars.

Holden loved to fuss around his Paramount office, cleaning out cupboards, rearranging artworks, ordering snacks from Balzer's, the nearby gourmet grocery. He sometimes sprayed the office with his favorite French perfume, explaining to Elinor Moller, "Women work better in a perfumed atmosphere."

When Holden opened his Paramount office, he went to the Califor-nia Map Company and bought a wall-size relief map of the world. After every trip in the United States or abroad, he stuck pins in the map to indicate his travels. He spent so much time doing it that Miss Moller remarked, "You know, I don't think you really like to travel. You just like to stick pins in that map."

He responded with the Holden grin: "You know that, and I know that, but let's keep it *our* secret."

Ardis sometimes accompanied Bill on his trips. When Bob Hope invited Bill to help entertain American troops in Greenland for a television special, Bill agreed, if Ardis could go, too.

After a long period of filmmaking, Bill decided to take Ardis on a Caribbean vacation. His personal lawyer, Robert Lerner, was son of the mercantile family that had established the Lerner Marine Institute on Bimini Island. Lerner and his wife, Jan Clayton, and the Holdens spent a week aboard the Lerner yacht; Bill studied fish life at the institute and dived with scuba gear off the reefs.

The Holdens and the Lerners spent a few days in Havana attending the bullfights and touring the nightclubs. At Sloppy Joe's, Bill discovered the Daiquiri and he enthused: "I want a whole bathtub of this, and I'm going to submerge myself in it!"

Early in the morning, the quartet returned to their seventh-floor suite at the Nacional Hotel. Jan walked into the living room and gasped. Bill was standing on his hands in the open window.

"Ardis!" Jan shrieked.

By the time Ardis rushed into the room, Bill had come inside, but she saw the open window and knew immediately what he had done. She lifted a large glass ashtray and hurled it at his head. Bill ducked, but not soon enough. The ashtray grazed his forehead.

Bill felt his forehead and saw blood on his hand. "You could have killed me!" he protested.

"Yes." Ardis nodded, recalling bullfight jargon: "You hooked to the right, and I thought you would hook to the left."

Another trip in the mid-1950s took Bill Holden around the world as salesman for Paramount's VistaVision, but the purpose of the trip was not entirely public relations.

Most of Holden's romances with his leading ladies ended with the completion of their movies together. Not so with Audrey Hepburn. He brought her home for dinner with Ardis, as he did with all his leading ladies. But he and Audrey found time to be alone, their dressing rooms being close together at Paramount. To Holden she embodied everything that he admired in a woman, and she was young, eleven years younger than himself. Audrey considered him the handsomest man she had ever known, and she was entranced by his manly charm and gentle humor.

With his marriage to Ardis growing more acrimonious, Bill once again considered another marriage. Audrey was receptive; she loved Bill and believed they could make beautiful babies together. But no. Bill admitted that he could never again be a father. When he was twenty-nine and Ardis had given birth to their two sons, both she and Bill agreed they wanted no more children. Their business manager, Andy Hickox, arranged for Bill to have a vasectomy. Cost of the operation: seventy-five dollars. Bill had been an outspoken advocate of vasectomy, arguing that all husbands should have them after two children. In later life he claimed never to have had regrets. But once he did.

An evening at the Encore, a jazz nightclub on the Sunset Strip. Joey Bushkin was playing piano with his combo, and Bill Holden was a fan of Bushkin's creative improvisations. He and Ardis hosted a table that included Audrey Hepburn and her date, Mel Ferrer, Alexis Smith and Craig Stevens, Herb Steinberg of the Paramount publicity department, and his wife Caroline.

"Isn't Joey great?" Bill said enthusiastically, leading the applause at the end of a session.

When the room returned to the usual nightclub clatter, Audrey tapped a spoon on her glass and said, "Ladies and gentlemen, I have an announcement." She turned her eyes to the beaming Ferrer and said, "Mel and I are engaged to be married." Everyone at the table greeted the announcement joyfully. Except Bill Holden. He remained grim-faced for the duration of the evening. A few days later, he asked Frank Freeman to send him on a globe-circling goodwill tour for VistaVision.

Parras, Mexico, 1968.

Bill Holden was filming *The Wild Bunch* under the erratic direction of Sam Peckinpah, and the waits between scenes were seemingly endless. Holden and Warren Oates sat on horseback awaiting their cues, and Holden occupied the time by spinning tales of his past to the younger actor. Among them:

"I really was in love with Audrey, but she wouldn't marry me. So I set out around the world with the idea of screwing a woman in every country I visited. My plan succeeded, though sometimes with difficulty. When I was in Bangkok, I was screwing a Thai girl in a boat floating in one of the klongs. I guess we got too animated, because the boat tipped over and I fell into the filthy water. Back at the hotel I poured alcohol in my ears because I was afraid I'd become infected with the plague.

"When I got back to Hollywood, I went to Audrey's dressing room at Paramount and I told her what I had done. You know what she said?

" 'Oh, Bill!' That's all: 'Oh, Bill!' Just as though I were some naughty boy. What a waste!"

16

Picnic: Goodbye, Harry

"How would you like to make history?" Harry Cohn asked exuberantly.

Holden was always suspicious of Cohn in such moods. "What do you mean, Harry?" he asked.

"How would you like to be the first actor to star in his own remake?"

"Don't tell me you're planning a remake of *Father Is a Bachelor,*" Holden said, smiling.

"No, dammit. *Golden Boy!*"

Holden pondered for a moment. "No, Harry."

"What do you mean, no?" Cohn demanded.

"I mean no. In the first place, I don't want to repeat something I did fifteen to twenty years ago. In the second place, *Golden Boy* isn't valid today. The whole social structure has changed since the Depression. Italian boys don't have to fight their way out of the ghetto anymore."

"You're a hardheaded bastard," Cohn muttered.

"You're right, Harry. Guess who I learned that from."

Columbia had only one more commitment with Holden, and Harry Cohn was eager to claim it while the star was hot. Cohn proposed six other projects. Holden's anger rose at being forced to work for a fraction of his worth, and he rejected them all.

When Cohn offered *Picnic,* Holden was ready to say no again. At thirty-seven, he considered himself too old to play Hal Carter, the bare-chested drifter who dazzles the women of a small Kansas town.

"Do it," urged Jack Gordean, who handled Holden for Charlie Feldman's Famous Artists agency. "It'll be an important picture, and it will mean you can say goodbye forever to Harry Cohn." Holden agreed to join the cast that included Kim Novak, Rosalind Russell, Betty Field,

105

Susan Strasberg, Arthur O'Connell, and a newcomer from the Broadway stage, Cliff Robertson. The director was Joshua Logan.

Holden immediately took young Robertson under his wing. During a lunch break in rehearsals, they drove in Bill's Thunderbird to his office at Paramount. Robertson watched in awe as Holden conducted business with his secretary, poured himself a beer, flirted with Anita Ekberg, traded quips with Billy Wilder. As he and Holden drove back to Columbia, Robertson marveled, "Is this what Hollywood is really like?"

"Look, Cliff," Holden said, "it's like this only as long as they think they can make money out of you. The studios will give you an office and almost everything you want. But as soon as your career starts to slide, they'll drop you like a hot potato. Remember that."

Robertson witnessed an example of Holden's independence during the rehearsal period. Jack Fier, a strutting martinet who acted as Harry Cohn's production manager and hatchet man, strode on the stage to announce Cohn's displeasure that some of the actors were reporting late. He finished the speech, whipped the air with the riding crop he always carried, then turned to leave.

"Tell Harry Cohn to stuff it up his ass," Bill Holden said.

Fier turned slowly, his eyes narrowing. "What did you say?" he demanded.

"I said, tell Harry Cohn to stuff it up his ass," Holden repeated.

As the others on the stage watched with trepidation, Fier stepped challengingly toward Holden until they were face to face.

"I'll say it to you again, Jack," said Holden. "Tell Harry Cohn to stick it up his ass. Furthermore, I don't give a shit. I've got mine. I've made a bundle, and I've put it away, and no tinhorn tyrant like Harry Cohn can scare me anymore."

Fier studied him with a mixture of awe and disbelief, blinked, and said, "I love ya, baby." He made a quick retreat out the stage door.

Josh Logan rehearsed the cast for two weeks, then the *Picnic* company flew to Hutchinson, Kansas, for six weeks of locations. The film workers were housed at the Baker Hotel, which was the site of a Holden escapade that has been related in many versions. Ronald Reagan offers this account:

"They were up in his suite after a day's shooting, late afternoon before they went to dinner. It was an old-fashioned hotel with big windows all the way to the ceiling, the kind that opened up on hot summer days. Bill just strolled over, and they looked—Josh almost died. Bill was standing on his hands on the window ledge!"

Logan in his autobiography describes Holden as hellbent on martinis in his fourteenth-floor suite. The director asked if he could perform a gymnastic feat for the movie. Holden described his Suicide Bridge escapade, then demonstrated his skill by hanging out the window by his elbow. The acrophobic Logan couldn't watch, and Holden resisted Rosalind Russell's entreaties to re-enter the room. Only if Logan watched would he do so. Logan watched, and Holden climbed back in.

Rosalind Russell's interpretation, from her posthumous autobiography:

Holden was entertaining her and a few others in his tenth-floor suite. He enjoyed showing off his prowess while drinking, and he suddenly leaped out the window and hung by his hands from the sill. Despite pleas to return, he began lifting his fingers until only two kept him from falling. "If we don't pay attention to him, he'll stop this nonsense," Miss Russell reasoned, and they all left for her suite. Holden next tried dangling from her window—"he was strong as an ox, stubborn as a monkey, and luckier than anything."

Cliff Robertson provides another account:

Holden was serving drinks and playing phonograph records for visitors in his suite: Robertson; Rosalind Russell; Miriam Nelson, the choreographer; and Joseph Steele, publicist for the film. Holden and Steele were arguing, and Holden said, "You think you know me pretty well, don't you?" Steele nodded and Holden said, "Do you think I would do this?" He went to the open window and stood outside on the ledge, poised as if to leap.

The others in the room were panicked. Robertson had heard of Bill's exploit on Suicide Bridge and realized he was getting the reaction he wanted. Robertson himself climbed out the window on the other corner of the room and shouted to Holden the old burlesque line, "Meet you round the corner in a half an hour." Bill was amused, and he stepped inside.

With most of his leading ladies, Bill Holden maintained a closeness, often an intimacy. Kim Novak was an exception.

Terrified in her first starring opportunity, she remained aloof from the rest of the *Picnic* company, refusing dinner invitations with the wan explanation "I don't think I would have anything to contribute." Seeking spiritual strength for her challenge, she prayed nightly in Hutchinson's Catholic church. Bill Holden, whose offers of help had been declined, grumbled, "She'd be better off if she spent more time learning her lines and less time reciting her rosary."

Holden himself had been terrified by a scene he would have to perform in the film: the mutually seductive dance by Hal and Madge, a highlight of the play.

"I can't do it!" he proclaimed to Miriam Nelson, who had come from Hollywood to choreograph the dance. "I'm a lousy dancer."

"You don't have to be Gene Kelly," she argued. "It's just a little ad lib dance to 'Moonglow.' "

Logan, who realized that the dance was a crucial sequence in *Picnic,* worried about his reluctant star. He took Holden and Miss Nelson to roadhouses and induced them to dance to the jukeboxes.

"C'mon, Bill!" Logan urged. "Wiggle your ass a little!"

"If you want a wiggling ass, you'd better get Brando," Holden grouched.

After two weeks of rehearsals, the dance was scheduled to be filmed one evening in Hutchinson. Logan filmed the long shot of Kim descending to the landing platform of the park lake, then ordered the camera moved in for the dance. Suddenly the Kansas sky exploded, and hail the size of golf balls poured down. The deluge continued until the park became a quagmire. Filming was impossible, and the company returned to Hollywood, where the dance would be staged.

The delay heightened Bill Holden's anxiety. He marched into Harry Cohn's office and announced, "I can't do it!"

"Can't do what?" said the startled Cohn.

"I can't do that fucking dance. I'm a lousy dancer; I'll look like a fool. How can I make it a big love scene with Kim Novak? She's a pain in the ass."

"Can't argue with you there, pal. But you've got to do it."

"On one condition."

"What's that?" Cohn eyed him suspiciously.

"I get a stunt check."

"You think doing a dance deserves a stunt check?" Cohn exploded.

"This one does. I'll put a price tag on it: eight thousand bucks."

Cohn acceded rather than risk a delay in production. The boat landing had been reproduced on the Columbia ranch in Burbank, and the dance was scheduled one evening. "I'm sure as hell not going to do this sober," Bill said. "What do you drink, Kim? Miriam?" From his dressing-room bar he produced the favorite drinks of the principals in the dance production. James Wong Howe, the cinematographer, devised a plan to circle the two dancers with the camera, filming them mostly from the waist up. He focused on the sensuality of the young lovers, their eyes fixed on each other, their passion mounting.

The scene played magnificently on the screen, especially with the addition of the haunting *Picnic* theme by George Duning as counterpoint to "Moonglow." The music became America's number-one hit record, and women everywhere dreamed of dancing in the moonlight with William Holden and being seduced by the railroad tracks.

Early one evening, Bill Holden completed the final scene of *Picnic.* He and Josh Logan went to Harry Cohn's office to announce the end of filming. Cohn was uncharacteristically expansive; Holden was resentful. He had been paid a total of $38,000 for *Picnic.* His current rate was $250,000 per film.

"Well, I never thought I'd see the day!" Holden remarked.

"What do you mean?" Cohn asked.

"I mean it's been sixteen years of being tied to this goddam place, and tonight it's over. Thank God!"

"Now, listen, Bill, it hasn't been so bad."

"Not for you and Columbia it hasn't! For me? That's another matter. All the suspensions. Working for fifty lousy bucks a week."

"What do you mean? I never paid you fifty bucks a week!"

"The hell you didn't!"

"No, I paid you twenty-five bucks a week. Paramount paid you the other half."

Holden laughed ruefully and said to Logan, "See what I mean?"

"Come on, Bill," Cohn said cajolingly. He reached into his desk and added, "I got a bottle of Scotch here to celebrate with."

"What is it—poison?" Holden asked.

Cohn poured three glasses of whisky. Holding his own glass high, he announced, "Here's to your next picture at Columbia!"

When Holden told me this story in 1965, he added, "I swore I would never work for Columbia again. A year later I was on a plane to Ceylon to make *Bridge on the River Kwai*—for Columbia!"

Stalag 17. The Moon Is Blue. Executive Suite. Sabrina. The Country Girl. The Bridges at Toko-Ri. Love Is a Many-Splendored Thing. Picnic.

Film historians could not recall a star having so many box-office hits as did William Holden in the mid-1950s. His achievement was acknowledged by the theater owners of America who voted in the annual poll conducted by the *Motion Picture Herald*. Holden was named the seventh-biggest moneymaking star in 1954, fourth in 1955, and number one in 1956. He was followed by John Wayne, James Stewart, Burt Lancaster, Glenn Ford, Martin and Lewis, Gary Cooper, Marilyn Monroe, Kim Novak, and Frank Sinatra.

Success brought a flood of requests for interviews, and Holden tried to accommodate all. He generally liked reporters. "After all"—he grinned—"I got my name from a newspaperman." Holden was always conscientious in interviews, never seeming bored, always trying to supply fresh answers to the same old questions. The Hollywood Women's Press Club voted him the Golden Apple as the most cooperative male star in 1951 and 1955. On the second occasion, he told the women, "Being voted the most cooperative actor is strange, inasmuch as I've been away from Hollywood for nine months of the last year. Maybe I'd rate better if I just stayed away all the time."

On February 27, 1956, a new accolade: William Holden appeared on the cover of *Time* magazine, a rare achievement for a film star.

Time reporter Ezra Goodman spent weeks researching the article, which was written by an editor in New York. Goodman was impressed by Holden's staid upbringing, his business sense, his conservatism, as evidenced on the wall of his studio office: the coat of arms of his ancestor George Washington, presented by the National Society of the Sons of the American Revolution.

Goodman detected another side of Holden: the daredevil to whom "Warm up the ice cubes!" was a battle cry.

Billy Wilder told Goodman, "I would not paint [Holden] exactly as a sort of Jekyll and Hyde type, but he's a very tense man and drinks to pull himself together and to go on the set for the next scene. His drinking is to overcome his natural inhibitions. Deep down in his heart he is an inhibited boy who feels very uncomfortable to act. He is the exact opposite of the ham. He was sort of pushed into acting. He drifted into the profession slightly against his own will. At heart he's a wonderful hot-rodder. He would rather have been a race driver. He's a goddam good driver."

Time editors could not believe that Holden was so normal, and one of them went to South Pasadena to interview Mary and William Beedle, hoping to uncover some dark secret about their son. The effort failed. The *Time* story cited Holden's image as an ordinary citizen but added that "the gray flannel suit has a scarlet lining, and though Bill generally keeps it hidden, he is secretly proud that it is there. He has a savage temper and is no respecter of persons. The studio grips can catch it if they talk too much on the set, and so can the director. When Bill gets too tense, which is frequently, he drinks to relax, and he drinks too much. 'It costs him $18,' says a friend, 'to get an edge on.' Before he does a scene, he usually takes a few belts."

Holden was incensed by the article, and he banned any further contact with *Time* and its reporters. He had always trusted the press to give him fair treatment. The *Time* experience convinced him he had trusted too much. He would not make that mistake again.

Even though he was the most sought-after leading man in Hollywood, Bill Holden understood the transitory nature of the film business and its dependence on youth. The lesson was underscored when he competed for the role of Bick Benedict in *Giant.*

Holden realized the importance of *Giant.* The Edna Ferber novel had been a huge bestseller, and George Stevens, then at the peak of his career, was planning his customarily meticulous production. Holden had several conversations with Stevens about the film and he felt encouraged. Then one afternoon Bill learned that Rock Hudson had been cast as Bick Benedict. Stevens had reasoned that in the telling of the dynastic story it would be easier to age younger actors in the latter scenes than to make older actors seem younger in the early scenes.

Depressed at losing an important role to a younger actor, Bill Holden decided to take a steam bath at the Universal studio gym. Rock Hudson, who had learned of his casting in *Giant* two hours before, was in the steam room. He was aware that Holden had been in contention for the Bick Benedict role. Having never met Holden, Hudson tried to remain inconspicuous, a difficult task since he was six feet, four inches tall and naked.

Holden, who was also naked, recognized Hudson and congratulated him on winning the *Giant* role.

"I wish you a lot of luck with the picture," Holden said. He added with an edge to his voice, "It's a *very* good role."

Holden was thirty-seven years old, Hudson was thirty.

17

The Bridge on the River Kwai

Although neither was a failure, *The Proud and the Profane* and *Toward the Unknown* broke the string of Holden hits. *The Proud and the Profane* was a war movie which Holden enjoyed mostly because of the Virgin Islands location and Deborah Kerr, whom he found to be delightfully free of pretense. *Toward the Unknown* was a story of supersonic test pilots, produced by Holden's own company, Toluca Productions.

John Wayne, Burt Lancaster, Kirk Douglas, Alan Ladd, and other stars had formed their own production companies as a means of guiding their own film destinies and earning more money. Both factors appealed to Bill Holden, and he incorporated Toluca Productions, Toluca Enterprises, and Toluca Publishing.

At first Holden enjoyed his position as corporate president. He auditioned songwriters, supervised a record album, bought film properties, developed *Toward the Unknown.* After the film was completed, Holden told Hickox, "It's goddam boring sitting behind a desk. Dissolve the companies."

Holden had neither the patience nor the artistic drive to be his own producer. Nor was there need. Every studio in Hollywood sent him scripts, eager for his approval. Among the projects proposed to him in 1956 was *The Bridge on the River Kwai.*

The project had a complicated history. Pierre Boulle had written a novel in French, an allegory about the insanity of war. The central figure was a British colonel, a prisoner of the Japanese in Thailand, who in a demented sense of duty helps his captors build a vital railroad bridge.

Carl Foreman, rebuilding his career in Europe after being blacklisted in Hollywood, bought an option on the book for £300, against a purchase price of £3,000. Alexander Korda declined the film, telling

Foreman, "That colonel is either insane or a traitor." Sam Spiegel agreed to produce it, and he made a deal with Columbia, for which he had produced *On the Waterfront.*

Foreman wrote the first script, creating the role of an American who escapes from the prison camp and returns to help blow up the bridge. Spiegel sought Humphrey Bogart for the part.

Harry Cohn, who felt his onetime absolute power over Columbia Pictures threatened by Spiegel's independent production, refused to release Bogart from another Columbia commitment. Spiegel's anxiety was growing. A year before the scheduled start of production, he had entered a contract for the building of a railroad bridge in Ceylon. As the completion date neared, he had neither director nor stars.

After considering Howard Hawks, John Ford, and other Hollywood directors, Spiegel decided on an Englishman, David Lean. Laurence Olivier was asked to play Colonel Nicholson, but he declined, saying, "I can't imagine anyone wanting to watch a stiff-upper-lip British colonel for two and a half hours." Alec Guinness also refused on the grounds that he was committed to a London play; besides, he and David Lean had clashed on *Oliver Twist* nine years before.

The persuasive Spiegel convinced Guinness to accept the role. The producer's next choice for the American Shears was Cary Grant. But Spiegel feared that American audiences, who had rejected Grant in a serious role in *Crisis,* might expect him to play comedy in *The Bridge on the River Kwai.* Spiegel then considered William Holden.

The location in Ceylon intrigued Bill Holden, and he accepted the secondary role of the American sailor Shears. Since *Kwai* was his first independent contract with Columbia, he wanted the best possible terms. His advisers arrived at a formula that seemed ideal: a $300,000 fee, plus 10 percent of the gross receipts, payable at a maximum rate of $50,000 a year.

Holden was elated. He was paying U.S. income tax at the maximum rate of 90 percent. By deferring his earnings from *Kwai,* he would be assured of an annuity of $50,000 a year when his earning capacity as a movie actor had dwindled.

Columbia executives had cautioned Holden that he might be subjected to criticism because of Carl Foreman's association with *Kwai.* Holden was unconcerned. He considered himself an anti-Communist, but he had refused to take part in the Red hunt of the early 1950s. He had seen innocent lives ruined by the Red hunters.

When Columbia announced the casting of Holden in *The Bridge on the River Kwai*, he was telephoned at his Paramount office by Hedda Hopper.

"You're not really going to make that picture for Sam Spiegel, are you, Bill?" the columnist demanded.

"Hell, yes!" Holden answered. "It's one of the best scripts I've ever read."

"Yes, and you know who wrote it."

"Sure. Carl Foreman."

"A damned Red."

"I don't know anything about his politics. All I know is he has written a crackling good script."

"Bill, you can't do it! We can't let those Commies get their feet back in the industry now. And you especially. You're one of the pillars of the community. You're respected as a solid, straight-thinking American. I'm telling you, Bill, you can't do that picture!"

Holden exploded. "Goddammit, Hedda, since when are you or anybody else telling me what I can or cannot do? I've seen what you vigilantes have done to Larry Parks and a lot of other people. Well, don't start meddling in my life, because I won't stand for it!" He slammed down the phone.

It was the only time Elinor Moller had heard her boss lose his temper, and the outburst resulted in a permanent estrangement between Holden and Hedda Hopper. In the end, Columbia had second thoughts about Foreman. The *Kwai* script, on which Calder Willingham, Michael Wilson, and Pierre Boulle also worked, was credited only to Boulle.

Bill Holden arrived in Colombo, Ceylon, on Christmas Day 1956. He checked in at the Galle Face Hotel and went to the room of Bill Graf, veteran Columbia Pictures hand who was overseeing *Kwai* production for the company. He was bearing a package filled with small boxes, and he told Graf's wife Betty, "I bought these in Hong Kong and Singapore for members of the company, and I need to get them wrapped. Can you help me?"

Holden and Mrs. Graf sat down at a table, and she wrapped the packages while he wrote cards. After she finished the last present, a gold cigarette holder, he handed the package back to her: "This one's for you."

Except for Spiegel and the Grafs, Holden knew none of the *Kwai* company. David Lean had brought his own crew from England. Working with a non-Hollywood crew for the first time, Holden soon learned the English habits, including the traditional tea break. He found Lean businesslike and cordial, Guinness businesslike and aloof. Holden was amused by Sessue Hayakawa, who told stories about his days as a silent-film Hollywood star. Holden was closest to Jack Hawkins, who shared a love of booze and good times.

Geoffrey Horne, who had studied at the Actors Studio in New York and had made one previous film, was the only other American actor in the company. On the first day of filming, Holden realized that Horne was nervous and told him, "Good luck, I know you're going to do a great job." Holden often provided helpful suggestions and sympathetic support. But at times he seemed to regard the virile twenty-four-year-old actor as a rival. One day Holden was asking Jack Hawkins and Alec Guinness about an English director with whom he was considering a film. When Horne volunteered that he had worked with the director, Holden snapped, "I don't need any advice from someone as young as you who knows less than I do."

Jungle sequences were filmed deep in the Ceylon interior at Kitulgala. Despite the oppressive weather and the housing in a native shack, Bill Holden never complained. One day he and Horne were playing a scene in the river while elephants were being worked upstream.

"Ah, the glamorous life of a movie star!" Holden mused. "Here I am on an island in the Indian Ocean, standing up to my navel in a filthy river, dodging elephant shit the size of cannonballs!"

Younger actors grumbled about Lean's long preparations for scenes and the excessive number of takes. Holden never questioned the director's judgment. After several weeks of filming, Lean disappeared into his tent. When he emerged, he told Holden, "I've been rethinking your character. Shears is too nice, too willing a hero. He should be mean, cowardly, cynical, so when he does return for his act of heroism, it will have more meaning." Holden readily agreed to refilming, even though it meant extending his stay in Ceylon.

The revised Shears, who resembled Sefton of *Stalag 17*, became more significant to the events of *The Bridge on the River Kwai*, as evidenced by the scene in which Shears and the Canadian Joyce (Geoffrey Horne) refuse to abandon the wounded Warden (Jack Hawkins) on the mission back to the River Kwai.

WARDEN
What are you doing? I didn't give orders for a halt.

SHEARS

We all need it. . . .

WARDEN

We're still five hours' fast march from the objective. Maybe six. Come on!

SHEARS

If you keep walking on that foot, you'll bleed to death.

WARDEN

Yes. You're going to leave me here.

SHEARS

If you stop, we stop.

WARDEN

You can't study the layout of the bridge after dark. You've got to get there before sundown.

JOYCE

But, sir—when the job's done, who knows if we can return by this route, or whether we could find you if we did?

WARDEN

If you were in my shoes, Joyce, I wouldn't hesitate to leave you here—and you know that.

SHEARS

He doesn't know it, but I do. You'd leave your own mother here if the rules called for it.

WARDEN

You'll go on without me, and that's an order! You're in command now, Shears.

SHEARS

I won't obey that order. You make me sick with your heroics. There's a stench of death about you—you carry it in your pack like a plague. Explosives and L pills, they go well together, don't they? And with you it's just one thing or the other—destroy a bridge or destroy yourself. This is just a game, this war. You and that Colonel Nicholson, you're two of a kind. Crazy with courage—for what? How to die like a gentleman, how to die by the rules. When the only important thing is how to live like a human being!

I won't leave you here to die, Warden, because I don't care about your bridge. I don't care about your rules. If we go on, we go on together.*

---

*Grateful acknowledgment is made for permission to quote from the filmscript of *The Bridge on the River Kwai*, copyright © 1957 by Columbia Pictures.

The prison camp sequences were filmed at a location seven miles out-side Colombo, and the movie company returned every night to the Galle Face Hotel. One evening Holden, dressed in his prison costume, entered the hotel with Spiegel, who like Holden was covered with dust from the location. The hotel manager asked them if they would mind waiting before crossing the lobby. The reason: Chou En-lai, the premier of China, was expected to arrive for a reception in the hotel.

Holden and Spiegel watched the procession of Chinese dignitaries enter the hotel, then the two men went to their rooms to clean up. Holden telephoned Spiegel: "I've got an idea, Sam. Why don't we try to meet Chou En-lai? We could tell him we're a couple of average Americans and show him that Americans are not ogres, after all."

Spiegel readily agreed. He was as curious as Holden to meet the leader of a nation that had been totally isolated from the United States. The overture was made through the hotel manager, and Chou re-sponded that he would be delighted to have the two Americans join his party.

"I recognize you," said the Chinese leader to Holden in reasonably good English. "I saw you in a film, though I can't remember what it was."

Chou neglected the other guests to talk at length with the two Americans. As they left, he told them, "If you ever come to China, let me know."

Holden was hungry for letters from home, and he read with excitement Ardis' account of the family Christmas with the Beedles. "She'd better get her ass over here," he grumbled. Yet when he was given a forty-five-day break in filming, he did not return to California. He spent the time in Hong Kong, where he had bought an apartment and had made investments.

Ardis came to Ceylon in March, and the reunion was joyful, for a time. The old tensions returned, and Ardis was especially critical of Bill's drinking—prompting him to drink more.

One night after dinner in the hotel, Bill and Ardis joined Jack and Doreen Hawkins, Bill and Betty Graf, and a few others in the Hawkinses' suite. After several brandies, Holden was telling stor-ies in an energetic manner. Sweeping his hand for a punch line, he knocked the glass from Ardis' hand. The drink spilled down her white dress.

"This dress is ruined!" she exclaimed.

Bill turned to her and raged, "Goddammit, go out and buy six more dresses! I'll pay for them!"

The party ended soon afterward amid quiet embarrassment. The next day each guest received a bottle of champagne with a note: "If there's anything I hate, it's a nasty drunk—Bill."

The entire *Kwai* company was invited to a reception at the Japanese embassy, and all were urged to attend. The Ceylonese government had been reluctant to permit filming of a movie portraying the Japanese as sadistic captors, and insisted that Columbia secure the approval of Japan. Bill Graf convinced Tokyo that *Kwai* was anti-war, not anti-Japanese, and Ceylon granted its permission.

Sam Spiegel, David Lean, Bill Holden, and other members of the cast and crew attended the reception in the embassy garden, which the Japanese had lighted with colorful paper lanterns. The buffet tables were laden with delicacies, and native dancers entertained the guests. The most popular attraction was the gilly-gilly man and his cobra-charming act. Holden, drinking sake from a tall glass, watched with fascination. When the act was over, he picked up the cobra and wrapped it around his neck.

The onlookers were shocked and frightened. Sam Spiegel turned white. Afterward Spiegel said to Holden, "I don't give a goddam what you do after this picture is finished. But don't ever do something like that while you're here!"

Bill strode away angrily, and Ardis hurried after him. "Where are you going?" she said.

"I'm going to find the gilly-gilly man," he said.

"What for?"

"I'm going to buy his cobra and put it in Spiegel's room!"

"Bill! You can't do that! He'll have a heart attack!"

"That's the general idea."

She realized he was serious, and she grabbed his arm. "Bill, I have never told you not to do something. I'm telling you now. If you do this crazy thing, I'm leaving on the next plane." Bill abandoned his plan.

Ardis remained in Ceylon until the filming of the final sequence, the blowing up of the bridge. The climactic scene of the film had been planned with great care. Spiegel had hired Sheffield Steel to build the bridge, International Chemical Industries to plan the explosives. He bought an ancient locomotive and six cars from the Ceylon Railroad; the train was to be destroyed in the explosion.

Lean ordered the multiple cameras to roll, and the train started lumbering toward the bridge. Nothing happened. The train continued over the bridge to the other side of the river and toppled over a hill.

On the second try, bridge and train erupted in a glorious explosion. The filming of *The Bridge on the River Kwai* was over. But none of the company could leave Ceylon until the film had reached London and was safely processed.

"Where is the bridge footage?" Spiegel cabled from London. Neither Lean nor Graf dared tell him that the film was lost. Frantic messages were dispatched along the air route to London. Finally, after two weeks of anxiety, the bridge explosion footage was discovered sitting in the blazing sun on the runway of Cairo airport. Miraculously, it was unharmed.

Released in December of 1957, *The Bridge on the River Kwai* proved an immense success and won seven Academy Awards, including best picture, direction, writing, photography, editing, score, and acting —by Alec Guinness.

"I feel terrible," Guinness remarked later to Holden. "I received the award, while you were the star."

"You deserved it, Alec, you were great in the picture," said Bill, adding with a grin, "You keep the Oscar; I'll keep ten percent of the gross."

Holden's *Kwai* deal became well known, and it was generally considered among the best ever accorded a film star. Too good, declared the Internal Revenue Service, which claimed that such deferment of income would not defer taxes. Holden would have to pay taxes on the amounts accrued, even though not paid to him. His attorney, Deane Johnson, studied applicable cases and argued that the IRS was wrong. The IRS finally agreed with him.

Neither Holden nor his advisers had counted on *Kwai*'s enormous prosperity—$30 million in the first release. Columbia was in an ideal position, earning more in interest from the Holden fund than it paid him annually. Holden discovered that after commissions and taxes, he actually kept only $9,000 out of the $50,000 paid to him annually.

By 1979, Columbia was holding more than $3 million of Holden's deferred earnings from *The Bridge on the River Kwai*. With income still mounting, more than sixty years would be required to repay him and his heirs under the existing contract. Deane Johnson negotiated a settlement. Terms of the settlement were secret, but the amount was reportedly $600,000, of which Ardis received half. Thereafter, Holden would receive his ten percent of gross earnings from *Kwai* without the $50,000 limitation. He willed the income to the industry charity, the Motion Picture and Television Fund.

18

Sophia, Duke, and the Big Decision

"Never con a con man."

Bill Holden gave the advice to Carl Foreman as they entered a partnership to produce *The Key* for release by Columbia Pictures. It was the same advice he gave to others over the years on how to deal with Bill Holden. Sometimes he said, "Never crap a crapper," or "Never bullshit a bullshitter." The message was clear: Holden had been through the studio wars, had witnessed every possible doublecross, so don't try to deceive him.

"Don't worry," Foreman assured him. "I find it hard to lie."

Carl Foreman's career had improved from his blacklist days, even though he had been denied writing credit and a share of the profits of *The Bridge on the River Kwai*. Columbia Pictures had agreed to finance him in the production of a series of films to be made in Europe. The first was *The Key*, based on the Jan de Hartog novel *Stella*. Holden welcomed another overseas assignment and agreed to the terms: $250,000 plus 10 percent of the gross receipts.

Sophia Loren and Trevor Howard were the co-stars, Carol Reed the director. Holden was uncomfortable in the early filming because of the clubby relationship between Reed and Howard. Because Howard could not remember his lines, Reed allowed him to improvise. Holden, who had been disciplined to adhere to dialogue as written, was thrown off balance, uncertain of his cues. As a result, Howard dominated their scenes together. Holden's assurance returned after Howard completed his role.

Holden was impressed by Sophia Loren's professionalism, as well as her raw sensuality. He was determined to get her to bed. So was Carol Reed. Both failed because of the bodyguards provided by Miss Loren's husband, Carlo Ponti.

The Key failed to achieve popularity, but it helped establish a lasting friendship between Bill Holden and Carl Foreman. They were distant politically, but they shared other things, including the agony of failing marriages.

At the conclusion of *The Key,* Holden presented Foreman with a slender volume by Cyril Connolly, *The Unquiet Grave.* The inscription: "To Carl—an unquiet man in an unquiet time from an unquiet friend —Bill."

Why was Bill Holden attracted to *The Unquiet Grave?* It is an esoteric book, full of classical allusions and modern aphorisms, cynical in tone. Possibly its observations appealed to Holden, then forty and at a crossroads in his life.

> There is no pain equal to that which two lovers inflict on one another. This should be made clear to all who contemplate such unions. . . . It is when we begin to hurt those whom we love that the guilt with which we are born becomes intolerable. . . .
>
> In the sex-war thoughtlessness is the weapon of the male, vindictiveness of the female. Both are reciprocally generated, but a woman's desire for revenge outlasts all her other emotions. . . . Yet, when every unkind word about women has been said, we still have to admit, with Byron, that they are nicer than men. . . .
>
> Life is a maze in which we take the wrong turning before we have learned to walk. . . .
>
> It is the fear of middle-age in the young, of old-age in the middle-aged, which is the prime cause of infidelity, that infallible rejuvenator. . . .
>
> I am forced to admit that anxiety is my true condition, occasionally intruded on by work, pleasure, melancholy or despair.

Whenever Bill Holden quoted philosophy, he was more succinct. He often cited the remark: "One should always treat a whore like a lady and a lady like a whore."

During a noisy movie-industry party at Marty Rackin's Bel Air house, Richard Quine wandered into the library. To his surprise, he found William Holden and John Wayne lamenting with each other over a near-empty bottle of cognac.

"I hate being a picture actor!" Holden complained.

"Goddammit, so do I!" Wayne agreed.

Together they listed the elements they hated: the makeup, the hair dye, the costumes, the indignity of exposing emotion before a hundred people, the adoration of strangers. "I'll be damned if it isn't a job for sissies," Wayne grumbled.

They had more in common than a distaste for the unmanly aspects of their profession. Both had been born in the Midwest and had grown up in the conservative Pasadena-Glendale area. Both had become actors more or less by accident, had achieved stardom early, had been forced to rebuild their careers after falling from grace. They shared the same agent, Charlie Feldman, to whom they were devoted.

Wayne and Holden had become Hollywood's most successful male stars. When Holden wrested the title of box-office champion from Wayne, Holden received a telegram: "Sneak!" It was signed by John Wayne.

Co-starring John Wayne and William Holden in a film seemed impossible, but it was accomplished by Martin Rackin, a quintessential hustler.

He was a street-educated New Yorker whose writing career began as ghost for Robert Ripley's newspaper cartoon *Believe It or Not.* He submitted jokes to radio comics, then moved to Hollywood and became famous for his fast talk and glib scripts. After working on movies for Martin and Lewis, Rackin formed a partnership with John Lee Mahin, a distinguished screenwriter. They paid one dollar to option a book about a cavalry raid of the Civil War, *The Horse Soldiers.* The Mirisch Company agreed to provide $3.5 million in financing if Rackin could deliver an important director and two top stars.

John Ford was the key to Rackin's scheme. When Ford agreed to direct the film for $200,000 plus 10 percent of the net profits, the rest was easy. John Wayne was always willing to work for his longtime mentor. Bill Holden joined the project at the urging of his friend Marty Rackin.

Undistinguished in other respects, *The Horse Soldiers* marked the beginning of big-money deals for Hollywood stars. Holden and Wayne received $750,000 apiece as well as 20 percent of the profits. The final contract involved six companies—United Artists, Mirisch, Mahin-Rackin, Ford, Wayne, and Holden—and had twice as many pages as *The Horse Soldiers* script.

The deal seemed in jeopardy when Paramount Pictures sued Holden to prevent him from making *The Horse Soldiers,* claiming he was committed to a Paramount film. But a federal judge refused to grant an injunction, and production plans continued. The suit further embittered Holden against his onetime employers.

As details of the massive production took shape, John Lee Mahin became concerned. "You know, Marty," he told his partner, "I think we'd better do some more work on the script. It needs fixing."

"Don't worry about it," said the ever-confident Rackin. "We've got John Ford, John Wayne, and William Holden. That's enough."

Mahin didn't think so. Neither did John Ford. When he and Rackin were conferring aboard Ford's yacht in Honolulu, the director remarked, "You know where we ought to make this picture?"

"No," said Rackin. "Where?"

"Lourdes. It's going to take a miracle to pull it off."

Filming of *The Horse Soldiers* began in late October of 1958 in southern Louisiana. Most of the company were quartered in the town of Natchitoches, near the location sites. Rackin and Holden stayed in Shreveport and drove to the set every day. Holden enjoyed the detachment, having learned how Ford liked to control the lives of those on his film locations. For John Wayne there was no escape. Ford, who never let Wayne forget that he had been elevated from prop man to star by John Ford, badgered his protégé continually. Ford, a onetime heavy drinker who had been forbidden alcohol by his doctors, was especially critical of Wayne's drinking.

"Jesus, Marty, the old man is driving me nuts," Wayne complained to Rackin. "You gotta get me outa here."

Rackin devised a convenient lie which he told to Ford: "They've been complaining about the dailies in Hollywood; Duke's teeth are photographing yellow. I've got to take him to a dentist in Shreveport and get his teeth cleaned. We'll be back tomorrow."

The ruse worked, and Wayne enjoyed a night of carousing with Holden and Rackin, removed from the baleful gaze of John Ford. The following morning, Rackin drove the two actors to Natchitoches in his rented Thunderbird. Fearing Ford's wrath if they were late, Rackin pushed the car past a hundred miles per hour on the country roads. Wayne glanced at the speedometer and commented, "You know, Marty, if we all die in a crash, you'll get third billing." Rackin slowed down.

They arrived late at the location, and Ford realized that the trip had concerned more than dental hygiene. He kept the two stars working under the hot Louisiana sun all day.

Newcomers to the Ford team often became targets of the director's abuse. Not so with Bill Holden. Ford treated him respectfully, though with a watchful eye. One afternoon Ford noticed Holden in deep conversation with the leading actress, Constance Towers. "Well, it's started," Ford commented, anticipating a romance. However, Holden was merely giving advice to the actress in her first film.

Miss Towers noticed the contrast in the two stars. Holden left the location immediately after he was released. Wayne remained, sometimes for an hour or two, signing autographs and talking to local youngsters. "How the devil does Duke do it? That would drive me nuts," Holden remarked.

One night Holden was dining with Rackin and Mahin at a Shreveport restaurant when a burly oil worker called from the bar, "Hey, Holden, c'mon over here! I want you to meet my girl."

Holden ignored him until he called again, "Hey, Holden, come here!"

Holden swung around and fixed his cold blue eyes on the man. "Look, buster," he said, "I haven't worked my ass off for twenty-two years so somebody like you can address me as 'Hey, Holden.' You can call me 'Bill' or you can call me 'Mr. Holden.' Don't call me 'Holden.' Now I'm talking to friends at this time. When I'm finished, I may come over and meet your girl." He returned to his conversation with Rackin and Mahin. By the time he finished, the man and his girl had disappeared.

The Horse Soldiers moved to Natchez, Mississippi, amid a growing sense of failure. Ford, realizing the script's shortcomings, became more dyspeptic, his direction more perfunctory.

Ford always provided work for over-the-hill film workers, and he had employed an aging stunt man, Fred Kennedy, as a bit player. Kennedy needed money, and he pleaded with Ford to be allowed to double for Holden in a saddle fall. The director realized that Kennedy was overweight and out of condition but finally agreed to let him do the stunt.

"I want you to play a trick on Fred," Ford told Constance Towers. "When he takes his fall, you rush in and give him a big kiss."

The camera rolled and Ford called "Action!" Kennedy galloped his horse and fell off exactly on his mark. Miss Towers dashed to him on cue, took Kennedy in her arms, and screamed, "This man is dying!" He had broken his neck in the fall and was dead before he reached a hospital.

The tragedy plunged John Ford into black despair. He blamed himself for allowing Kennedy to take the hazardous fall, and he had no heart to continue the location shooting. The company returned to Hollywood, and Ford filmed the final battle in a single day in the San Fernando Valley. He hurried through the rest of the film and left immediately to nurse his guilt in Honolulu. Marty Rackin was faced with the task of assembling a film that lacked important story points and a stirring climax. As for Bill Holden's share of the profit from *The Horse Soldiers*, there was none.

In the late 1950s, the accountants, lawyers, and business managers of Hollywood made a startling discovery. Congress had passed a law exempting Americans from income taxes while they worked outside the country. The purpose of the law was to encourage American investment in foreign countries as well as to foster economic growth in non-Communist nations. Nothing in the law said that it couldn't be applied to movie stars.

The exodus began: Clark Gable, Van Johnson, Audrey Hepburn, Kirk Douglas, Burt Lancaster, Yul Brynner, David Niven, Deborah Kerr, Alan Ladd. Not all were Americans, but all had established their movie fame in Hollywood.

When Andy Hickox pointed out the monetary advantages of living abroad, Bill Holden leaped at the suggestion. "Where would you suggest I live?" he asked.

"Switzerland seems like the most advantageous place," said the business manager. "Taxes are low, living is good, and the location is central to wherever you might make movies."

"Great!" said Holden. "I'll go look for a house right away."

Bill Holden was ready to leave. After his travels—he was averaging 100,000 miles a year—he found Hollywood stiflingly provincial. He was appalled to return from the political and economic ferment of newly emerging nations and find his friends talking about grosses of the recent films and the latest gossip from Hedda and Louella. His own interests were distant; he had invested in a radio station in Hong Kong, an electronics company in Japan. He had continents to explore.

There were personal concerns as well. Perhaps if he and Ardis removed themselves from the pressures of Hollywood they could rediscover the contentment they had known in their early marriage. Virginia had grown up and married, and now the Holdens had only West, who was fifteen, and Scott, thirteen. Bill was disappointed with their progress in California schools. His European friends had told him the value of education in the Swiss schools, where students were drilled in English, French, and German.

The basic motive was money. In Shreveport he had seen oil millionaires by the dozen, men who did little work and reaped enormous tax-favored incomes. It galled Holden to be forced to hand over 90 percent of his income to the government. He had been scrupulously honest in his tax dealings, not even deducting expenses for his cars, his home, entertaining the press and visiting dignitaries.

Holden flew to Switzerland and found a house at St. Prex, near Lausanne, that seemed ideal. He telephoned Andy Hichox: "This is where I want to live; I'm going to buy it."

On August 29, 1959, Bill and Ardis and their two sons boarded a Pan American jet clipper for the new polar-route trip to Europe. Holden told reporters, "We are taking up residence in Switzerland because of my film commitments in Europe over the next three years and not necessarily because of high U.S. income taxes." The severing of his American ties was complete; he had sold the Toluca Lake house for $120,000, $20,000 more than he had paid for it.

During the next three years, Bill Holden, once the solid citizen of Hollywood, became the object of calumny and vituperation. Film industry guilds and unions, including the Screen Actors Guild, attacked him for fostering "runaway production" during a time when Hollywood was already depressed by the competition of television. Members of Congress assailed him as a millionaire tax evader taking unfair advantage of laws intended to help average American wage earners abroad. The new Attorney General, Robert F. Kennedy, cited Holden as an example of how the rich perverted the tax laws. Kennedy's wife Ethel was heard to call William Holden a traitor for choosing to live in Switzerland to avoid taxes.

Holden was bewildered by the fury of the attacks and incensed that he was singled out as villain. When I saw him in Stockholm in 1961, he was defiant.

"I'm living the kind of life I think is best for me and my family," he said. "I will continue to do so, no matter what laws are changed or what anybody says."

When I asked him about the criticism of his own union, the Screen Actors Guild, he softened his attitude: "I'll tell you a story that expresses my point of view. Two psychiatrists are riding in an elevator to their offices. When the first one arrives at the fifth floor, he slaps the other one across the face and leaves. The second psychiatrist proceeds calmly to his own floor. The elevator operator is perplexed, and he asks his passenger about the incident. 'Oh, yes,' the psychiatrist says, 'that's *his* problem.' "

He added: "What the senators and the Guild are talking about is *their* problem. It couldn't bother me less. They talk about the American stars who are living in Switzerland. Well, who are they? David Niven? He's English. Deborah Kerr? She's English. Peter Ustinov? He's English. Noel Coward? He's English. Audrey Hepburn? She's Dutch-English. They mention Ava Gardner. But wait a minute, she's living in Spain, isn't she? So who does that leave? Me, Bill Holden. That's all.

"It seems to me that Americans have always been noted for moving around, for being unafraid of new challenges, new frontiers. Now certain people are trying to tell us to stay home and not work abroad. It's a form of isolationism. Why did President Kennedy propose the Peace Corps, if not to get Americans to live and work in foreign countries?

"They can change the laws any way they like. That won't make my life any different. Living in Switzerland has been the most rewarding experience of my life."

Congress changed the law, placing a $25,000 limit on tax exemption for Americans working abroad. By that time Holden had made two films in Europe for $750,000 apiece. The tax-free $1,500,000 was more than he could have amassed during a decade of working in the United States. Deprival of the tax exemption made no change in Holden's mode of living. He felt alienated from his onetime friends and associates of Hollywood, contemptuous of the smug attitudes of main-current America. The glow of patriotism he had felt during and after the war now dimmed. He felt himself a citizen of the world.

19

Africa

Bill Holden's friends could never understand his attachment to Ray Ryan. The two men seemed totally unalike: Ryan the big blustery Irishman, wearing his wealth like a badge; Holden a man wary of all pretense, scornful of the show-off aspects of a movie star's life. A confirmed loner, Holden nonetheless found vast amusement in the company of Ray Ryan.

His background was surrounded by legend, and Ryan seemed to relish the mystery attached to his career. Born in Watertown, Wisconsin, in 1905, he had become an oil wildcatter in the early 1930s. His Ryan Oil Company, based in Evansville, Indiana, drilled more than a thousand wells in sixteen states. His biggest operations were in Texas, where he became associated with H. L. Hunt, Clint Murchison, and other high-risk entrepreneurs. During World War II, Ryan owned a California factory supplying airplane parts for the air force. After the war, he speculated in Palm Springs real estate, buying the El Mirador Hotel and launching a resort community, Bermuda Dunes.

Ryan had investments in Las Vegas, and it was widely rumored that he had close ties to the underworld. He did nothing to discourage such rumors, nor did he deny legends about his gambling. Among them: that he had won $243,000 in gin rummy from H. L. Hunt during an Atlantic crossing; that he had bet $50,000 apiece on twelve college football games on a single Saturday.

Bill Holden met Ray Ryan in Palm Springs and discovered that the brash gambler could be entertaining—and useful. Ryan advised Holden on investments that inevitably proved profitable. Holden began flying around the country with Ryan in his private plane to scout oil ventures and other investment possibilities.

During a trip to Dallas, Holden walked into Ryan's hotel suite as Ryan was opening his suitcase. Inside were piles of hundred-dollar bills —$400,000 worth.

"My God, aren't you worried about carrying around all that money?" Holden asked.

"Yeah, it does get a little heavy," Ryan replied. He never disclosed what the money was for. At one time he acted as carrier for Hunt and Murchison, who made huge bets on athletic contests and wanted the wagers kept secret. They knew they could trust Ray Ryan.

Ryan had always wanted to see Africa, and he found a ready companion in Bill Holden. In January of 1959, they left for Kenya, where they were joined by a business associate of Ryan's, Carl Hirschmann, a Swiss banker.

The three hunters arrived in Nairobi, bought expensive outfits, and acquired licenses to shoot the "big four"—elephant, rhino, lion, buffalo. They embarked into the veldt in grand style, with two white hunters, a small arsenal of weapons, two dozen carriers and trackers, stocks of gourmet food, and cases of whisky. Bill Holden had scarcely hunted since his high school days on the Mojave Desert, and he was thrilled by Africa's savage beauty and atmosphere of danger. But when he fixed his gunsight on a huge bull elephant, he found he could not squeeze the trigger.

"I can't kill an animal like that," he said, laying down his rifle.

Ryan had no such reluctance. He continued amassing trophies until one day he fired his rifle and the telescopic sight dislodged, tearing a gash in his head. The nearest hospital was at Nanyuki, fifty miles away.

"That would be a good place to rest," suggested a white hunter. "A nice hotel there, the Mawingo. Many safaris stop at the Mawingo."

The name meant Cloudland, and the place seemed halfway to the sky, nestled on the slopes of the majestic Mount Kenya, 17,000 feet high. The hotel had been built on a lavish scale during the early 1930s as a private residence for a wealthy and eccentric Englishwoman. When she tired of Africa and a lover, she gave the place to him and returned to England. Later it was bought and remodeled by Jack Block, who operated the famed New Stanley Hotel in Nairobi. Nanyuki had been dangerous country during the 1950s when the Mau Mau were massacring white settlers. Kenya was on the brink of independence in 1959, and the Mau Mau had been pacified. Their chief, Jomo Kenyatta, was destined to become the new nation's leader.

Years later, Bill Holden recalled the birth of the Mount Kenya Safari Club, telling how he, Ryan, and Hirschmann returned to the Mawingo Hotel, "and we used to sit there watching the sunset after a marvelous day out in the fresh air. We'd say time and again how great it would be if someone would only take over the place. It could be among the most beautiful spots on earth.

"Bob Ruark was there at the time, and he finally said after about three nights, 'I wish you bastards would either put up or shut up.' I suppose it was in the back of our minds in any case; between us we had nine children, and this would be a great place to bring them and our friends. So we negotiated with the Blocks and eventually bought."

Robert Ruark, who had become a latter-day Hemingway with his books and newspaper writings about Africa, gave this report in a column:

Now what really happened is this. It was last spring. We were drawn together by whisky. I had come with a Spaniard named Ricardo Sicre from elephant hunting up north, and we ran into this Holden, who needed a shave, and this Ryan, who needed a shave and haircut, and this Hirschmann. Holden, Ryan and I all had the gout, and a telescope had kicked back and durned near took the top off oilman Ryan's head. Someone stole the horns off one of their buffalo, to make snuffboxes out of, and we were sitting around sulking in the lobby of the Mawingo Hotel.

"Thees a nice place," Ricardo said. "Very pretty. But no action. No girls. No music. Nothing bot scenery. Me, I like mountains but you look at a mountain only so long."

"I like Hong Kong myself," actor Holden said. "There you got action and mountains."

"I am a Palm Springs kid myself," Mr. Ryan said. "There you got action and scenery. But I am kind of all shook up by this Africa."

"I happen to know who owns this joint," I said. "And what it'll sell fór. Why don't you buy the joint and provide the action?"

Mr. Holden looked at Mr. Ryan, who still needed a haircut. Mr. Ryan looked at Mr. Holden, and then they both looked at Mr. Hirschmann.

"Let's buy it," they said like a Greek chorus.

The three travelers bought the Mawingo Hotel, Ryan and Holden providing 45 percent apiece, Hirschmann 10 percent. They soon discovered a major drawback. Holden recalled: "We had big plans for bird sanctuaries, but the problem was we had no control of the grounds. The hotel was a public house, and anyone could come along and use it as a picnic ground, if they liked. Monday was cleanup day—all the bottles and trash from people bringing along their orange squash and a brown paper bag full of lunch. So we turned it into a club, so that we had enough control to be able to get on with the bird and wildlife sanctuary, and manicure the grounds, plant gardens, and so on."

They named it the Mount Kenya Safari Club, and promoter Ryan devised a way to attract attention. Honorary memberships, which included a gold car and wall plaque, were issued to Winston Churchill, Clark Gable, Lily Pons, the Duke of Manchester, Walt Disney, Joan Crawford, John Wayne, Jack Dempsey, Norman Vincent Peale, Lyndon Johnson, Everett Dirksen, Prince Bernhard, Conrad Hilton, John Ford, Bob Hope, Henry J. Kaiser, and many more. Most of them never saw the Mount Kenya Safari Club.

With fierce ambition and a prestigious if invisible membership, the new owners aimed to make the Mount Kenya Safari Club the showplace of East Africa. To the big white English manor house were added rows of white bungalows. A kidney-shaped swimming pool was built in front of the main house, with acres of clipped grass sloping to a rushing stream. Beyond was the magnificence of Mount Kenya, often obscured, but some days seeming to be just outside the hotel windows.

Bill Holden contributed his energies everywhere. He supervised the damming of streams to create trout-laden ponds. He designed the bungalows. He choreographed native dances to entertain guests at nightfall. He imported a chef from Vienna and tried to teach the natives kitchen cleanliness. Somehow they couldn't remember to wash their hands before starting work, so Bill ordered them to wear white cotton gloves. That made some of the chores difficult.

"One day," Bill related, "I walked in the kitchen and found one of the workers wearing his white gloves—and opening pea pods with his toes."

Bill hired a hundred workers for the hotel, soon found he had three hundred to support, since all brought their relatives. He shut down hotel operations three times to get rid of the hangers-on; each time they returned.

Despite the elegant facilities and a drumbeat of publicity, the Mount Kenya Safari Club operated at less than one-quarter occupancy in its first three years. To most American tourists in the early 1960s, Kenya seemed distant and dangerous, the specter of marauding Mau Mau still vivid in their minds.

Bill Holden remained undiscouraged. He had never intended to make a profit from his African venture. Even if he lost money, as he would surely do, he had gained immeasurably. He had discovered in Africa his spiritual home.

In 1976, he summed up his feelings during an interview with *Africana* magazine:

"There are two things that happen to you when you come to Kenya. You can regenerate yourself here, and you can reconstitute yourself. A few years ago, the centers of Europe were the places to go to enrich yourself culturally. It's still important for many Americans who must find their cultural roots. But, in my opinion, once this has been done, there's little to be had from Europe in terms of plain enjoyment.

"Kenya offers the opportunity for a much deeper cultural experience. It is, after all, the cradle of man, as Leakey and others have shown. And because the concept of learning and the quest for knowledge is so much more intense than it was, say, two generations ago, this is of great interest to people. On top of all that, you have this marvelous climate and an infinite variety of landscapes within a relatively small area."

He could thus intellectualize about the appeal of Africa, but his motivations went deeper. He had found something far more meaningful than the vocation of film acting. And Africa was the ideal setting for a man to whom danger and death had held a lifelong fascination.

Bill once rhapsodized to a friend: "Every day in Africa might be your last. That sense of anticipation keeps you thrillingly alive!"

20

The Expatriate

Before the Holden family departed for their new home in Switzerland, Ardis, West, and Scott underwent $3,000 worth of French lessons so they would have an acquaintance with the language. Not Bill. He claimed he was too busy.

"But how will Bill understand what's being said in Switzerland?" Billy Wilder asked.

Answered West: "He'll just snap his fingers at me and say, 'Translation.'"

Throughout his travels, Bill Holden made no effort to learn the language of the country he lived in or visited. It was not his style. He brought an American curiosity to foreign lands, but it did not extend to studying the languages or exploring social issues. He was ever the traveler, moving on to another place when his curiosity was fulfilled.

He had no intention of becoming a Swiss. He shipped his furniture from Toluca Lake to St. Prex, so he could live in familiar surroundings. He gutted the four-bedroom house overlooking the Lake of Geneva and had it rebuilt more in Californian than Swiss style. He socialized not with Swiss intellectuals or businessmen but with other expatriates: Noel Coward, Yul Brynner, David Niven, Norman and Erle Krasna, Deborah Kerr, and Tony Bartley. He raced his Bentley as swiftly on the Swiss highways as he had his Ferrari on the Palm Springs back roads.

Richard Gehman wrote of how Holden was speeding on a long, steep hill outside Lausanne-Ouchy "at his customary breakneck seventy miles an hour. As he pulled out to pass a lumbering truck, another truck appeared over the crest of the hill. A head-on collision seemed inevitable. 'Cross your fingers,' Holden threw over his shoulder to his wife, Ardis, who was seated in the back with a friend. 'They *are* crossed; I cross them every time I get into this car,' Mrs. Holden said. Holden gunned the motor and cut in, barely avoiding a crash. While his wife and her friend shakily lighted cigarettes, Holden gave a wild, boyish laugh."

Bill was delighted when visitors came from Hollywood. When Cliff Robertson was making a film in Europe, Bill urged him to spend a day or two in Switzerland. Robertson flew to Lausanne and registered at the Beau Rivage Hotel. Bill was waiting for him in the bar.

Holden greeted his Hollywood friend warmly and ordered him a drink. Bill was being interviewed by a visiting reporter, and he was obviously guarded in his replies. When the reporter left, Bill told Robertson, "I don't trust a lot of these reporters; they speak with forked tongues. You tell them something, and they print something else."

After more drinks, Bill said, "C'mon, I'm going to take you to Geneva to meet a friend of mine, a real character named Ray Ryan." Holden and Robertson sped along the highway in Bill's Bentley. Robertson contemplated why Bill Holden would own a Bentley and not a Rolls-Royce; the only difference was the radiator. Then Robertson realized that the Bentley cost a hundred dollars less and was faintly less ostentatious. Thus an acceptable extravagance for the expatriate Golden Boy.

As they drove, Holden talked about his life in Switzerland. "You know, I've got my sons in school here," he said. "One of them speaks English and French; he's bilingual. The other speaks English, French, and German; he's trilingual. It's terrible."

"Why is that?" Robertson asked.

"Hell, I'm not even lingual."

They arrived in Geneva, met Ray Ryan, had more drinks and a lavish dinner, which Ryan paid for from a roll of hundred-dollar bills, and went on to visit the Norman Krasnas. Robertson never did meet Ardis. He surmised that she and Bill were having another of their arguments.

The move to Switzerland had not improved the relationship between Bill and Ardis; in fact, the old antagonisms intensified, sometimes violently. One evening at the Krasna house in Switzerland, Bill climaxed an argument by hitting Ardis across the face with his hat. Bill once called Krasna in a panic: "Ardis has left the house! Where could she go? What can I do?" He and Ardis had argued again, and she had disappeared. Bill called the local police.

Furious with Bill, Ardis had gone to Erle Krasna, who had sequestered her in the Krasna guest house. Ardis stayed there until she decided Bill had been punished enough.

"Bill was always complaining about Ardis," observes a longtime friend. "He complained about how she spent money, how she said such cutting things. But here's the point: he never stopped talking about her."

Another friend adds this comment: "Ardis was married to one of the world's most famous and most attractive men. Beautiful women wanted to go to bed with Bill, and many did. Ardis was married to a man who drove like a maniac when he was sober and hung out of windows when he was drunk. Bill had a fierce temper, and much of the time it was directed at Ardis, the closest target for his frustrations. Bill would disappear for a month or two in Africa or the Orient, and he seemed to welcome the long movie locations that would keep him away from his wife and sons. Yet with all his transgressions, Ardis always took him back. She never stopped loving him."

Holden often admitted his reliance on Ardis. On a film location he told a publicist this story:

A farmer was the envy of his neighbors. Each year he seemed to know exactly the right crops to plant, so that his harvests were greater than anyone else's. Then one winter the farmer's wife died. In the spring his crops were stunted, the barn burned, his cattle sickened. Year after year, it was the same story. One day a neighbor asked him what went wrong. "When my wife died," the farmer replied, "I lost everything."

Bill Holden added, "If I were to lose Ardis, I would lose everything."

The World of Suzie Wong was Bill Holden's first film after moving abroad. It involved a location in Hong Kong, and that was enough to make him overlook the improbabilities of a soggy script about an American painter and a Chinese whore. Jean Negulesco was the director, and the producer was Ray Stark, whom Bill had known as an agent with Charlie Feldman at Famous Artists Agency.

Filming began in Hong Kong, with interiors to be completed in London. Producer Stark found Holden to be of enormous help in dealing with Hong Kong officials, who recognized the American star's help in bringing investment and tourism to the colony. Bill delighted in showing Stark the sights and pleasures of the city.

One night they were crossing the bay on the Kowloon ferry, returning to the Peninsula Hotel after a ceremonial dinner at the home of producer Run Run Shaw. Both Holden and Stark were drunk. When the ferry docked, Holden suggested, "Let's walk to the hotel."

"No, let's take a rickshaw," said the producer. In a playful mood, he made the rickshaw driver sit in the seat and started pulling him toward the hotel.

Bill grabbed Stark angrily. "Don't ever let me see you do that again!" Bill snapped. "This rickshaw is how that man makes a living and supports his family. That's his dignity. Don't ever harm a man's dignity."

The company completed Hong Kong filming and returned to London, where trouble began. France Nuyen, who was repeating her Broadway role as Suzie, began to pine for Marlon Brando, her lover in far-off California. Gossip columns reported that Brando was romancing a Filipino-Hungarian actress, Barbara Luna. The distressed France Nuyen began overeating, and soon she was bulging out of her silken cheongsams. She was fired and replaced by Nancy Kwan, daughter of an Englishwoman and a Chinese architect. Trained in the English ballet, she had been discovered in Hong Kong by Ray Stark and had appeared in the U.S. road company of *The World of Suzie Wong*.

Next, Stark fired Jean Negulesco. The producer telephoned Richard Quine in Hollywood and asked him to take the next plane to London.

Quine, who had known Holden slightly at Columbia and had worked with Stark on a film version of *Funny Girl* when it was intended for Judy Holliday, arrived at London airport twenty-four hours later. Holden, Stark, and John Patrick, the scriptwriter, greeted him, and they motored to the Connaught Hotel for an all-night discussion of the film. Quine was driven to the Elstree studio, where a huge Hong Kong street had been erected, and he was induced to start directing immediately. Quine realized he was being coerced, but he was enjoying it. He also realized the company had to work fast. Locations had to be reshot in Hong Kong before the monsoon season.

One Sunday evening, the *Suzie Wong* principals enjoyed a rare evening out in London. Holden, Stark, Quine, Patrick, and Miss Kwan were joined by the visiting Charlie Feldman. The only night spot they could find open on Sunday was a third-class dance hall near the Dorchester Hotel. After a few drinks, Bill noticed two black girls dancing together in front of the tinny orchestra. He rose and introduced himself to the dancers. He started dancing with one of them, conversing animatedly.

Ava Gardner, who was also making a film in London, entered the dance hall with a party and sat in a booth. When the dance number ended, Bill greeted Ava warmly. After a brief conversation, he said, "Excuse me," and he left to dance with the second black girl.

When he returned to his own table, Ray Stark told him, "Bill, are you crazy? You could have danced with Ava Gardner, one of the most beautiful women in the world!"

"Yes," said Bill, eyes twinkling, "but look how happy those two girls are."

The World of Suzie Wong company completed interior scenes and flew immediately to Hong Kong. On the night of their arrival, Ardis and Bill joined Stark and Quine for dinner in the Marco Polo Room of the Peninsula Hotel. After coffee, Holden said to Quine, "C'mon, buddy." Quine followed him out of the restaurant, presuming they were headed for the men's room. Instead, Bill took him to a Vespa motor scooter parked outside the hotel. Bill revved the engine and said, "Get on."

"What the hell are you doing?" Quine demanded.

"You gotta see Hong Kong before you can make this picture—right? So you're going to see it. Get on!"

Quine clung tightly to Holden as they roared into the drizzly night. They visited bar after bar in Kowloon, consuming large quantities of Johnnie Walker Black Label and dancing with bar girls pursuing Suzie Wong's profession. At two-thirty in the morning, they rode to the waterfront, where Bill awakened a family who owned a motorized sampan.

"We want to go to the Hong Kong side," Bill said, adding a few words in Cantonese and a flash of currency for persuasion. Another tour of the bars, ending in the incongruously named Maxime's, where Quine played piano and Bill the bongos with a jazz band composed of Italians. They returned to Kowloon by the sampan, boarded the Vespa, and rode back to the Peninsula Hotel.

"Okay, now you've seen Hong Kong," Bill said. The two men showered and dressed and reported for the start of the Hong Kong locations for *The World of Suzie Wong*.

The Counterfeit Traitor was an ambitious film produced by William Perlberg and written and directed by George Seaton in Berlin, Hamburg, Copenhagen, and Stockholm. Holden was on his best behavior, especially since Ardis often visited the locations and Scott Holden had a minor job in the film company. Only once did Holden rebel.

The film company had arranged to shoot in the Hamburg railroad station late Saturday afternoon when traffic was light. Hamburg police were assigned to keep people behind roped-off areas and avoid disruption of filming. A middle-aged man laden with packages refused to detour on his passage to the train. Two policemen pulled him back and beat him with nightsticks, breaking his legs.

"Goddammit, that's atrocious!" Holden raged to Seaton and Perlberg. "We have no right to block people's access to the trains. We have no right to disrupt their normal lives. You let those Gestapo cops beat that poor bastard to a pulp. Well, I want no part of it. You can make the goddam picture by yourselves."

Holden started to leave for the Atlantic Hotel, and George Seaton stopped him. Seaton and Perlberg talked to Holden for an hour in the terminal office until they convinced him to resume work.

The Counterfeit Traitor was scheduled to conclude in Stockholm, but the northern winter descended before Seaton could finish. The production was suspended until the following June, when the Stockholm sequences would be completed.

Members of the production company noticed a change in Holden when they reassembled in 1961. He looked haggard and puffy-eyed, and he missed the first day of filming because of his appearance.

Bill enjoyed entertaining members of the Hollywood press who visited the location. First to arrive were Erskine Johnson of NEA and his wife Isabel. He instructed her in the Swedish custom for drinking aquavit: "First you entwine your arms, touch your noses together and look into each other's eyes. Then you toss the aquavit down in one gulp and follow with a slug of beer." By the end of the evening, Holden seemed so loaded with aquavit that Mrs. Johnson bet her husband five dollars that he would not appear on the set in the morning.

To Johnson's amazement, Holden was before the camera at 9 A.M. Bill commented, "The last thing I remember was sitting on the toilet at three-thirty. That's where I was when the assistant director called me at seven A.M."

Bill took my wife Pat and me out to dinner on our first night in Stockholm and introduced us to the aquavit custom, resulting in the alltime hangover of my life. After another evening of much drinking, Bill's attorney, Deane Johnson, who was visiting him on business, forbade him from dining with members of the press.

When we met for an interview in Bill's suite at the Grand Hotel, he was serious, even somber as he defended himself against the attacks of the Screen Actors Guild, Congress, and the Kennedy administration. He smoked almost constantly as he paced the room and talked about his life abroad.

"I make pictures abroad because that's what interests me," he said. "That's where I can do some good. The stories I look for are ones that show an American in an international situation. They're the ones that make money, and I'm not out to make producers lose. I've tried strictly American themes like *Toward the Unknown* and *The Horse Soldiers*. They don't sell. But something like *Suzie Wong*, which most of the critics deplored, is headed for ten million dollars' profit."

He talked about his life in Switzerland and how well his sons were doing in school; he planned for them to take two years of college in the United States, then earn degrees in Europe with the possible goal of representing American companies on the Continent.

"These past few years of moving about the world have been more rewarding than anything I have known in my life," Bill said. "It is one thing to read about the far-off places where news is happening; you really get an understanding when you've been there.

"Switzerland is an especially stimulating place to live. People of all nationalities live there, and international meetings of all kinds are held in Geneva. The Swiss themselves are a marvelous people. They haven't had a war in six hundred and fifty years, and they practice what has been well called 'unconditional nonaggression' toward other people's lives.

"We like it there. We are going to stay."

Joel McCrea and Frances Dee were passing through the Geneva airport after he had completed a film in London. They encountered their old friend Bill Holden, who was himself en route to London for a film with Leo McCarey.

"You don't sound very enthusiastic," said McCrea. "Leo's a great director."

"I know, Joel," said Bill. "But I just can't get excited about making pictures anymore."

With *Satan Never Sleeps*, Leo McCarey attempted to recapture his *Going My Way* glory. Holden and Clifton Webb were miscast as Catholic priests combating the Communists in rural China. The locations were filmed in England on sets built from *The Inn of the Sixth Happiness*. For the female lead, Holden insisted on giving another chance to France Nuyen, whose career had languished after her firing from *The World of Suzie Wong*.

Bill drank heavily during *Satan Never Sleeps*. To his amazement, Leo McCarey drank more: two quarts of brandy a day. The film reflected the condition of its two major participants, and it was the first in a series of failures for William Holden.

21

Capucine

Germaine Lefebvre was born in Toulon, France, on January 6, 1935, the daughter of a businessman who wanted her to teach school or work in a bank. Germaine had other ambitions. Most of all, she wanted to escape the stiflingly strict Catholic atmosphere she had endured all her life.

"I have always been a dreamer," she once told an interviewer. "I started as a kid to dream of being somebody else, of making something of myself.

"The chance did not come until I was seventeen and a half. I was working for an uncle, and I had to give my money to my parents. I was so frightened I did not know where to turn. Then one day I stole the money—it was mine, not theirs—and I went to the big town, Paris. They tried to bring me back and put me in a home for delinquents, but I would not go. They did not press it because of gossip and embarrassment in such a town as Toulon, so I did not return."

She became a fashion model, dropping her name, which she always hated, and calling herself merely Capucine, the French word for nasturtium. Against her parents' wishes, she married an actor, then divorced him eight months later. Capucine began earning the top modeling fee of seventy dollars an hour. She was ideally suited to show the new styles of Paris designers; she was an angular five feet, seven inches, with the long, straight nose and high cheekbones of an early Picasso.

She moved to New York to improve her English and make higher fees as a model. One of Charlie Feldman's scouts spotted her in a restaurant, offered a trip to Hollywood and a screen test. Gregory Ratoff directed the test, which resulted in a contract with Famous Artists Agency at $150 a week. Almost immediately she became Charlie's girl. Feldman supervised her publicity and found her roles in his own films or those involving his clients: *Song Without End, North to Alaska, A Walk on the Wild Side*. And then *The Lion*, with William Holden.

Ever since acquiring an interest in the Mount Kenya Safari Club, Holden had tried to induce a Hollywood company to star him in a film that could be shot in Kenya, using the club as a base. His dream was to establish complete studio facilities to accommodate any visiting filmmakers. He sought a deal with Darryl Zanuck for *Roots of Heaven* but failed. Then 20th Century–Fox signed with him for *The Lion*, agreeing to spend $100,000 to build a sound stage and other permanent facilities.

The film company had trouble with the animals from the beginning. None of the local lions responded to direction, and a docile movie lion named Zamba was shipped by air from Hollywood. One morning Holden remarked to the animal's trainer, "You really ought to be more careful about keeping Zamba locked up. I saw him walking on the lawn in front of the club last night. Nearly bumped into him."

"Not Zamba," said the trainer. "He was safely in his cage." Bill suddenly realized he had had an encounter with another, untrained lion.

"Where can I keep the pythons?" the snake trainer asked Holden.

"How about your bathtub?" Holden suggested. The arrangement worked well until one of the pythons turned on the hot water faucet and the snakes wriggled in panic. "The pythons are loose!" screamed a woman, racing through the hotel lobby. A visiting reporter saved the situation by breaking the bathroom window and turning off the faucet with a broom handle.

The Mount Kenya Safari Club, unaccustomed to a large number of guests, was straining to meet the challenge. And failing. After working before the camera all day, Holden returned to the club and tried to restore order. He worked in the office and kitchen until midnight, delivering room service orders himself.

With Jack Cardiff as director, *The Lion* company was mostly British. On Guy Fawkes Day, Bill decided to create a celebration for them, as well as the British who had remained in Kenya after the Mau Mau rebellion. He intercepted a truckload of fireworks en route to Tanzania and staged a dazzling display. During the celebration a Kikuyu child fired a Roman candle onto the roof of the club, setting it afire. Bill grabbed an extinguisher, climbed to the roof, and put out the blaze.

Despite his efforts to maintain morale, tensions rose in *The Lion* company. English members of the crew directed their scorn at the handful of Americans, who were being paid at a higher scale. The friction turned to violence in the club bar one night, and a full-scale donnybrook began. The alarmed manager ran to Holden's cottage.

Holden jumped into his Land Rover and drove it up the front steps and into the lobby. Pulling a pistol from under his belt, he said to the startled movie crewmen, "All right, fellas, let's stop this shit." The riot was over.

Ardis came to the Safari Club while *The Lion* was being filmed. There was a noticeable tenseness between them, like combatants in an uneasy truce. After two weeks, the truce was broken, and Bill and Ardis argued fiercely. She left Kenya, and the movie workers guessed that Capucine was the reason. Bill and Capucine gave no visible evidence of affection, being totally businesslike on the movie set. Once Bill commented on Capucine's penchant for telling long, boring stories: "She's so marvelously ornamental—when her mouth is shut."

With Ardis gone, the attraction toward Capucine proved irresistible. Now Bill felt a double guilt: that he was betraying both Ardis and his close friend Charlie Feldman. In fact, Charlie had wearied of Capucine and was willing to have Bill take her off his hands.

When *The Lion* was completed, Bill began a drinking binge. He had contracted hepatitis, and alcohol aggravated his condition. He left the Mount Kenya Safari Club on a stretcher and flew to Italy, where he was treated at the famed Montecatani health spa. Under doctors' supervision, he ate a special diet, exercised, took hot baths, and drank large amounts of mineral water. Over the years Holden became a familiar visitor at Montecatani.

His recuperative powers amazed his friends. After the Italian cure, he returned to Switzerland with his customary vigor, racing his motorboat across Lake Geneva and speeding his Bentley along the alpine highways. He never stayed long. Always he had an excuse to leave Ardis and the boys. The Safari Club needed his attention, and there were other investments: an apartment building and radio station in Hong Kong, a restaurant in Kyoto, an electronics firm in Tokyo, a diamond mine in South Africa, a racetrack in Puerto Rico. There were new lands to be visited, new cultures to be savored.

"We only pass this way once," he remarked, "and I want to see and hear and feel and smell as much of life as I possibly can."

22

Crack-up in Paris

Bill Holden once told Ryan O'Neal, "I remember the day I arrived at Orly Airport for *Paris When It Sizzles*. I could hear my footsteps echoing against the walls of the transit corridor, just like a condemned man walking the last mile. I realized that I had to face Audrey and I had to deal with my drinking. And I didn't think I could handle either situation."

Paris When It Sizzles was the product of expediency. Marty Rackin, Holden's buddy from *The Horse Soldiers*, had become head of production at Paramount, which had commitments for one picture apiece with William Holden and Audrey Hepburn under their old contracts. Irving Lazar put together a package for his clients Richard Quine and George Axelrod: Axelrod would write, Quine direct, and both produce an American version of *Henriette*, a 1952 film by Julien Duvivier. The script seemed well suited for Holden and Hepburn. He would play a screenwriter working on a deadline in Paris, acting out his script fantasies with his secretary (Hepburn) until they fall in love.

Filming took place in the summer of 1962, with Paris living up to the title of the movie. Bill moved into a baronial house on the Avenue Foch and for a time seemed the same steady professional of his Hollywood years. He gave a lighthearted interview to Art Buchwald on the subject of movie kissing.

"I've kissed some lovely women in the movies, such as Audrey Hepburn, Grace Kelly, Barbara Stanwyck and Deborah Kerr, to name a few, and I've kissed some women I haven't enjoyed playing a love scene with at all. . . .

"There was one actress who used to eat garlic for lunch every day and then expected me to kiss her in the afternoon. But I decided the hell with it and I refused. The director ordered me to kiss her so I told *him* to kiss her. He said it wasn't his job to kiss her; it was my job. I said he was the director and I wanted him to show me how to do it. But he refused. They called the producer and he said I had to kiss the girl. I told *him* to kiss her. He said it wasn't his job to kiss her. I said I wouldn't kiss her unless she stopped eating garlic. The actress, who by this time loathed me, said she'd eat whatever she liked.

"They finally had to write the kiss out of the script. There's just so much an actor can do for his art.

"Another time an actress I was working with was three months pregnant and kept getting sick on the set. It was quite a frightening experience. She'd get sick, then we'd play a love scene, she'd get sick, then we'd play a love scene.

"In this case I liked the girl, so I went through with it, but it was the hardest scene I have ever had to play.

"One actress had a bridge in her mouth and was afraid I'd hurt her tooth. We finally took it out and put it in a jar before we did the scene.

"Let's face it, it's pretty difficult to kiss someone who is a stranger. I don't think anyone in movies enjoys playing a love scene. Kissing someone is an intimate act, and when you have to do it in front of people it's not easy. . . ."

Billy Wilder was in Paris filming locations for *Irma La Douce,* and Holden visited his old friend. He also met Jack Lemmon, whom he had known slightly when both were under contract to Columbia. Lemmon seemed highly agitated, and Holden learned why.

"I'm getting married," said Lemmon, who had long been courting the actress, Felicia Farr. "Felicia is flying in tomorrow morning at four-thirty, and I'm nervous as a cat."

"I know just the thing for you," Holden said. "Leave it to Bill."

That evening Holden conducted Lemmon on a tour of Paris nightlife, leading him to bistros, night clubs, and bars that offered a wealth of food, drink, and entertainment. Holden delivered the happy, relaxed bridegroom to the airport, then returned to the Avenue Foch for an hour's sleep before reporting to the studio.

Bill had always drunk during films, but never as he did on *Paris When It Sizzles.* He started drinking early and continued through the day. Dick Quine was astonished at the change in Bill since *The World of Suzie Wong,* three years before. "Bill was like a punch-drunk fighter, walking on his heels, listing slightly, talking punchy," the director recalls. "He didn't know he was drunk."

Some mornings Bill arrived on the set at the Bologne studios with a bush baby on his shoulder and a wide grin on his face. Quine took one look at his star and announced, "Wrap the company." The director realized Bill would be useless for filming that day.

Quine hoped to keep Bill under control by maintaining closer surveillance on him. The director arranged to rent the house next door to Bill's on the Avenue Foch. It was a three-story place with a top-floor terrace overlooking the garden. A tree stood near the terrace, and Quine discovered by climbing into the tree he could peer into Bill's bedroom and determine if he had gone to bed.

One night Quine tried his maneuver, perching in the tree, which swayed toward Bill's house. As he was straining for a view into the bedroom, Quine heard a familiar voice: "Hi, buddy."

Quine gazed down and saw Bill sitting beside a small pond. He was lighting candles and floating them on the water. Candles always held fascination for Bill.

"Hi, Willie," Quine said sheepishly from the treetop.

"What are you doing?" Bill asked.

"Just getting a little air."

"Oh? Well, you'd better get some sleep. We've got a lot of work to do in the morning."

Paul Clemens and Eleanor Parker visited Paris, and they were alarmed by Bill's condition. He invited them to dinner at his house, and he greeted them with the bush baby on his shoulder. During dinner he sat at the head of the table, facing three-quarters to the side, seemingly in a trance. He returned to the conversation, talking as animatedly as ever, then fell silent again.

At the end of a day's shooting, Quine and Axelrod accompanied Bill to the studio parking lot, hoping to send him home safely in a limousine. The three men were discussing the next day's work when Bill glanced up at Audrey's second-floor dressing room. "Oh," he said, "I forgot to say goodnight to Audrey." He started climbing up the outside wall.

"Bill, don't do that!" Quine shouted.

"Bill, get down!" Axelrod yelled.

Nothing would dissuade him. Audrey heard the commotion and came to the window. "You stop that, Bill!" she exclaimed. He continued ascending the wall, finally reaching Audrey to give her a kiss on the cheek. Then he lost his grip and fell backward, landing with a thud on the hood of a Citroen. He limped the next day but was otherwise unhurt.

Ardis arrived from Switzerland and tried to reason with Bill, but her efforts ended in fierce arguments. Audrey Hepburn was warm and sympathetic, and the nearness to her only made Bill drink more. Paramount executives became alarmed by reports of bizarre happenings on *Paris When It Sizzles* and the slow progress of filming. Marty Rackin flew to Paris and tried to straighten out Bill. He stayed for seven weeks and accomplished nothing. Even Charlie Feldman's fatherly persuasion could not dissuade Bill from his downhill slide.

Karl Tunberg arrived in Paris to show his script of *The Seventh Dawn* to William Holden. A veteran Hollywood scenarist who was producing movies abroad, Tunberg realized that if William Holden agreed to appear in *The Seventh Dawn,* financing would be assured.

Holden had expressed interest in the Malaysian adventure drama and had invited Tunberg to his house in Paris. Tunberg approached the massive iron gates of the Holden address and heard a wild jungle cry. He gazed around and saw no wild animal. The cry again. Tunberg gazed upward to the iron gate and saw Bill Holden hanging from its height like a drunken orangutan.

When Holden climbed down, Tunberg could see that he was totally drunk. "C'mon inside," Bill said genially.

Tunberg presented his script, and Bill tossed it aside.

"I'm sure you put a lot of work into it and it's a beautiful script," Bill mumbled. "But you see, I'm not going to do any more pictures. I hate being an actor. I hate the bastards who run the business. I hate everything about it. And now I'm going to bed."

He climbed the stairs unsteadily and disappeared. Dick Quine had been present during part of the conversation, and he tried to explain that Bill had been having problems with his marriage and other matters. Tunberg departed with a sense of failed mission.

Quine himself had been drinking, out of anger and frustration over Holden's behavior, also, his friends believed, because of a broken romance with Kim Novak. One night in the garden of Holden's house, Quine became so enraged that he grabbed Bill by the throat.

"You cocksucker, how dare you do this!" Quine screamed. "How can you behave like such a monster? It's unfair to me, it's unfair to everyone who works with you, it's unfair to yourself. You're torturing your family and everyone who loves you. For God's sake, Bill, why do you do it?"

Bill smiled wanly like a small boy being chastised. Quine released his grip.

"I don't *want* to do this," Bill replied helplessly.

Quine persuaded Bill to enter the Château de Garche, a hospital for alcoholics, for an eight-day treatment. George Axelrod telephoned Tony Curtis in Hollywood and told him that the film was in desperate trouble because of Holden's drinking. Would Curtis fly to Paris and play a guest role to keep the film company occupied until Holden's return? Curtis agreed.

At the end of the treatment, Bill Holden returned to the movie set refreshed. He acted as if nothing had happened, and no one dared remind him. Quine and Axelrod tried to hurry the production along, and they rearranged the script, eliminating physical scenes that Bill obviously couldn't handle.

Finally, one sequence remained, with Bill appearing in a Dracula costume. Bill announced he was going to Switzerland for the weekend.

"Please don't go, Bill," Quine urged. "We've got this one sequence to do, then you'll be free to do whatever you want."

"I've got to go," Bill insisted. "I'm taking delivery of a new Ferrari."

"Then please don't drive the car," Quine pleaded.

Bill returned to the studio the following Monday with his arm in a splint. "I ran into a wall," he said sheepishly. Quine shortened the Dracula sequence because of the injured arm, and *Paris When It Sizzles* was completed.

Except for a few gossip-column items, news of Holden's behavior went unreported in the press. The film was uniformly panned, and several reviewers noted Holden's haggard appearance. Said A. H. Weiler in *The New York Times:* "Mr. Holden shows signs of strain and a decided lack of conviction before this pseudo-merry chase ends." Judith Crist in the *New York Herald Tribune* commented that Holden "is not Cary Grant even though he tries and he tries and he tries. And *Paris When It Sizzles?* Strictly Hollywood—when it fizzles."

After the completion of *Paris When It Sizzles,* Holden resumed drinking. When he entered the Château de Garche again, his health seemed ruined. Unable to leave his business to care for his friend and client, Charlie Feldman sent Capucine. Holden was delighted to see her; and her presence, as well as his remarkable recuperative powers, helped bring a swift recovery.

Holden was eager to return to work and restore his reputation. He met with Karl Tunberg in London, sober. Bill reached agreement with Tunberg for *The Seventh Dawn* and flew off to Africa, leaving details in the hands of Charlie Feldman.

Tunberg soon discovered he had a co-producer: Charlie Feldman. Feldman insisted that Capucine would be the leading lady. Tunberg argued that the script called for a Eurasian. "What the hell, we'll make her look Chinese," said Feldman, departing for Cap d'Antibes.

Tunberg was convinced that *The Seventh Dawn* would be ruined by the casting of a onetime Paris model as a Eurasian agent for the Communists. When Holden returned from Africa, he agreed, and so did the director, Lewis Gilbert. At a meeting in Holden's suite at the Connaught Hotel, the three men vowed to make a stand against Feldman.

When Tunberg complained that Feldman refused to accept his telephone calls, Holden said, "I'll get through to Charlie." He placed a call to Cap d'Antibes and said in a thick German accent that William Holden had been seriously injured. Feldman quickly came on the phone, and Bill said, "Charlie—Karl, Lew, and I are agreed that Cap isn't right for the role. If you insist on her, we'll all take a walk. Understand?"

Tunberg flew to Japan to seek actors for *The Seventh Dawn*. While there, he read the news that Capucine had been cast in the movie. He tried to reach Feldman, who remained incommunicado. Tunberg called Lewis Gilbert, who admitted that he had been forced to renege on his stand against Capucine. Bill Holden remembered nothing about the agreement. He was drunk again.

"Hey, buddy, you need some sun," Bill Holden said to his friend Richard Quine. "A couple of weeks in the sunshine will make you healthy again. Come with me. I've got it all planned."

Quine was too weak to argue. For weeks he had been working furiously to bring some semblance of order to *Paris When It Sizzles*. After editing the film in Hollywood, he had returned to Europe for dubbing of new lines by the stars: Holden in Munich, Audrey Hepburn in Paris. He had contracted influenza and was recovering in the American Hospital in Paris when Holden arrived for a visit.

"I can't take two weeks off, Bill," Quine replied.

"Then just a few days," Holden insisted. "The sun will do you good. Bake you out."

"All right—a few days."

"Good! I've already got the plane tickets."

Assuming that he would spend a few days in the south of France, Quine packed a few clothes and accompanied Bill to the airport. Quine became suspicious when he boarded the jet and learned that the first stop would be Hamburg.

"Bill," said Quine, "Hamburg is not on the way to the Riviera."

"Don't worry about it," Holden said confidently. "We just have three more stops before we get off."

"Three stops! What are they?"

"Beirut, Tehran, and New Delhi."

The jet was already rolling down the runway. "My God, where are you taking me?" Quine demanded.

"Just some nice quiet place where we can get some sun. Let's have a drink."

Quine realized he was powerless, and he relaxed and observed what it was like to travel Holden-style. At Tehran, Bill went to the transit lounge and purchased a five-pound tin of caviar. He stepped into a phone booth and called a diplomat friend in Bangkok. "I'm coming there with some Iranian caviar," Bill said. "Can you locate me some baked potatoes and sour cream?"

The baked potatoes and sour cream were at the Erawan Hotel when Holden and Quine arrived for an overnight stay. The exhausted Quine asked, "Where are we going, Bill?"

"Not much farther," Holden replied with a smile.

They reported to the airport the next day for a flight to Kuala Lumpur. When Bill learned that President Sukarno of Indonesia was also flying to Kuala Lumpur, he changed his and Quine's flight to the jet carrying Sukarno. "When you're in this part of the world," Bill explained, "you go where the safety is."

When they arrived in Kuala Lumpur, Bill announced, "We're almost there." Their destination was Port Dixon, on the Strait of Malacca. A hotel owner had loaned Holden the use of a beach house and a two-seater Thunderbird. For a few idyllic days, Holden and Quine enjoyed the swimming, water skiing, Malaysian cooking, and restful seaside life. Quine announced he would have to return to Hollywood to complete the film.

"Okay, buddy," Bill said. "I've got to stay here to make a movie. You've got to see Singapore and Hong Kong on the way home. I'll make all the arrangements."

The Seventh Dawn proved to be another rugged location, involving swamps, snakes, and fights with parangs, the Malayan machetes. Holden drank heavily throughout the filming. The dalliance with Capucine on The Lion became a romance that Holden made no effort to keep secret from the others in the film company.

At the end of production on The Seventh Dawn, Holden collapsed from excessive drinking. He was flown to Switzerland, where he was immediately hospitalized.

23

Transitions

For days Bill Holden lingered in a semiconscious state in a Lausanne hospital. Both Capucine and Ardis were present, their mutual concern for Bill overcoming the embarrassment of their meeting. Bill suffered convulsions so severe that Ardis feared he would have brain damage. She remained with him during the worst periods. By happenstance, Capucine was always in the room when Bill awakened. She had helped him through the paroxysms of drying out before, and now he called her "my Florence Nightingale."

After his release from the hospital, Bill announced to Ardis that their marriage was over. He moved out of the St. Prex house and took an apartment in Lausanne. The gossip columns predicted that Bill would marry Capucine.

Bill was guarded when he visited Los Angeles in August of 1963 for the birth of his first grandchild, the daughter of Virginia, who had married Dr. Aly Baylor. Bill confirmed to Harrison Carroll of the *Herald-Examiner* that he and Ardis were living apart: "It's been that way since I went to Malaysia to do my last film, but there has been no discussion about signing any papers or any court action. I hope it won't come to that. I just want to be on my own for a while to think things out."

"It's true I'm having a romance with William Holden," Capucine told columnist Sheilah Graham. "I will not lift one finger to make him get a divorce. That is not my business. And if his wife wants to fight to get him back, that is her business. But their marriage has been on the rocks for years, and everyone knows that."

Capucine told Earl Wilson that her romance with Charlie Feldman had been over before she started one with Bill Holden. She added, "I don't know whether I want to get married. I've been a bachelor for a long time. I love it. Even if he asked me tomorrow I'm not sure I'd say yes." She denied being a homewrecker: "I didn't break anything that wasn't broken before."

To Liz Smith she complained, "I'm a little sick of people saying, 'Close friends tell me you and Bill are now just pals.' Or, 'Close friends say you and Bill will marry.' Or, 'Close friends say you should get credit for helping him stop drinking.' Honestly, I'm not going to take an ad on the latter. He is the one who stopped. I wouldn't say I had a little white cap and was his nurse; I think that's between us, not a public matter. Of course, Bill is the first one to kid around and say, 'Well, Capucine was waiting for me and she had a gun pointed at my head.' "

Bill and Capucine accepted Sam Spiegel's invitation to steam across the Atlantic in the 500-ton Spiegel yacht *Malahane.* The producer was planning a Christmas party in Barbados, and he was sending his yacht from the south of France.

It should have been a heavenly voyage. Bill and Capucine were the only passengers aboard the *Malahane,* which was fully staffed and carried a French chef and a supply of new movies. But for ten days Bill and Capucine had no one else to talk to and nothing to look at but endless ocean.

When they arrived in Barbados, Sam Spiegel recognized that the flame that had been so visible between Bill and Capucine had been extinguished in the Atlantic crossing. Three days later she left for Hollywood. The romance never resumed, but, as always, Bill remained friendly with the woman he had loved. She would always be his Florence Nightingale.

For almost two years, Bill Holden remained away from films—by far his longest absence from the screen, except for the war years. Partly it was his own choice; he felt the need to recover his health and straighten out his personal life. Also, as his interests ranged worldwide, he became more dissatisfied with the profession of film acting. On visa and immigration forms he always entered his profession as "businessman." He was furious when an official at the Rome airport crossed out "businessman" and wrote "actor."

The movie offers weren't coming at the rate Holden had known for ten years. During the mid-1960s, Hollywood was undergoing another of its periodic depressions, and fewer films were being made. The studios had become leery of overseas production after watching costs rocket out of control on *Cleopatra.*

Bill Holden was no longer hot. His last five films—*Satan Never*

Sleeps, The Counterfeit Traitor, The Lion, Paris When It Sizzles, The Seventh Dawn—had been failures. The Golden Boy had lost his gleam at the box office. He had also lost his popularity with millions of Americans who had seen the onetime solid citizen of Hollywood abandon his country for the high living and low taxes in foreign lands.

Most damaging to Holden's career was the talk among Hollywood producers that his drinking could balloon a production's budget.

Bill Holden claimed to be unconcerned whether he ever made another movie. His fortune had been assured, and he was more interested in prowling the world for new adventure. Africa held a mystical attraction for him. He loved to climb into his Land Rover and prowl the limitless plain, with only a pistol for protection.

The Mount Kenya Safari Club had become a headache. Despite the widespread publicity, not enough tourists were attracted to the place, and it was losing $140,000 a year. In April of 1965, Holden and Ray Ryan decided to close the Safari Club and sell it. The sale did not diminish Bill's love affair with Africa. He moved forward with plans to establish an animal reserve adjacent to the Safari Club.

Bill Holden was in Bangkok when he heard the news: His brother, Dick Beedle, was missing in Peru. Dick had been working in Peru for Gooch Laboratories, the family company. A former air force pilot, he had been flying a light plane from Lima to Pisco, on the coast 125 miles southeast, and had radioed that he was out of fuel.

Bill immediately telephoned his parents, who had retired to Palm Springs. "I'm leaving right away, I'll be there tomorrow," he said.

After consoling his parents, he flew to Peru, accompanied by Ardis. They met Dick's wife in Lima, and Bill conferred with government officials who told him an extensive air search had found no wreckage. Dick's plane had probably fallen into the ocean.

Bill returned to California with feelings of grief and guilt. Twenty years after Bob had been downed at sea, the same had happened to Dick. Bill felt that in his own selfish pursuits he had paid too little attention to Dick, just as he had failed Bob during the war.

New Year's Eve 1964. Bill Holden was in Beverly Hills, staying at the home of Charlie Feldman, who was producing a movie in Europe. At loose ends, Bill noticed an invitation on Feldman's desk. It was for the biannual New Year's party given by Charles Lederer, the screenwriter and close friend of Billy Wilder. Bill decided to go.

Ordinarily Bill hated big Hollywood parties, but this one was different. It was a congenial crowd that included a lot of old friends: Fredric March, Dean Martin, Groucho Marx, Arthur Lake, Claudette Colbert, plus new faces like Steve McQueen and Shirley MacLaine. Of all the beautiful women at the party, Bill was most attracted by a slender blonde named Patricia Stauffer. She seemed different from the others, fresh-faced and glowing, without the competitive air of Hollywood beauties Bill had known. Her date for the evening offered no objection to Bill's attentions; he was Eli Robbins, a Beverly Hills social figure who was eighty-three years old. Bill followed them to Pat Stauffer's house, and a new and ultimately enduring relationship began.

Everyone called her Peep, a childhood name she had acquired when her younger brother couldn't pronounce Patricia. Bill, who always applied a name of his own choosing to intimates, changed Peep to Winker, and that was the name he always used. She had been born Patricia Morgan, daughter of a Los Angeles stockbroker and reared in the old-line society that sniffed at the nouveau riche of Hollywood. She attended private schools, University of Southern California pre-med, the University of Madrid, the Los Angeles Art Center, and Columbia University before becoming a model for Anne Klein sportswear in New York. She attracted the discerning eye of Ted Stauffer, onetime husband of Hedy Lamarr, operator of Hollywood cafés and Acapulco hotels. After two years of marriage and a daughter Melinda, Ted and Pat separated and were divorced five years later.

Pat Stauffer was the kind of woman Bill Holden favored: willowy, sensual, and independent. Unlike all the other women he had been involved with since leaving South Pasadena, she was not an actress. That intrigued him. Although she was always perfectly groomed, she was not obsessed with her own appearance. Nor was she overwhelmed by his fame or by the movie business in general. He admired her bright, alert mind, her perception of the sham of the movie world.

Like all women, Pat Stauffer was overwhelmed by Bill Holden. Not merely because he was exceptionally handsome. She also found him tender and thoughtful. Pat Stauffer became an important part of Bill's life, visiting him on movie locations, traveling to Hong Kong and Africa, sharing his good times and enduring his miseries. It was a relationship that would continue, with interruptions, for the rest of his life.

Alvarez Kelly was Holden's first movie after the two-year lapse. Jack Gordean, who had taken over as Holden's agent after Charlie Feldman sold Famous Artists to devote full time to producing, put together a package with another client, Edward Dmytryk, as director. As with *The Horse Soldiers,* the script was based on an actual Civil War incident.

Holden met in Hollywood with Dmytryk, whose first film as a director had been *Million Dollar Legs,* in which Holden had played a tiny role. The meeting was formal and businesslike. Holden had misgivings about the director's Communist background (he had served a prison sentence as one of the Unfriendly Ten, later recanted). Dmytryk was concerned about Holden's reputation as a boozer.

Holden made no attempt to conceal his drinking problem. He told Dmytryk of his cure: "The French have an intelligent way of doing it: they let you drink some wine." That made Dmytryk even warier. The drunks he had known could not tolerate *any* alcohol.

Both men expressed concern about the script, which had not improved after several rewrites. Dmytryk hoped that the strong cast, headed by Holden, Richard Widmark, and Patrick O'Neal, would be able to surmount the script's shortcomings.

Daniel Taradash was dispatched to Baton Rouge, Louisiana, to doctor the script. He was alarmed to discover that Bill Holden couldn't remember the new lines. "Dan, you take the script too seriously," Holden said to the writer, who didn't appreciate the comment.

Taradash noted that Bill seemed world-weary and unenthusiastic about filmmaking—so different from the Holden he had known on *Golden Boy.* The writer said to Bill, "Why do you do it, Bill? Why come down here to Louisiana to make a picture you're really not interested in? You've got all the money you can ever use, you've had a great career. You obviously don't need to continue. What's making you go on?"

Bill replied, "I want one to go out on."

During the *Alvarez Kelly* location, Deane Johnson paid a visit to Holden. The attorney brought divorce papers to be signed, but admitted that Ardis had not yet agreed to a settlement. Nor would she, for years to come. She told friends that she still loved Bill and was willing to wait for him to return to her.

Richard Widmark and Bill Holden, both with reputations as loners, drew close during the filming of *Alvarez Kelly.* They found they had much in common, except politics. Widmark was a liberal Democrat, and he considered Holden a conservative. They avoided talking about politics—or acting. Like Holden, Widmark did not enjoy being categorized as an actor.

Widmark noted that when Holden was sober, he seemed like a steady member of the Establishment. But after a couple of drinks, Bill started to giggle and laugh and flirt with the girls. He always insisted on driving, and his speed terrified Widmark. One night when they went to the local restaurant run by a man called Fat Jack, Holden swore he would drive no more than fifteen miles per hour. He kept his word. Then as Holden and Widmark approached Fat Jack's, the car struck a column in front of the restaurant. Then another, and another, until the entire portico came tumbling down.

Holden and Widmark were dining in Fat Jack's one night when Steve McQueen entered with a group from the *Nevada Smith* company, which was also filming in Baton Rouge. McQueen sent a waiter with an invitation for Holden and Widmark to join his table. "Fuck him," Bill replied, indignant at the presumption of a Johnny-come-lately. "Let *him* join *us* if he wants to." He fumed through the dinner, then passed McQueen's table on the way out of the restaurant.

"Would you like a drink?" McQueen asked.

"Sure!" said Bill, sitting down at the table. That was the last Widmark saw of Bill for the rest of the evening.

The nightly boozing continued, and Bill often appeared on the *Alvarez Kelly* set with a fierce hangover. He climbed on his horse and took a solitary ride through the bayou country. He returned refreshed, willing to face what he realized was an imperfect script. He expressed his feelings one morning when he was plagued with a throbbing headache and a recalcitrant horse. He rolled up the script and tried shoving it in the horse's rear. *"That's* where it belongs!" he said.

Widmark realized that even with a hangover, Holden never lost his competitive spirit. He never indulged in upstaging, but he was always alert and challenging to other actors. As a result, both did their best work.

Widmark contracted the flu in the middle of the location and was confined to his motel room. Knowing that Widmark had once played the drums, Bill bought him a snare drum to occupy him during his recovery. Afterward, when the two actors were leaving for the location in early morning, Bill insisted that Widmark play a few licks on the drum before they departed.

One day Bill announced, "I've got four days off; I'm going to Paris." Alarmed by possible delay in the film, Widmark talked him out of the trip.

"Then I'll go to New York," Bill said.

"No, Bill, it's just too risky," Richard argued.

"Chicago, then."

"Bill, I've got a better idea. I've got the weekend off. Let's go to New Orleans."

Holden and Widmark, accompanied by Harry Carey, Jr., drove to New Orleans. They dined at Brennan's, and daiquiris put Bill in a playful mood. At the end of the elegant meal, he said, "I want to show you my trick." He grabbed the edge of the tablecloth and gave it a sharp jerk. The trick didn't work. China, glassware, and silver crashed to the floor. Bill apologized to the management as he left.

Next stop, the Playboy Club. The three actors created a stir as they joined the raucous Saturday night crowd. Bill began charming the bunnies, and Richard played drums in the band. Ever the competitor, Bill resented Widmark's assuming the spotlight, and he disappeared. Widmark later found him asleep on the pool table.

Bill quickly revived, and after a few more drinks told his companions, "We're going to continue the party at my suite, and the bunnies are coming, too." When Widmark arrived at Holden's hotel suite, he found a half-dozen of the Playboy Club hostesses sitting uncomfortably around the edges of the living room. Bill's bedroom door was closed, and the sound of a running shower could be heard. Finally the bedroom door opened, and Bill appeared, clad only in a towel. He stood on a coffee table, shouted "Whoopee!" and returned to the bedroom. The party was over.

Holden never failed to arrive on the *Alvarez Kelly* locations, but some mornings his eyes were bloodshot, his face puffy. He was unable to remember dialogue, and Dmytryk was forced to reduce his scenes to short takes. The result was damaging to a film already handicapped by a poor script.

Holden contracted salmonella in Louisiana, and *Alvarez Kelly* suspended for six weeks while he recovered. The film was completed in Hollywood.

Richard Widmark and William Holden always felt close after *Alvarez Kelly*, though they rarely saw each other. Widmark observes, "That four months of being constantly together on a film location was the equivalent of ten or fifteen years of friendship."

In 1963, *The Bridge on the River Kwai* was being released again in Japan, where it had been an enormous success despite the depiction of Japanese prison camp brutality. Sam Spiegel enlisted Bill Holden to attend the reopening in Tokyo, and the pair met in Stockholm for an SAS flight over the North Pole. Spiegel had heard reports of Bill's drinking, and he was relieved when Bill ordered only wine during the long flight.

The arrival at Tokyo was chaotic. Immigration officers told Spiegel and Holden they could not enter the country without visas. They had only passports. Columbia Pictures representatives tried to convince the bureaucrats that the two visitors were very important personages. The immigration officers said no exceptions could be made.

The Tokyo press had been primed for Holden's arrival. Photographers standing behind the barricade flashed their cameras at the Hollywood star, who grew increasingly annoyed with the delay. Finally, higher authority was reached, and the two Americans were allowed to pass through the gates. The flashes continued as Holden hurried to the waiting limousine.

Holden and Spiegel were ushered to adjoining suites in a mid-city hotel. The producer was starting to open his luggage when he heard Bill say over the telephone, "I want a double martini."

"Oh, my God!" Spiegel said quietly. His fears were justified. Bill started on a binge that continued throughout the visit to Tokyo. The festivities for the *Kwai* reopening had been thoroughly planned, including many interviews, dinners given by Sessue Hayakawa, and a reception with the Crown Prince. Some events had to be canceled with the excuse that Mr. Holden was ill. The experience was both shocking and saddening to Sam Spiegel, and his relationship with Bill Holden was irreparably damaged.

24

Death on the Autostrada

"All his life," observes Paul Clemens, the artist, "Bill Holden had a romance with death."

It had started when he was a boy, with backyard stunts that exasperated his mother. The feats on Suicide Bridge, the dangling from high windows, the obsession with speed, the fascination with wild and dangerous places, the insistence on doing his own movie stunts, the heavy drinking—all bore out Clemens' analysis. Miraculously, he had inflicted no serious harm on himself or anyone else. His luck changed on the night of July 26, 1966.

Valerio Giorgio Novelli, forty-two, lived with his wife, their thirteen-year-old son, and his aged parents in a small apartment in Prato, on the outskirts of Florence. Novelli sold textiles to support his three-generation family. On a warm July night he was driving his Fiat 500 on the autostrada that connected Florence with the Tyrrhenian coast. He was en route to Torre del Lago, where his wife and son were vacationing.

At 10:15 P.M., the headlights of another car suddenly appeared behind Novelli's Fiat. In an instant the tiny car was struck, the impact hurling it into the opposite lane of traffic, where it landed on its back. By the time Valerio Novelli arrived at the hospital in Lucca, he was dead. The police report: "Multiple fracture of the skull as a result of overtaking on the highway."

Another Italian autostrada fatality, but the news was printed throughout the world. The driver of the car that struck Novelli's Fiat was William Holden.

After the accident, Holden remained isolated in his suite at La Pace Hotel in Montecatani, where he was undergoing one of his drying-out periods. He saw only his Italian lawyers, Luigi Velani and Adorni-Bracessi, the American consul from Florence, police investigators, and an inspector from the public prosecutor's office. Gradually the story of the fatal evening was pieced together.

Holden had enjoyed a pleasant dinner with some American friends and had drunk only a couple of glasses of wine. Two of the guests were Sarah West, twenty-three, and Susan West, twenty, daughters of a New York businessman who was vacationing in Italy with his family. The two young women were granddaughters of the writer Anita Loos. After dinner, Sarah and Susan wanted to visit friends at the sea resort of Viareggio. "I'll take you in my new Ferrari," Holden volunteered.

He was driving his silver-gray Ferrari, registered in Switzerland, along the autostrada at a fast speed—Italy had no speed limit. Suddenly the Fiat loomed before him, driving slowly in the left-hand, passing lane. Holden sounded his horn, he told police, and tried to swerve to the right. But it was too late. The Ferrari, which was impounded in accordance with Italian law, had only a dented left fender. Neither Holden nor the West daughters suffered any serious injury. The Fiat was totally wrecked.

How fast was Holden driving? The only indication came from Giorgio Gamba, a Prato industrialist, who said he was speeding his own Porsche faster than a hundred miles per hour and he had been passed by Holden's Ferrari shortly before the crash.

Cynics on the Via Veneto in Rome predicted that a rich, famous foreigner like William Holden would have no trouble avoiding a penalty from the Italian system of justice. But on August 13, the deputy public prosecutor of Lucca, Angelo Antofermo, announced, "Mr. Holden has been informed through his lawyer that he has been formally charged with manslaughter."

The penalty under the Italian penal code: a sentence of six months to five years in jail. If death had been caused by an automobile accident, the sentence could be no less than half the maximum of five years, although it was usually suspended.

Holden was permitted to claim his Ferrari and to leave Italy. He returned to Switzerland, and for more than a year he endured the uncertainty of his fate in Italy. Finally, on October 26, 1967, a court in Lucca found him guilty of manslaughter and sentenced him to eight months in jail, the sentence suspended. Since it was his first offense in Italy, the sentence was not entered in criminal records. Holden's lawyers had reached an out-of-court settlement with the widow of Valerio Novelli for $80,000, part paid by a London insurance company, part by Holden.

Bill Holden rarely talked to anyone about the Italian accident. It had made him deeply ashamed and, more than any other event, contributed to the disquietude of his later years. Always he was susceptible to guilt. This time the guilt was overwhelming.

A few friends offered their sympathetic help. One was Frank Sinatra, who proposed using his considerable influence in Italy if Bill desired it. Bill never had occasion to accept the proposal, but he was extremely grateful to Sinatra.

Bill Holden needed to work. Charlie Feldman provided the opportunity in a James Bond movie, *Casino Royale*. Feldman had acquired rights to the Ian Fleming book following the immense success of the Bond films starring Sean Connery. Feldman employed five directors, an all-star cast, and $12 million in a vain attempt to match the Connery films. Feldman paid Holden only $40,000 for his brief appearance, but Bill made no complaint.

The Devil's Brigade was David L. Wolper's entry into feature films after a distinguished career as a television documentarian. Wolper assembled a notable cast—Holden, Cliff Robertson, Vince Edwards, Michael Rennie, Dana Andrews, Claude Akins, Carroll O'Connor, Richard Jaekel—and Andrew McLaglen was scheduled to direct the World War II adventure in Utah, Hollywood, Italy, and England. It was Wolper's first experience in dealing with Hollywood actors, and, in the case of Bill Holden, it proved to be unnerving.

On the Utah location, Holden's demeanor was totally professional. He had an immediate rapport with Andy McLaglen. They had met when Bill was still named Beedle and going to school in South Pasadena and Andy lived in nearby La Canada. That was when Bill's prime ambition was to join the motorcycle drill team of Andy's father, Victor McLaglen.

The director found Holden to be a great help in maintaining morale on a location that involved complex logistics and occasional danger. A climactic scene required the major actors to charge through a battlefield with bombs exploding all around them. One actor threw down his helmet and refused to risk such danger. When Holden walked calmly through the battle area, the other actors followed his example.

The Devil's Brigade was filmed on a mountaintop that could be reached only by truck on a winding road or by helicopter. Wolper, McLaglen, and the principal actors were delivered by helicopter. At the end of a day's work, one of the stars asked for the helicopter because he was traveling to Los Angeles to appear at the Academy Awards presentation. But instead of flying only to the bottom of the mountain, he commandeered the helicopter to take him to the Salt Lake City airport. Holden and McLaglen were stranded. Holden uncomplainingly rode down the mountain standing up in the back of a pickup truck.

An important scene called for the actors to scale over the top of a cliff. Doubles were used for the actual climbing, but McLaglen wanted closeups of the principals as they reached the summit. That meant hanging on to solid rock with a four-thousand-foot drop below.

"Forget it!" said one of the stars.

"Come on, it's not so hard," Holden said cajolingly. He demonstrated by hanging over the cliff. The other actors joined him.

Holden drank only wine during the Utah location, remarking to Cliff Robertson that he could no longer tolerate hard liquor. Ardis came to Utah for a few days, and Bill continued his good behavior. After Ardis departed, Pat Stauffer arrived for a visit. He started drinking vodka, and when Pat objected, they argued and she returned to California. Bill claimed to Robertson that he still wasn't drinking. But Robertson observed that each morning on the way to the location Bill had his driver stop at a liquor store.

"When he was sober, he was not exactly an introvert, but he was very quiet," McLaglen recalls. "When he was drinking, his whole personality changed. He became garrulous, talkative, loud, outgoing. His performance, which at most times would be a hundred percent, became inept. He tottered on his feet, steeling himself to say the dialogue. If I saw that he was laboring, I would put my arm around his shoulder and walk him around. 'Do you think you can do it?' I asked him. 'If you can't, we'll do it tomorrow.' He smiled and said, 'That's a deal.' Usually he made it through. I had to reshoot only one scene because he was drunk."

Holden was able to steel himself for the important scene: the return to camp of his American-Canadian soldiers after a drunken brawl in a saloon. One of the actors cracked, "Bill was the only one in the scene who was *really* drunk."

His drinking worsened in Italy. He seemed totally out of control, as evidenced by the machine gun incident.

The Devil's Brigade was filming in San Lucia, a small Italian mountain town that had been devastated in World War II and had remained as it was as a reminder of German destructiveness. McLaglen used the town for a scene in which the Americans and Canadians slogged up a river that flowed through the heart of the town.

Holden and the other actors were required to wade through the fast-flowing frigid water holding their weapons above their heads. A line of curious townspeople peered down at the movie company from a bridge. Suddenly Holden looked up at them and shouted, "What the fuck are you staring at?" He opened fire with his machine gun.

The Italians screamed and ran for cover. The sound of the blank shots echoed through the granite ravine, electrifying the other actors and the film crew. All stared in astonishment at Holden, whose rage was now directed at himself.

Bill's embarrassment was devastating. He began downing a bottle of vodka before reporting to location in the morning. David Wolper arrived on the set one day to find Holden missing. "I'll go back to the hotel and find him," said the producer. As he was driving back to the hotel, he noticed Holden's Bentley parked outside a bar. Wolper found his star totally drunk.

Wolper telephoned a United Artists executive in Paris. "What can I do?" Wolper asked desperately. "I've got a week and a half to shoot, and Holden is too drunk to work."

"Don't worry, I've dealt with this before," the executive assured. He dispatched a Paris doctor to administer injections and arranged for a warm and sympathetic Italian beauty to come to the location from Rome to assist in the recovery. The prescription worked, and Bill was able to finish the Italian location and go on to London for the completion of *The Devil's Brigade.*

Throughout the filming, Holden had been urging Wolper, "You've got to come to Africa, David," and the producer had tentatively agreed. But he changed his mind after the Italian episode.

On the last day of filming, Wolper, his wife, Deborah Kerr, and Bill Holden lunched at the Dorchester Hotel. Bill mentioned confirming the trip to Kenya, but Mrs. Wolper said she didn't feel well enough and her husband was too tired. She had been instructed to make the excuse by Wolper, who, because of childhood experiences, was unable to deal with drunks.

Wolper noted the crestfallen look in Bill's eyes. When they returned to their hotel room, Wolper remarked sadly to his wife, "He didn't believe us."

25

The Wild Bunch

William Holden's film career continued its precipitous descent. He was fifty when *The Devil's Brigade* was released, and some reviewers noted that he looked all of his age and more. Commenting on the hackneyed nature of the film, Vincent Canby wrote in *The New York Times,* "There is hardly a character, a situation or a line of dialogue that has not served a useful purpose in some earlier movie or television show. Now with the passage of time, the characters, the situations and the lines have begun to look very tired and very empty, like William Holden's eyes."

The men who ran the American film companies, to whom William Holden was merely an expatriate actor with a boozy reputation, no longer considered him for starring roles. To them he seemed to be more interested in his African adventures than in making movies.

Indeed, Holden was spending more time in Africa. After selling his interest in the Mount Kenya Safari Club, he bought a 1,250-acre ranch next to the property and established a game ranch with Don Hunt, a Detroit accountant who had gone to Africa on a hunting trip in 1962 and remained to become a game catcher and conservationist.

"We're planning to raise elands on the ranch," Bill explained to me during a Hollywood visit. "They're a large antelope which make good eating. Kenya is a protein-poor country, and this could be an important contribution to the Kenyans' nutrition. They average five pounds of meat per year, while the average American consumes one hundred and twenty-five pounds of meat."

He also told me about his other interests, for which he made three globe-circling trips a year. "I usually come to California first, to check on business matters and visit my parents. Then I stop in Tokyo for a couple of days; I've got an electronics company there. I go to Hong Kong, where I own a radio station; we're applying for a television license. Then to Singapore, where I have other interests. From there I go to Bombay. No, I have no businesses there because the government won't allow it. From Bombay it's only five hours to Nairobi."

But Bill's pride and his sense of competition would not allow him to turn his back on films, despite his worldwide interests. He had been king of the mountain, and he still wanted that "one to go out on."

Sam Peckinpah had nurtured the script of *The Wild Bunch* during the three years he was unable to find work after the fiasco of *Major Dundee* (he had walked off the film after a series of battles with the producer). He sold his new project to Warner Brothers and began assembling a cast of hard-bitten adversaries on the Mexican frontier. His first choice for Pike Bishop, the outlaw leader, was Lee Marvin. But Marvin was tied up in the extended shooting of *Paint Your Wagon.*

The producer, Phil Feldman, brought up the name of William Holden. Kenneth Hyman, Warners production chief after Seven Arts had bought the company, was reluctant. He was well aware of Holden's reputation for unreliability. But although Holden had not had a hit movie in ten years, his name still had credibility with film customers in the United States and especially abroad. And, considering his past salaries, he was available at a bargain rate: $200,000, plus 10 percent of the gross after $10 million. Holden was signed to head a cast that included Ernest Borgnine, Robert Ryan, Ernest O'Brien, Warren Oates, Strother Martin, Ben Johnson, Albert Dekker, and L. Q. Jones.

From the outset of the location shooting in the remote Mexican town of Parras, Peckinpah seemed intent on converting the actors into his own variety of wild bunch. He exhibited a unique talent for roiling the atmosphere and infuriating the cast and crew without losing their respect for him as a filmmaker. He drove everyone hard, especially himself, fired those who displeased him, ordered take after take of seemingly unnecessary scenes, spent long hours striving for visual effects, stormed and ranted hourly.

Peckinpah had become notorious for excoriating Charlton Heston, James Coburn, and Richard Harris on *Major Dundee,* and veterans of that film were waiting to see how Sam would handle Bill Holden. The tone was set on the first day.

Bill was not required for the first day's shooting, but he appeared on the set, as was his custom. L. Q. Jones, Strother Martin, and Albert Dekker were playing a scene in which they exited from a house following the first shootout. Peckinpah made the actors perform the action again and again. As midday approached, the temperature and the atmosphere on the set grew more heated.

Holden watched intently as Peckinpah continued berating the actors under the sweltering sun. Then Holden turned on his heel and started to leave.

"Where are you going?" the director demanded.

"If that's the way things are going to be on this picture, I want no part of it," Holden replied calmly. When he started work three days later, Peckinpah screamed at everyone except Holden.

Holden had worked with every kind of director during his thirty years in films and had never clashed seriously with any of them. The same with Peckinpah. Bill's attitude, as always, was "Bill Holden is ready." He uncomplainingly performed whatever physical action Peckinpah requested. He even acceded to the director's request that he wear a mustache to give his handsome face a harder look.

Bill was drinking beer only. Other members of the cast wondered how long he would last, especially as the working conditions worsened on the remote locations. He never faltered. Even during the Saturday night poker session, when the other players were slugging down whisky, Bill remained with Heineken, his favorite beer.

One night a serious poker match was being held in Bill's rented house. The players were Bill, Peckinpah, Warren Oates, Strother Martin, Ernest Borgnine, and stunt men Billy Hart and Buzz Henry. In the middle of heavy betting, Bill suddenly emitted a rebel yell and threw his beer bottle to the ceiling. The other players stared at him in astonishment.

"Wowee!" Bill exulted. "I've been drinking this goddam beer for five weeks, and at last I'm drunk!"

Bill never complained during the long waits while Peckinpah was planning shots. He occupied the time by spinning yarns to Warren Oates: how he had to leave South Pasadena and his father's fertilizer business because he smelled bad; how he and Glenn Ford competed with each other; how he fucked his way around the world after Audrey Hepburn refused to marry him.

Even though he was the leading actor in *The Wild Bunch*, Holden never played the star. He spent as much time talking with stunt men and gaffers as he did with the other actors. He was given a private house with a staff, but he shared it with his fellow workers, hosting dinners two or three times a week. He also shared the house with Pat Stauffer for a time. When Ardis appeared unexpectedly on the location, Bill enlisted the help of the still photographer Bernie Abramson to spirit Pat to another house and out of Ardis' view.

C. C. Coleman, Jr., whose father had been assistant director on *Sabrina* and other Holden films, was starting his own career as an assistant director on *The Wild Bunch*. He received an early education from Bill Holden. When Peckinpah told him to assemble the principal actors, Coleman shouted, "Get Mr. Holden! Get Mr. Borgnine! Get Mr. Oates!"

Shortly afterward, young Coleman felt a punch on his shoulder. He turned and faced a stern Bill Holden. "Son," Bill said firmly, "don't you ever call my name again."

As the long weeks wore on and the company moved to a remote location at Torreón, tempers wore thin. Robert Ryan chafed at working only two days in five weeks. A Democratic activist, Ryan wanted a brief vacation so he could campaign on behalf of Robert F. Kennedy's presidential campaign.

"Can't let you go," said Peckinpah. "I might need you."

For ten days, Ryan reported to the set in makeup and costume. He never played a scene. Finally he grabbed Peckinpah by the shirtfront and growled, "I'll do anything you ask me to do in front of the camera, because I'm a professional. But you open your mouth to me off the set, and I'll knock your teeth in." Peckinpah did not further provoke Ryan, who had been a boxing champion in college.

Ernest Borgnine complained about the road leading to the location; it was covered with a powdery dust that choked the actors as they were driven to work. All of his complaints to Peckinpah were unavailing.

One day as he was being driven to the location, Holden found Borgnine and his driver parked beside the road. "Breakdown?" Bill asked.

"No, I'm not going another inch until Sam does something about this road," Borgnine declared.

Soon Peckinpah appeared in his limousine, and Borgnine told him, "Get this road watered down or I'm going to beat the shit out of you."

A few minutes later, two water trucks appeared. Holden said admiringly to Borgnine, "You son of a bitch! You got something all of us wanted. How did you do it?"

"Just said the magic words," Borgnine replied.

Bill learned that Charlie Feldman had died. William Beedle, Sr., had died in 1957 and Charlie had become a second father to Bill. It was a severe loss to him. Together with Ben Johnson, Bill left the location to attend the Feldman funeral in Hollywood. When he returned, he announced to his fellow actors, "We're going to have a wake for Charlie."

Bill had taken most of his clothes to California. He left the clothes and filled his suitcases with steaks he bought at the Farmers' Market. The location workers, who had not tasted fresh meat in weeks, were ecstatic. Bill himself barbecued the steaks, and Ben Johnson made red-eye gravy and baked biscuits. Warren Oates sat on the kitchen floor with his feet propped against the warped oven door. Through all the toasts to Charlie Feldman and other departed friends, Bill drank only beer.

United by the miserable living conditions and their love-hate relationship with Sam Peckinpah, members of *The Wild Bunch* cast formed a close-knit band. There was one outsider, a young actor we'll call Raoul White. From the outset of production, his behavior appalled the other actors and members of the crew. He lingered in his dressing room after his call to the set, keeping the rest of the cast waiting. He talked about his prowess as an actor and lover, flipping his pistol like a wild west show performer. He bawled out minor crew members who were afraid to talk back. He was, in the words of assistant director C. C. Coleman, "an arrogant prick."

Bill Holden chose to ignore White, and most of the other actors followed his example. As the weeks ground on, White's conduct became more intolerable. The showdown came in the climactic scene of the shootout between Holden's Wild Bunch and the Mexican bandits.

Holden, Borgnine, Oates, White, and other Bunch members were stationed on horseback in a cave, from which they would charge out to battle. Outside were four hundred bandits engaged in a drunken celebration, their chief reveling with whores atop a parapet.

The Wild Bunch were mounted on horseback within the closely confined cave. The atmosphere was tense, because of the potential danger of the gallop out of the cave and the battle to follow. White began twirling his gun.

"Don't do that, Raoul," Holden cautioned. "If that blank went off, one of us could get powder burns, or the wad could hit somebody's eye."

White ignored him. He continued flipping the gun. Then he took aim outside the cave and fired. The shot reverberated through the cave, deafening the actors and spooking the horses.

"Goddammit, don't do that!" Holden shouted. "You're going to stampede these horses!"

White, a wild grin on his face, fired again. And again.

Behind the camera outside the cave, Sam Peckinpah was astonished. Crew members stared at the cave, from which gunsmoke was drifting. The extras, most of them teenage soldiers of the Mexican army, reacted nervously, and some began pulling the bolts of their rifles. Rumors had circulated that live ammunition had been issued among the blanks.

Everyone stared at the entrance to the cave. Suddenly Raoul White came flying out, landing spread-eagled in the dust. Bill Holden stepped into the sunlight, followed by Ernest Borgnine.

Holden grabbed White by the hair and dragged him up twenty steps to a platform where they could be seen by everyone. He shook White and held him before the crowd. "I want you to apologize to these people for being a stupid son of a bitch," Bill demanded.

White shook his head defiantly. Bill grabbed him by the throat and started squeezing. "I apologize," White gasped.

Holden dropped him to the ground. "All right," Holden announced, "let's get back to work and finish this goddam picture."

The Wild Bunch finally ended, on a sour note.

The last two weeks were filmed at Torreón, an improvement over the primitive Parras. Everyone was pleased that the long ordeal was over, and Bill Holden announced he was giving a party for the cast and crew. Peckinpah, who felt that he should be the one to give the "wrap" party, refused to attend.

When *The Wild Bunch* was first previewed in Kansas City, it ran 190 minutes. The audience was perplexed by the intricate plotting and appalled when blood actually spurted from the impact of bullets. The Warner Brothers–Seven Arts sales executives, all trained in traditional film marketing, expressed despair.

Peckinpah reduced the film to 143 minutes, plus an intermission. *The Wild Bunch* played early engagements at that length, then the distributors insisted that it be trimmed to two hours and fifteen minutes. The train battle was eliminated, as well as brief connective scenes that helped explain the plot.

Critical opinion was almost equally divided between those who considered *The Wild Bunch* a near masterpiece and those who found it gory and repugnant.

Judith Crist, *New York:* "The film winds up with a shootdown that is the bloodiest and most sickening display of slaughter that I can ever recall in a theatrical film, and quotes attributed to Mr. Holden that this sort of ultra-violence is a healthy purgative for viewers are just about as sick."

Vincent Canby, *The New York Times:* "The first truly interesting American-made western in years. . . . After years of giving bored performances in boring movies, William Holden comes back gallantly."

Warner Brothers–Seven Arts did little to support *The Wild Bunch*, and the staid members of the Academy of Motion Picture Arts and Sciences declined to nominate Holden or any of the actors in 1969. Despite its lack of acceptance, *The Wild Bunch* was an important, pivotal film for Bill Holden. It demonstrated to the film community that he had the discipline and the resolve to attempt a complex, mature characterization and carry it off.

26

African Interlude

For David Seltzer, the assignment seemed like a dream. He was going to Africa to produce, direct, and write a television documentary with William Holden, an actor he admired.

Seltzer was twenty-six, and he had risen fast as a maker of documentaries for David Wolper. During the filming of *The Devil's Brigade*, Holden had sold Wolper on the idea of making a series of television documentaries to inform Americans of the growing danger to wildlife, native populations, and the environment of Africa and other lands. Wolper made a contract with CBS for nine specials with the title *William Holden: Unconquered Worlds*.

The first of the specials was called *Adventures at the Jade Sea*. Holden had proposed a tour around Lake Rudolf, the 150-mile stretch of jewellike water in the remoteness of northern Kenya. The region would provide a graphic example of the depletion of animal life and the precarious existence of native tribes.

The expedition was assembled: eleven white men and sixty natives and tons of equipment. Holden insisted that the trip would be made realistically, by foot wherever possible or by land vehicles. No flying to the locations. David Seltzer agreed. He sought a documentary flavor of real African life, not a Hollywood version. From the outset Holden seemed to accept Seltzer as an equal, even though Bill was old enough to be his father.

Holden started drinking beer or Campari and soda the day the expedition set out for Lake Rudolf. By the time Seltzer was ready to begin production, his star was out of control.

Seltzer was appalled and frightened. The man who had seemed so calm and rational in their early conversations was now acting like a caricature of a temperamental movie star. "My life doesn't depend on this picture," Seltzer said, threatening to leave.

170

Holden continued drinking. The worst came when the party visited the El Molos, a tribe of two hundred sickly, starving natives leading a doomed existence on the shore of Lake Rudolf. Holden had brought medicines, and he himself applied sulfa to the children's sores and wiped their diseased eyes with Vaseline. He had made friends with Father Joseph Poletti, an Italian priest who ministered to the tribe.

One day when Father Joseph was present, the drunken Holden raged at Seltzer: "If you took all the Seltzers in the world and put them in a pile, what you'd have is a pile of shit!"

The young filmmaker was dumbfounded, literally. He was so shocked by Holden's outburst, especially in front of a Catholic priest, that he couldn't speak. He felt himself growing sick, not only from the public humiliation and the damage to his self-esteem, but from the intense heat, which was making him physically ill.

At breakfast in the tent the following morning, Holden was sober. "Well, David, what are we going to do today?" he asked cheerfully.

Seltzer did not reply.

"David, we have to discuss our plan for today," Holden said.

No answer.

"I am *sorry* if I behaved badly, David. Now snap out of it. We've got work to do today, and we have to talk about it."

For two days Seltzer was unable to speak. Then he regained his equilibrium and was able to function again. During the four-month safari, he was afforded an extraordinary, closeup view of William Holden. His conclusions:

Holden was going through a difficult period in his life; it was his fallow period between *The Bridge on the River Kwai* and *Network*. He resented me, resented my youth. I became a kind of son figure to him, and was part of the reason for his rage. He felt that he had failed as a father. . . .

He seemed to me like an immensely lonely man. He felt that he had been afraid all his life. He never felt like an artist, he never had the satisfaction of doing a good piece of work. . . .

He complained about being recognized. When he was asked for his autograph in the city, he would say afterward, "Why can't these goddam people leave me alone?" But if he wasn't recognized at an African barbecue, he'd put a monkey on his head until people gathered around. . . .

He claimed to have a feeling about Africa, but he never

learned the language, which is the easiest in the world. And he had no real feeling for the natives. He liked to play practical jokes on them, like putting on a gorilla mask and driving his Land Rover through a village. . . .

I think of him as exploding with laughter or exploding with rage. When he was angry, he would point his finger and shout, just as he did in the movies. But when he laughed, it was like a narcotic.

The rages continued intermittently, but Holden could also exhibit fatherly concern. Seltzer was stricken with a severe sunstroke, and he became delirious with a fever of 105 degrees. Holden would have flown him to a hospital, but the airplane had been grounded because of lack of fuel. The expedition carried a refrigerator that was used to store the film; Holden ordered the film removed so ice could be made to pack around Seltzer.

"But the film will be ruined in this heat," protested one of the crewmen.

"So what?" Holden replied. "Take the film out!"

Holden himself packed the ice around the unconscious Seltzer. After two days he began to recover, and soon he was able to resume his duties. Whenever he appeared bare-headed, Holden shouted, "Where the hell is your hat?"

Seltzer was astonished that a movie star would have so little regard for his own comfort and safety. Holden never complained about the oppressive heat, the insects, or the primitive living conditions. He hurtled over the rough terrain in jeeps and Land Rovers, pursuing antelopes and zebras. He walked into a compound and tried his hand at calming a wild eland. The effort failed, and Holden was forced to retreat like a defeated matador.

Holden and Seltzer remained united on one stand: they would not cheapen their film. They ignored instructions from Hollywood: "Give us more tits and ass."

An important sequence of *Adventures at the Jade Sea* was filmed among the Samburu tribe, who were engaged in the ages-old ritual of circumcision of teenage sons of the village chief. David Seltzer remembers:

"The ritual took place on a mountaintop, and we were camped on the side of the mountain—no tents, just canvas beds to sleep on. It was a night of full moon, and the sounds of restless animals could be heard. Also the chant of the natives in their village five miles away.

"I studied Bill's face in the light of the campfire, and his gaze seemed far-off. It was the only time I ever saw his face look peaceful."

They parted friends, and later Holden tried to make amends for his treatment of Seltzer in Africa. He arranged for Seltzer to be represented by Jack Gordean, and the young man found himself on a client list that included Holden, John Wayne, Barbara Stanwyck, and Richard Widmark. A couple of years after the African trip, Holden sent an urgent message for Seltzer to join him in Hamburg.

"I've got something that's really hot," Bill said excitedly. "It's movie footage smuggled out of Russia by a refugee."

Night after night, they studied reels of film, and they came to a disturbing conclusion: The view of Russian life was entirely favorable. Holden and Seltzer began to suspect an elaborate ruse to present an uncritical view of Russia on American television.

Holden confronted the so-called refugee over dinner. "We've begun to think that perhaps life in Russia is not as sweet as these films suggest, that maybe they were designed to make us think so."

The man's wife became enraged, but he quieted her and said, "I'm ashamed to admit that you are right." Holden closed the matter without rancor.

In 1969, Holden organized another television safari, this time to Somalia, where he hoped to capture and relocate leopards endangered by the proliferation of wart hogs. Harvey Bernhard, who came from Hollywood as executive producer, was astounded by Holden's total lack of fear.

At Tella in Somalia, where the heat was 140 degrees, the expedition came to a fort where the Mulla had repulsed attacks by the British for forty years. Holden carried a mine detector to see if he could locate artifacts from the final bombing by the British in 1920.

The visitors were greeted by seven red-bearded sheiks who were guarding the ruined mosque. They warned that the place was filled with cobras. Bernhard dashed back to the plane for snake boots and weapons. Holden walked calmly into the mosque in his shorts and walking shoes. No cobras were seen.

The journey took the travelers to the Red Sea, where Bernhard, Holden, and his partner Don Hunt slept on the beach. Their only provisions were a bag of limes and a case of gin. The natives dug huge lobsters out of the mud and threw them on the campfire. The three men squeezed lime juice onto the cooked lobsters and ate them between swallows of gin.

At such times Bill Holden supplied stories from his adventures in Africa and Hollywood. Once he told Alan Landsburg, who was executive in charge of the television series, about a tribe of tall warriors in northern Kenya who remained virtually naked. Their only adornment was a wooden cap painted orange, fastened over the tip of the penis. That was for protection from the ground when they sat on stools they carried; they also used the stools as headrests for sleeping.

Holden was visited in Africa by a famous beauty with a reputation as a courtesan, and they flew by small plane to the remote village of the tall naked warriors. When she stepped out of the plane, Bill related, she viewed the cluster of bare natives and murmured, "Ahhh, smorgasbord!"

During the Somalia expedition, Holden had hoped to locate a herd of rare and threatened white eland, but a revolution in the country forced the filmmakers to leave. The footage was never assembled, and CBS canceled *William Holden: Unconquered Worlds*.

27

Marking Time in Films

After the relentless violence of *The Wild Bunch*, William Holden chose a sentimental movie about a father whose son is dying of radiation poisoning. Terence Young wrote *The Christmas Tree* and directed it in Paris, Corsica, and Nice, with Holden, Virna Lisi, André Bourvil, and young Brook Fuller in the major roles.

Holden behaved professionally throughout the filming until the Nice location, when the script called for him to play a scene with a bare-breasted Virna Lisi.

"It's vulgar, unnecessary, and entirely out of keeping with the rest of the picture," Holden argued.

Director-author Young countered that the scene would add a touch of realism to balance the sentiment.

"Bullshit! You're pandering to the audience!" Holden exclaimed, and he disappeared into his dressing room. And remained there drinking.

No amount of entreaty would convince him to emerge. Young, fearing loss of the entire enterprise because of his star's onset of South Pasadena puritanism, was desperate. A telephone call was made to Pat Stauffer in California. The call came at 4 A.M. At nine that evening she was on a flight to Paris. She arrived in Nice and helped to negotiate a compromise: the scene would be filmed with a more subtle treatment of the nudity.

The Christmas Tree was William Holden's fifty-fifth starring film, and the only one not distributed by a major film company. Although it appeared at the Radio City Music Hall, it did not receive a wide release from Continental Distributing. Most of the critics were repelled by the treacly, far-fetched script. Judith Crist in *New York* magazine called it "an obscenity" and predicted "There won't be a dry eye—or a full stomach—in the house." Yet Joseph Gelmis in *Newsday* appreciated

Holden's turn from his cynical roles of the previous decade and termed his performance "anguished and tender and altogether brilliant."

The Wild Rovers was a western written and directed by Blake Edwards and filmed in Arizona and Utah. During his early career as a writer at Columbia, Edwards had met Holden, but the pair did not become acquainted until preparation of *The Americanization of Emily* (both dropped out of the project before filming). Edwards' career had foundered after *Darling Lili,* starring his wife, Julie Andrews; and a western seemed ideal for a comeback. Holden was co-starred with Ryan O'Neal as a pair of wandering outlaws.

Julie Andrews, who was present on the locations, recalls: "Bill actually held out his hand and gave the picture to Ryan, but I'm not sure Ryan realized it."

Ryan O'Neal was a young television actor trying to make the difficult transition to feature films. He was intensely curious about Bill Holden, who seemed so battered by his years as a movie star. O'Neal pondered his own future. If he were to become a star in films, would he end up like Bill Holden? Whenever possible, O'Neal spent his off-camera time with Holden, pumping him for information. The best time for that came when the *Wild Rovers* company moved from Arizona to Utah. While the others flew to the new location, O'Neal drove Holden in Bill's Mercedes 500. They drank Heinekens continually and had to make regular stops to relieve themselves alongside the highway.

O'Neal maintained his barrage of questions.

"You seem so out of love," the young actor said. "You have homes in Switzerland, Africa, Hong Kong, yet you never seem contented anywhere. Who did you ever love? You've worked with some of the most beautiful, intelligent women in the world. Surely you must have fallen in love once."

"Yes, I did," Holden replied. "I fell in love with Audrey Hepburn."

"Perfect!" O'Neal exclaimed. "That's the one woman I would have chosen. Did she love you?"

"I think so. She wanted to get married, but I was already married. Besides, she wanted children, and I couldn't have any more." He told the story of his vasectomy.

Holden also related the story of his discovery as an actor, his initial interview with Harry Cohn for *Golden Boy,* how Cohn terrified him and left him dripping with sweat after every conversation. When O'Neal remarked that *Submarine Command* was a favorite picture of his, Holden commented, "It's a funny thing, I don't remember a thing about making *Submarine Command.* I was drunk through the whole picture. The only thing I remember is when Don Taylor and I jumped off a ship and swam to a submarine. We did it as joke on the director, John Farrow, who thought the stunt was being done by doubles."

"When did you start drinking—I mean *really* drinking?" O'Neal inquired.

"During the war," Holden replied. "I was stationed at some God-forsaken base in Texas, where the wind blew dust in your face all day. Hank Greenberg, the baseball player, was my roommate, and there was nothing for us to do but go out and get drunk every night. That's when it started."

"What did you drink?"

"Anything and everything."

"Did you ever figure up what it cost you?"

"Sure. My accountants kept track of my liquor bill. I don't remember the amount of liquor I consumed, but it was enough to float my motorboat in Switzerland."

Bill seemed to have a bottomless store of anecdotes, which he delighted in telling to O'Neal. Among them:

During the filming of *The Bridge on the River Kwai*, Holden and Jack Hawkins found relief from the staggering heat of Ceylon by standing under a waterfall in the jungle. The two actors wondered why film workers were shouting at them and soon found out: Holden and Hawkins were covered with leeches. "Not the kind you can get off with matches," Bill added. "These were big enough to require flamethrowers."

Ticks were another hazard in Ceylon. One had bored into Holden's knee, and it defied the efforts of doctors to locate and remove it. Bill endured constant pain in the knee for three years. Then one evening at the dinner table in Geneva, he'd had enough. "You bastard, I'm going to get you!" he exclaimed, jabbing a fork into his knee. With repeated probing, he located the head of the tick and pulled it out.

During the making of *Paris When It Sizzles*, Holden related to O'Neal, George Axelrod had engaged Marlene Dietrich for a guest appearance requiring a half-day's work. The scene called for her to emerge from a limousine and enter a fashion salon to choose a fur coat. As Holden was conversing with Axelrod outside the salon, the assistant director emerged to report concernedly, "We're in trouble; Miss Dietrich wants to keep the coat—and it's a white ermine!" Axelrod said confidently, "Don't worry, I can handle this." He returned white-faced from his conversation with Miss Dietrich and announced, "She gets the coat—and the limo."

During the filming of *The Wild Rovers*, Ryan O'Neal was nominated for an Academy Award as best actor for his performance in *Love Story*. The young actor was scornful: "Paramount must have bought the nomination. I don't think I'll go."

"Stop that shit!" Holden reprimanded. "That nomination was voted for you by your fellow actors in the movie business. That means a lot, maybe even more than the award itself, and you should respect it!"

"Okay, maybe I *will* go," O'Neal relented. "But tell me about your Oscar. Where is it? Africa? Switzerland? Hong Kong?"

Bill seemed sheepish. "The Bay of Naples," he admitted.

"What?"

"Yeah. I threw it in when I was on Sam Spiegel's yacht with Capucine."

Fired from his post as head of production for Paramount, Marty Rackin hustled his way into independent filmmaking. His first effort was an ill-advised remake of *Stagecoach*. Rackin sought his friend Bill Holden for another western, *The Revengers*, and the deal was made.

While the film was being prepared, Rackin suffered a heart attack and was told to remain in the hospital for six weeks. He feared *The Revengers* would be taken away from him, but Holden told the backers, "I'll do the picture when Marty's ready, not before."

When Holden first met the director, Daniel Mann, he said, "I've got to tell you something: you once threw me off one of your sets."

Holden related how he had entered the Paramount stage where Mann was directing *The Rose Tattoo*. An intense director, Mann ordered the intruder ejected. When informed it was William Holden, Mann snapped, "I don't care who it is; tell him to get the hell out of here."

Recounting the incident, Holden added, "You were absolutely right. I had no business intruding on your set. I respected you for that."

The relieved Mann commented, "Bill, you're a generous man. I think we're going to work well together."

They did, despite a confused and hackneyed script. The film was made in Mexico, and Holden and Ernest Borgnine found themselves working in Parras, the same location used for *The Wild Bunch*. One day they were playing a scene in the same cave where the actor had fired his pistol. Holden and Borgnine looked at each other and muttered almost in unison, "I thought we said we were never coming back to this Godforsaken place."

Holden drank only beer during *The Revengers*, but in such quantity that he was often drunk, though not out of control, by the end of the day. He was sympathetically attentive to Susan Hayward, still recovering from the sudden death of her husband, Eaton Chalkley. Scott Holden, who was seeking a career as an actor against his father's wishes, had a small role in the film, and Bill helped coach him. Bill sometimes joined members of the company in the cantina after the day's work, but he spent most of his non-working time by himself.

Mann directed a crucial scene in which Miss Hayward was nursing the wounded Holden back to health. The director was delighted with the result, and he complimented the actress. Then he went to Holden and exulted, "Bill, that was a wonderful scene. You gave it just the kind of depth and quiet emotion that I was looking for. You really came through."

"Thanks," Holden replied.

"Don't you enjoy having done a good piece of work, knowing that you have used all the resources at your command?" the director continued. "Isn't it a pleasure to make use of yourself to communicate feelings to a great number of people?"

"Not really, Danny," Holden replied. "All the rough edges have worn smooth. I don't get much out of it anymore. It's just a job."

Breezy was the third film directed by Clint Eastwood, the first in which he did not appear. Holden played the role of a middle-aged businessman who falls in love with a high-spirited girl. Universal insisted on a tight shooting schedule and a $700,000 budget, and Holden agreed to work for a minimal salary in return for a large percentage of the profits.

Crucial to the film was the casting of the girl, and Holden agreed to appear with all of the candidates in the tests. Kay Lenz, a nineteen-year-old actress who had appeared in a few television films, was chosen. Holden, who was fifty-three, helped assuage her nervousness and demonstrated how to hit marks effortlessly and how to avoid casting a shadow on the other actor.

Eastwood, who was at first awed by directing the veteran star, devoted most of his attention to Miss Lenz. One day Holden remarked, "I wish you'd talk to me more."

"Gee, Bill, that was an oversight on my part," said Eastwood. "I just thought that Kay needed the attention, and you didn't."

Holden smiled. "You know as well as I do, Clint, an actor needs all the help he can get."

The *Breezy* script included a love scene in which Miss Lenz would disrobe in front of Holden. Four years had passed since *The Christmas Tree*, and nudity in films had become commonplace. This time Holden did not object.

The actress was understandably nervous before the nude scene. Holden tried to reassure her: "Look, Kay, I've played love scenes a hundred times; there's nothing to it."

When Eastwood called, "Action!" Holden and Miss Lenz started disrobing. Holden stopped after removing his shirt, she continued. He stared constantly at her eyes, and when the scene was over, he told her, "Don't move." He put his shirt over her shoulders until a wardrobe woman arrived with a kimono. Afterward he asked a cameraman, "Was Kay nude?"

When asked to jump Holden asked photographer Philippe
Halsman: "Do you have a cane?" Bill proceeded to jump over
the cane eight times while holding the ends with both hands.
Copyright by Philippe Halsman

Finding a place for the Oscar
(photo: © Paramount Pictures).

Above: The Oscar at last (photo: Academy of Motion Picture Arts and Sciences).

Below: With another winner, Donna Reed, and Academy emcee Donald O'Conner, 1954 (photo: Academy of Motion Picture Arts and Sciences).

Above: Alec Guinness, Holden, Jack Hawkins in *The Bridge on the River Kwai,* 1957 (photo: © Columbia Pictures). *Left:* The Hamburg station scene, during which Holden became incensed because of police brutality. With Carl Raddatz and Helo Gutschwager, *The Counterfeit Traitor,* 1962 (photo: © 1961 Paramount Pictures and Perlsea Company). *Below:* Bill and Ardis on the *Kwai* location (photo: © Columbia Pictures).

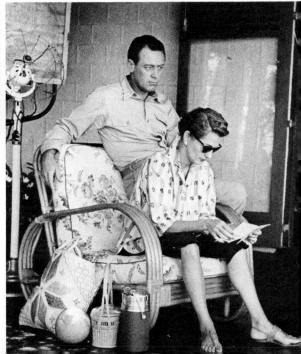

Holden proudly displays his new Ferrari to studio pals.
Pictorial Parade

During *The Lion* (1962).
Pictorial Parade

Above: Scene with Audrey Hepburn,
Paris When It Sizzles (1964). © 1963
Paramount Pictures, Richard Quine Productions,
and Charleston Enterprises

Right: On *Alvarez Kelly* (1966).
© Columbia Pictures

Below: With Capucine in *The Seventh
Dawn* (1964). United Artists

Above: Holden always remembered this moment with Frances Dee in *Meet the Stewarts,* 1942 (photo: © Columbia Pictures). *Right: The Bridges at Toko-Ri,* 1955 (photo: © 1954 Paramount Pictures). *Below:* Holden and Grace Kelly as husband and wife in *The Bridges at Toko-Ri* (photo: © 1954 Paramount Pictures).

With Kim Novak in *Picnic* (1956).
© Columbia Pictures

Kissing Audrey (1964).
© Paramount Pictures

Right: Ryan O'Neal played interrogator as well as co-star in *The Wild Rovers,* 1971 (photo: MGM). *Below:* Scott Holden played a small role in *The Revengers* (1972), which starred his father (photo: National General).

Ray Ryan and partner with African trophies

Director Clint Eastwood
and star contemplate
a *Breezy* (1973) scene.
Universal

Kay Lenz and Holden,
Breezy. Universal

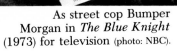

As street cop Bumper
Morgan in *The Blue Knight*
(1973) for television (photo: NBC).

Below: Holden and Faye
Dunaway were on better terms
in *Network,* 1976 (photo: MGM).

SECURITY ONLY

Glenn Ford's 1977 wedding to Cynthia Hayward. In front: Dr. Robert Schuller, Stefanie Powers, Holden, bride and groom. Back row: the James Stewarts, the Frank Sinatras, John Wayne. Wide World Photos

At the Board of Governors Ball, 1978. Frank Edwards

Lost in the Australian wilds
with Ricky Schroder, *The
Earthling* (1981). American
International

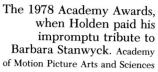

The 1978 Academy Awards,
when Holden paid his
impromptu tribute to
Barbara Stanwyck. Academy
of Motion Picture Arts and Sciences

Bill with his friend Bertie.
Frank Schaap

The last picture show,
S.O.B. (1981).
© Paramount Pictures

Holden didn't drink
on location during
The Earthling.
American International

"Tonight, my Golden Boy,
you got your wish."
Academy of Motion Picture
Arts and Sciences

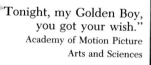

One of the last photographs of William Holden
Bob V. Noble

28

Personal

As his stardom continued, William Holden became more suspicious of the press. Once he had been every reporter's friend. But he had been stung too many times by interviewers who had seemed friendly and sympathetic, then had written about his drinking and his romances, two areas of extreme sensitivity to Holden. The bad press during the Italian autostrada tragedy had further embittered him against journalists. The number of reporters whom Holden trusted and would talk to dwindled steadily.

Holden employed few publicists during his career. When he was a young contract player, there was little need. The Paramount and Columbia publicity departments did an adequate job of creating attention for him. When his career faltered in the postwar period, Holden hired independent publicists—a practice the studios tried to discourage. The well-considered Jack Mulcahy and Larry Ginsberg handled his publicity for a brief time.

During the 1960s, Holden hired a large publicity firm as a favor to a former reporter who had gone to work for the company. The association ended on the day Holden received news of the Italian conviction. He was having a glum lunch with Deane Johnson and others at the Bistro in Beverly Hills when the senior partner of the publicity firm passed the table with little more than a nod. Holden fired his publicists that day.

Jay Bernstein was a press agent who had built a large Hollywood publicity office through large amounts of hard work and chutzpah. His ambition was to represent his childhood favorites, Susan Hayward and William Holden. After acquiring Miss Hayward as a client, he campaigned for Holden. By steering Jim Hutton as a client for Jack Gordean, Bernstein convinced Gordean to arrange a meeting with Bill Holden.

Bernstein arrived at Holden's Palm Springs house for what he had promised would be a ten-minute meeting. He stayed six and a half hours. During most of the conversation, Holden insisted, "I really don't like publicity, and I don't want a press agent." At the end of the meeting, Holden said wearily, "Okay, I'll hire you, but for one year only, no more."

Holden was alternately irritated by the young man's pushy ways and flattered by his idolatry. Holden's principal reason for hiring Bernstein was to publicize his African ventures, including the television documentary with Wolper. At the end of the *Wild Bunch* location, Holden said to Bernstein, "How would you like to go to Africa?"

"Sure—someday," the publicist replied.

"You're leaving tomorrow."

In Africa, Bernstein saw a different side of Holden—wild, unpredictable, competitive. After several drinks in the Mount Kenya Safari Club bar, Holden muttered to Bernstein, "You think you're so smart. I'm twenty years older, but I can beat you in anything. I'll bet you my interest in the club against five hundred dollars of your money that I can shoot a leopard before you do."

"No way. You could have a leopard tied up somewhere," Bernstein replied.

"All right, we'll think of something else. Lawn bowling! That's it!"

Holden insisted on staging the contest immediately. He ordered three Land Rovers to direct headlights on the club's bowling lawn. Despite his drunken condition, Holden won the bet in twenty minutes. Bernstein later realized Holden was serious about his side of the bet. The two men bet $5,000 on a matter concerning Holden's family. Bill lost and sent a check to Bernstein, who returned it. Holden sent it back with an angry note: "Do this once more and I'll never speak to you again."

The association of star and press agent ended after Bernstein persuaded his client to submit to a *TV Guide* interview about the African documentary. The writer promised to include nothing controversial, but his editors inserted such matters as the Capucine romance and the Italian tragedy.

"Jay, I'll be your friend, but I don't want you to be my publicist," Bill remarked. "I buried those things a long time ago. I don't need to pay somebody to dig them up for me."

In 1968, Andy Hickox retired after thirty years as Holden's business manager and tax accountant. That was disturbing to Bill, who maintained longstanding business relationships and did not like them to be disturbed. As a successor to Hickox, Deane Johnson suggested Frank Schaap, who had been doing accounting and tax work for Johnson as well as for Joan Bennett, Walter Wanger, and other Hollywood figures.

Holden interviewed Schaap and agreed to Johnson's selection. They formed an association that would last almost until Holden's death. It was a curious relationship between a movie star who was subject to periods of wildly erratic behavior and an accountant whose cool, businesslike manner contrasted to his wartime daring as a combat glider pilot.

Schaap soon learned the eccentricities of his new client.

Bill was exceptionally parsimonious, though subject to binges of extravagance. He always totaled a restaurant bill and complained to the manager if he felt he had been cheated. During the Arab oil crisis, he bought a diesel Mercedes as a means of beating the high price of gasoline. He once told Schaap that he had canceled one of the two telephone lines at his Palm Springs house as a needless expense.

"Okay, Bill, but that's the line that services the security system," Schaap commented. Holden rescinded the cancellation.

At other times he spent with little concern. An African buddy convinced him of big profits in buying seven custom-made British automobiles and reselling them. The company went broke and Holden lost $110,000.

Even when he had been victimized by supposed friends, Bill didn't renege. He instructed Schaap, "Pay the son of a bitch, but take his name off the Rolodex."

After being burned so many times, Holden became adamant in refusing loans to anyone. Yet he was liberal in other respects. A film writer, alcoholic and down on his luck, offered Bill rights to a story about a daring CIA agent. Bill agreed to payments totaling $10,000. The writer died after $6,000 had been paid for an uncompleted manuscript. Bill insisted on sending the remaining $4,000 to the widow.

Schaap learned that Holden had a passion for secrecy that bordered on paranoia. When the accountant remarked that Holden's business files were overwhelming the office, Bill said, "Let's burn them." He instructed Schaap to bring the files to Palm Springs in a station wagon and take them to the city dump to be burned with the help of ten gallons of gasoline. As an added precaution, Holden sent along his butler as witness.

Holden had an absolute horror of being sued and having to testify about his personal affairs in an open courtroom. Like most public figures, he was often threatened with lawsuits. He generally settled out of court, regardless of the merits of a case.

Holden compartmentalized his advisers. Jack Gordean handled the movie deals, Deane Johnson legal affairs, Frank Schaap accounting. Bill wanted none to venture into another's area. When Schaap volunteered to read the large number of scripts that came to the office, Bill replied, "Why don't you stick to what you know?"

Nor would Holden allow Schaap to visit his movie sets. "When I act," Bill explained, "I only want those people present who are supposed to be there."

Holden enjoyed knowing that he was a rich man. Periodically he said to Schaap, "Let's go over my investments," and the accountant recited the catalogue of property and stock Holden owned. The actor was impressed with affluent businessmen, and he listened to their talk in the steam rooms of spas where he went to dry out. He returned to Schaap with suggestions such as "I want you to look into offshore oil tracts," or, "Maybe we should buy some cattle as a tax shelter."

Schaap acted as intermediary between Bill and his two sons, who in the early 1970s were living in Holden's penthouse apartment in Geneva with charge accounts for living expenses. "I'm not going to give them another dime!" Bill ranted. "Let 'em go out and work for a living, the way I did." He often had blustery encounters with his sons. West, the elder, reacted defiantly, shouting back at his father. Scott was more of a diplomat, responding, "You're absolutely right, Dad." Ultimately Bill relented. It was easier for him to give his sons money than to establish a fatherly relationship with them.

Now in his fifties, Bill Holden began returning more often to California. Not to Hollywood, which he abhorred, but to his beloved desert. His visits to Hollywood were as brief as possible, long enough to conduct needed business. Characteristically, he did not stay at the Beverly Hills, Beverly Wilshire, or Bel Air hotels, the usual stopping places of celebrities. For a time he preferred the Continental on Sunset Strip. Later he favored the Beverly Hillcrest on Pico Boulevard, south of Beverly Hills. He liked its location, close to the airport, and the fact that he could move in and out of the hotel without running into fans or old friends.

In 1967, Holden bought a house on Driftwood Street in Palm Springs, a comfortable but somewhat gloomy Japanese-style place. It became his American headquarters, and he began filling it with his artworks from Africa and the Orient.

Bill and Ardis were finally divorced in 1973, ten years after they had formally separated. Their lawyers had made agreements several times during the ten years, but Ardis always balked, still clinging to the faint hope that Bill would return to her. She followed him to locations all over the world, and their meetings followed the same pattern: polite affection followed by bickering leading to shouting matches. At last Ardis conceded that their incompatibility was real and irreparable. Although the decision to divorce was entirely Bill's, Ardis placed part of the blame on Bill's mother. Ardis never spoke to Mary Beedle again.

Bill's freedom was expensive. Under California community property law, Ardis was entitled to half of his $8 million fortune. Even though he had no plans to marry again, Bill was willing to pay the price. With the divorce completed, the tensions between Bill and Ardis abated. They remained in contact with each other, and not merely because of the common concern for their sons. Ardis herself moved to Palm Springs, and her friends believed she did so to be close to Bill. In his later years, Bill dined weekly with Ardis during the periods when he was in the desert.

In middle age, Bill Holden clung to the habits of his earlier years. He still smoked cigarettes, though he realized they were bad for his health. His brand changed from Carltons to Kents or any cigarette that offered less tar and nicotine. He tried hypnosis, acupuncture, and other means to quit smoking. Nothing worked.

Bill loved his motorcycle with the same passion he had felt for the first machine he had known as a boy in South Pasadena. He bought a top-of-the-line Honda, black and powerful, and he roared over the desert roadways on it. Because the advertising offended him, he removed the Honda label.

Bill sometimes rode the motorcycle into Los Angeles, avoiding the freeway to journey by roads he had known in his youth. He happily spent six hours on a trip that required less than three hours by normal routes.

Irving Asher, retired as a film producer, lived next door to Mary Beedle in the desert resort of Indian Wells. One day Asher answered a knock on his front door and was confronted by a man in blue jeans, black leather jacket, racing helmet, and mirrored dark glasses. An oversized black motorcycle was parked at the curb, and Asher feared he was being accosted by a member of the Hell's Angels.

"Are you Mr. Asher?" the caller inquired.

"Yes," Asher replied.

"Well, I'm Mr. Holden."

Comments Phyllis Seaton, widow of George Seaton. "Bill Holden's struggle with alcoholism was heroic. No one ever fought it harder than he did—and lost."

Reporters and fellow film workers who saw him drink only beer or wine believed that Holden had conquered his drinking problem, and he tried to create that impression. In 1977, he told me that he had not drunk hard liquor for two years.

"I got started in the picture business with a hard-drinking crowd —guys like Brod Crawford and Duke Wayne," he said. "Booze was a way of life—macho. Then in my travels around the world I ran into a lot of would-be Hemingways. Can you imagine the consumption in the bars of Nairobi? There was no way I could keep up with those guys. Besides, it's expensive, not for myself, but the drinks I had to buy for others. One year when I was abroad, I kept my office at Paramount open. Everybody dropped in to have a drink on 'good old Bill.' When I got back to the studio, I discovered good old Bill had paid thirty-five hundred dollars for liquor when he hadn't been there."

The bitter truth was that he had not conquered his alcoholism and never would. In his desperation, he even turned to psychiatry, which he abhorred. After nine sessions with an expensive Beverly Hills psychiatrist, Holden angrily told Frank Schaap: "Pay that son of a bitch off; he's nothing but a goddammed quack bastard." Schaap concluded from Holden's remarks that the psychiatrist had invaded areas that Holden considered too private.

His alcoholism was a flaw of such excruciating pain that Bill could not discuss it with members of his family, his closest friends, or his lovers. When any of them brought the matter up, he replied brusquely, "I don't want to talk about it," or, "I can handle it." Or he would lash out: "Have you been spying on me? What I do is my own business!"

Friends learned not to mention Bill's drinking to him, for fear of losing his friendship. One weekend Marty and Helen Rackin picked Bill up at a sanitarium in Pasadena, and they drove to Palm Springs for a pleasant two days at Bill's house. The Rackins returned Bill to the sanitarium on Sunday evening, and no mention was made of the fact that he was undergoing treatment for alcoholism.

Bill invited the Rackins to the desert on another occasion. He greeted them with the mischievous look that he often had when he was drinking. "Bertie's missing," he announced.

"Who's Bertie?" Rackin asked.

"My pet python."

The news terrified the Rackins. Ardis arrived and saw their ashen faces. "Has that goddam snake gotten away again?" she asked Bill, who was delighted with the commotion he had caused. The four went out to a restaurant and when they returned, the butler announced that Bertie had been located. "Thank God. I wouldn't have slept here otherwise," said Helen Rackin.

Before going to bed, Bill insisted on showing films he had taken in Hong Kong twenty years before. Both Rackins were shocked by the contrast of the beautiful man in the movies and the rapidly aging Bill Holden who sat with them.

Bill appeared bright-eyed at breakfast despite the many drinks of the night before. He watched with great amusement as Bertie swam in the pool, then he excused himself and went to his room. He did not reappear. "Mr. Holden is taking a nap," said the butler, and after a few hours, the Rackins packed their belongings and were ready to leave.

"I'll say goodbye to Bill," said Marty, but there was no response to his knock on the bedroom door. For two days the producer tried to telephone Bill, but there was no answer. Finally Rackin, Jack Gordean, and Deane Johnson went to the desert and put Bill into a hospital.

Through the 1970s, the pattern was repeated with systematic regularity. For months beer would be his only drink, then suddenly and often seemingly without provocation, he started drinking vodka. At such times he sequestered himself, unable to bear the shame of having his friends witness his failure. He drank alone, without eating, staring heedlessly at a television screen. And when he had drunk himself into insensibility, someone always came to take him to a hospital or sanitarium.

That duty often befell Frank Schaap, the conscientious accountant who discovered Bill Holden required more than supervision of his investments and preparation of his tax forms. Again and again, Schaap hospitalized Holden, but Bill would never stay long enough for lasting treatment. He had remarkable recuperative powers, and when he felt well enough after two or three days, he left the hospital.

"I had a bad throat," he explained to friends. He always had some excuse; he never admitted that he had been treated for alcoholism.

Whenever Schaap confronted Bill with his drinking, Bill responded violently. He shouted so loudly in Schaap's office that someone in a neighboring office pounded on the wall. Once Schaap invented a story about a friend who drank too much and killed himself in an automobile crash.

Bill viewed Schaap suspiciously. "Why do you tell me that story?" Bill demanded.

"I thought you might find it interesting," said Schaap.

"Are you directing it at me?"

"Possibly."

"Well, that's not the way it's going to happen. You'll read about it in the papers: Bill Holden killed when a DC-Three crashes into the Himalayas during a blizzard."

Schaap learned to recognize Bill's subterfuges. The butler in Palm Springs telephoned Schaap that Holden had returned home the night before and had drunkenly forgotten to raise the garage door. His car had staved in the door. Later that day Schaap received a call from Bill.

"Frank, the damnedest thing happened last night," Bill said. "That beeper that I have to raise the garage door—it didn't work. Damned if I didn't go crashing right into the door. It's a wreck. Don't you think we ought to write the manufacturer and complain?"

"Sure, Bill, I'll do that," Schaap said reassuringly. "And I'll get the door fixed, too."

Pat Stauffer remained vigilant during Bill's withdrawal with the bottle. She saw through the excuses he instructed the servants to give: "He's out riding his motorcycle," or, "He doesn't want to be disturbed." Pat owned a house in Palm Springs near Bill's, and she made inquiries of the mailman, the gardener. If her suspicions were strong enough, she went to the house and confronted Bill. Excuses were useless, because he was drunk and unshaven, and he hated for anyone to see him without a clean shave.

"When you get like this, you lose all sense of responsibility," she lectured him. "One day you'll fall down in public and end up on the front page of the *Enquirer*. They will crucify you. Look at Errol Flynn. Is he remembered as a dashing romantic star? No. People remember what the doctor said when Flynn died: that he was a fifty-year-old with an old man's body. The same with you. The press will forget about the Academy Award. They'll just remember you as a drunk."

"I can handle it, Winker," Bill said weakly.

"Look at you! You're *not* handling it."

"I'll be all right, honest I will. I just need to get through this one period, Winker, then I'll be okay."

After a brief cure, he would be the same Bill Holden again. For weeks, months, he maintained his equilibrium. Then his private demons returned, and once more he vanished into an alcoholic stupor.

29

Television and *The Towering Inferno*

The mid-1970s were a lean period in Bill Holden's acting career. In youth-conscious Hollywood there were few roles for a star in his mid-fifties with a face that betrayed his violent periods of alcoholism. Choice scripts were rare, and the offers he received were often for productions that entailed smaller salaries and less important billing than he had enjoyed. It was a humbling time for Bill.

"Stop worrying about star billing or the most important part in the script," advised his old friend Fredric March. "Once you have been a star with an established name, you can always get featured parts at two hundred and fifty thousand a crack. Do two or more a year, Bill, and that means five, six, seven hundred thousand bucks. Even you could live happily on that."

Bill's pride made it hard for him to reduce his price or billing. He did what he could to maintain his career. He began spending more time in California, so producers would know that he was available. He attended meetings of Alcoholics Anonymous in Palm Springs and was able to spend months away from hard liquor. He spent periods at La Costa resort near San Diego undergoing the healthful regimen of exercise, diet, and massage. Although he never had a face-lift, he submitted to a tucking of the eyelids by a London surgeon who had performed the operation for several aging stars.

Bill had been associated with Jack Gordean since the *Golden Boy* time, when Gordean worked for Charlie Feldman. Regretfully, Bill ended his exclusive representation by Gordean and took on the giant William Morris Agency, which offered the prospect of better deal making. But Bill would not cut ties with his old friend, and he promised that Gordean would remain his agent in certain areas.

Since there was little action for him in feature films, Holden decided to try television. He had done little television during his career, reasoning that exposure on the home screen would erode his appeal in theaters. His most memorable appearance was on a hilarious 1955 *I Love Lucy* program in which he was hit in the face with a pie.

The Blue Knight was a popular novel written by Joseph Wambaugh, the cop turned author. Lorimar Productions bought the dramatic rights and persuaded NBC to attempt an experiment in network programming: a four-hour broadcast on four successive evenings. A major star was needed for the central role of Bumper Morgan, an over-the-hill cop relegated to street patrol on skid row. Lorimar learned that William Holden was available. Author Wambaugh objected to the casting, arguing that his Bumper Morgan was fat and unattractive, certainly not a character to be played by Bill Holden. He was overruled.

Holden was hesitant. The salary was far below his usual price in features, though the deal did offer a large share of profits from release in theaters overseas. Other actors had told him dire tales of the speed and lack of care with which television movies were made. But he realized that he was becoming a faded name to the American public, particularly the young audience who patronized motion pictures. He agreed to undertake *The Blue Knight*.

Producer Walter Coblenz and director Robert Butler visited Bill in Palm Springs. He voiced his apprehensions about a television schedule and admitted that he had no feel for the character of Bumper Morgan: "I sure can't relate to a guy that would put the street ahead of his personal life." He said that he wanted to wear no makeup, explaining, "I hate makeup, always have; I keep my face tan so I won't have to wear it." His decision was a wise one. Without makeup, he looked all of his fifty-five years and resembled a burned-out cop.

Coblenz noted that all the lights in Holden's house were equipped with dimmers. "Having been on movie sets all my life, I'm uncomfortable if the light isn't balanced," Bill explained.

Realizing that most stars have relatives or hangers-on they want hired on productions, Coblenz asked Bill if he wanted anyone special put on *The Blue Knight*. "No, that's your department," Bill told the producer. "You do the hiring."

Holden remained patient during the scriptwriting, which was being done on a crash schedule by E. Jack Neuman (an earlier script by Rod Serling had proved unsatisfactory). When Lee Remick was hired for the other leading role, Coblenz was worried because Holden's contract provided that only his name appear above the title. Miss Remick's agents wanted her named above the title as well. "If it's a problem, I'll relinquish my single billing," Holden volunteered. The issue was settled by giving the actress special billing below the title.

The Blue Knight was filmed on actual locations on the seamy side of Los Angeles. Most of the actors had worked only in television, and they didn't know what to expect from a film star of Holden's caliber. He surprised them by arriving on the locations each morning on his motorcycle. He was always prompt and was impatient with delays. When a button came off his police shirt, filming was halted while another button was sewn on. "You wonder why a production like this couldn't afford two shirts," he grumbled.

Holden appeared in almost every scene, since Bumper Morgan was the central figure with whom thirty characters interrelated. To speed the filming, Holden took each new actor to a corner of the set and ran lines while Butler was preparing the next shot.

Jamie Farr, who had attracted notice as Corporal Klinger on the *MASH* series, was coached by Holden in how to hold a gun: "When you're in a long shot, you hold it at your waist; in a medium shot, at your chest; in a closeup, near your face. The audience always wants to see the gun."

Farr confided that he was trying to get a better contract from his *MASH* employers. Bill cited his own disputes with the studios and advised, "If you think you're worth more, hold out for it. You'll get it." Farr followed Holden's advice and succeeded.

Holden had no trouble keeping up with the television schedule. When the crew remained noisy after the actors stepped before the camera, he remarked in an even tone, "Hey, fellas, it's our turn now. We've got a scene to do."

One day Holden was standing on a corner in Little Tokyo waiting for a scene when a woman stopped her car in front of him. "Officer, could you tell me how to get to Aliso Street?" she asked.

"Sure, ma'am," Bill replied, and he gave her detailed instructions.

The woman gazed at his name badge, said, "Thank you, Officer Morgan," and drove on.

Walter Coblenz observed the incident and commented, "You sure get to know the city working on this picture."

"I knew this city before you were taken off your mother's breast," replied Holden, who told about the high school boy who rode his motorcycle all over Los Angeles making deliveries for his father's chemical business.

Director Butler had worked with Holden once before, as an associate director when Edward R. Murrow's *Person to Person* show visited the Holdens' Toluca Lake home. Butler was surprised to discover that Holden, reputed to be a self-assured man of adventure, was in reality "strung as tight as a piano wire."

During one scene Holden uncharacteristically blew one line after another. The director called a halt and drew Holden aside.

"Bill, is there something I can help you with?" Butler asked.

"It's those words!" Bill complained. "People just don't talk like that!"

"Jesus, that's easy, Bill. Change the words. Say the lines the way you want."

Bill smiled. "Robert, that's the easy way," he said. He returned to the set and performed the scene perfectly.

Almost invariably Bill followed Butler's direction. During a scene of extensive dialogue, Butler suggested, "How about sitting down for it?" Bill replied, "No, that's a cliché." He said the lines leaning against a chair and the scene proved more effective.

Holden worked twelve- and fourteen-hour days with little complaint. At the end of a strenuous day, he seemed tired, and Butler asked if Bill would like to have a studio driver take him to his hotel in a limousine. Bill merely smiled and threw his leg over his motorcycle. To accept a studio limo was not part of the Holden code.

The Blue Knight was completed three days under schedule. The final scene was shot at a nightclub on South Vermont Avenue. Holden played a drunken scene with Vic Tayback, and for the first time during the production, Bill was drunk. No one else at the location realized it, but Butler noticed that Bill was having trouble with the keys of the old Chevrolet he was driving. "Is there some kind of problem?" the director asked. Bill shot him an angry glance. "It was the only time he seemed annoyed on the picture," says Butler, "and I think it was only because he was drunk."

A "wrap" party had been scheduled in the commissary of the Burbank studios. Bill vetoed it: "We don't have wrap parties in the studio commissary on a Bill Holden picture." He engaged a private dining room at Sportsman's Lodge with a fancy dinner and a dance orchestra. Bill stood at the door and greeted each arrival, exchanging anecdotes with his co-workers and melting their wives with the Holden charm.

The Blue Knight was well received on television, creating the trend to mini-series such as *Roots* and *Shogun*. Holden was nominated by the Television Academy as best actor in a special. He was reluctant to attend the awards ceremonies, but he was persuaded by Bob Butler. Bill spent most of the time in the theater lobby, and Butler had to fetch him when his category approached. Bill won the Emmy and made a gracious speech thanking his fellow workers.

The Blue Knight brought new attention to the Holden career, but he realized little profit from overseas. Because of its episodic nature, it did not lend itself to compression as a feature movie.

The Towering Inferno was a humiliation for Bill Holden.

"It's a lousy script," he argued with Pat Stauffer. "McQueen and Newman have all the action. I spend all of the time talking on the telephone. Winker, I don't want to do it."

She tried to persuade him to accept the film. So did the William Morris Agency. It was a $15 million production by Irwin Allen, who had proved with *The Poseidon Adventure* the box-office value of combining well-known performers in a spectacle of mutual jeopardy. *The Towering Inferno* was an upgrading of the formula, a co-production of 20th Century–Fox and Warner Brothers; the studios had combined forces because both had bought novels on the theme of fire in a skyscraper.

Paul Newman and Steve McQueen were induced to take the leading roles because of million-dollar salaries. Billing was a problem, but it was solved by having Newman's name at the right and slightly above McQueen's. That left no room at the top for William Holden.

"I don't think I can change their billing," producer Allen said to Holden during negotiations.

"Don't worry about it," Holden assured him. He agreed to accept the role of the builder of the faulty high rise. The salary was better than he had received in years: $750,000.

Bill discovered what it was like to be a third-billed star. His dressing room was not as lavish as those for Newman and McQueen. He did not receive the same attention from the director, John Guillermin. When the company went on location in San Francisco, it was Newman and McQueen who received the clamor of the fans, not Bill Holden.

He performed his work uncomplainingly—for a time. A particular source of irritation was Faye Dunaway, who had become notorious within the company for causing delays. Again and again, Bill was left waiting on the set while Miss Dunaway completed the styling of her hair or redid her makeup or talked on the telephone.

For two hours one day, Bill waited for her to appear for an important scene. When she finally arrived, he took her by the shoulders and shoved her against the sound-stage wall. "You do that to me once more," he muttered, "and I'll push you *through* that wall." Set workers noted that Miss Dunaway's punctuality improved thereafter.

21 Hours at Munich was a semi-documentary for ABC Television, based on the massacre of Israeli athletes by Arab terrorists at the 1972 Olympic Games in Munich. Filmways was producing the film on a $2.2 million budget and offered Holden $150,000 plus a percentage of the foreign sales. After *The Blue Knight,* Bill had no illusions about overseas receipts from television movies. But he liked the script, believed that the subject was important, and agreed to play the role of the Munich police chief, Manfried Schreiber. Bill and Jack Gordean met with the director, William Graham.

"I'll do the picture on one condition: I won't use a German accent," Bill told Graham. "Americans who put on phony accents sound ridiculous."

"I agree," said the director, "but sometimes it works. Like Marlon Brando in *The Young Lions.*"

"Well, I'm not Marlon Brando," Bill replied.

21 Hours at Munich was filmed in many of the locations where the events took place. The German government, still sensitive about the horrific events of 1972, was reluctant to provide cooperation. But the presence of William Holden in the cast and the assurances of the producers that no exploitation was intended helped change the minds of the bureaucracy. Permission was granted to use the Olympic sites, and government helicopters were provided, including some that had actually taken part in the assault against the terrorists.

When Bill Holden arrived in Munich for the movie, Filmways provided a lavish suite at the Four Seasons Hotel. Bill soon asked to be moved to The Residence, a more modest hotel with housekeeping facilities, where most of the production crew were staying. "I want to be available if you need me," he told the production manager, Frank Baur, an old friend from Paramount days.

Holden and Baur had been drinking buddies at Paramount, and after a day's work they had made their way along Melrose Avenue from Oblath's to the Melrose Grotto to Lucey's. In Munich they drank what they called the "Baur-Holden Special"—Polinaris mineral water with lime and lemon.

Bill would not drink beer, even though the Bavarian studios maintained a cooler containing German beer on the set. He told Frank Baur,

"The worst thing that happened to me was when a Japanese doctor told me I could drink beer. I'd drink a case of beer and end up as drunk as if I'd been on booze."

Despite thirteen days of rain, *21 Hours at Munich* was completed on its thirty-day schedule. ABC was so enthusiastic about the movie that it was scheduled opposite CBS's first running of *Gone With the Wind*. The result was a ratings disaster for ABC, and *21 Hours at Munich* was never repeated on the network. The film was banned in Germany, but oddly enough, the Arab world embraced it. The terrorist leader, played by Franco Nero, was so charismatic that Arabs proclaimed him a hero.

30

Stefanie

He called her Stef, and he always spoke of her in terms of admiration and endearment.

She was a new experience for Bill Holden. The women he had loved—Ardis, Audrey Hepburn, Grace Kelly, Capucine, Pat Stauffer—had followed the same pattern. They were willowy, extremely feminine yet strong-willed, sensual in a soft, delicate way, deferential to his masculinity, tolerant of his excesses.

Stefanie Powers was a generation apart from Bill. She had grown up in the postwar years amid changing attitudes of the relationship of men and women. She had the build of a tomboy, and she challenged the boys at their own games. As she matured, she developed her own sensuality, coupled with a strong desire to succeed.

Bill met Stefanie at La Costa resort in 1974, when he was undergoing another of his restorations to health, and she was attending a tennis tournament. Bill later recalled how they met again a few months later at a Beverly Hills bookstore:

"Stef had some books on medieval tapestry, and I had some literature on Southeast Asia, so I said, 'Let's trade information over lunch.' Well, we did. We talked about art and history and found we had many compatible interests. . . . And then I became anxious to show her some of my sandpiles."

The first was Hong Kong (when asked his favorite place in the world, Bill always answered, "Hong Kong, after the war"). The travels of Stef and Bill took them throughout the world in the next five years, during a much-publicized and mutually rewarding relationship.

Stefania Zofja Federkievicz was born in Hollywood on November 2, 1942, the daughter of a Polish immigrant and a mother of Polish descent. They divorced when their daughter was small, and her mother married a studio worker named Paul. Stefania adopted the girlhood name of Taffy Paul.

Her mother had had frustrated ambitions of being a dancer, and she wanted her daughter to have the career that she had been denied. Mrs. Paul drove Taffy to dancing school and to auditions for child actresses at the studios. Taffy never found acting jobs, but she was entranced by the studio life and begged to visit sets where her stepfather was working. She haunted the movie theaters of Hollywood Boulevard with her brother Jeffrey. She saw *Picnic* thirteen times and thrilled every time she watched William Holden in the sensuous dance with Kim Novak. During junior high school, Taffy decided she would become an Olympic swimmer, and she developed the broad shoulders and strong muscles she would carry into adulthood.

At Hollywood High School, boys discovered the bright, darkly beautiful cheerleader who could match them in arm wrestling. She discovered a world of learning and adventure outside the limits of Hollywood, California, by reading books, particularly *Gods, Graves and Scholars,* which had a profound influence on her. She dedicated herself to improvement and strove to substitute her slangy, Polish-tinged speech for cultured English tones such as she heard in *Lawrence of Arabia,* which she saw eight times.

Graduation from Hollywood High was almost prevented by a girlish prank. Tanked up on stout malt liquor at a sorority party, she and four friends staged an act of defiance against authority by sawing down a twenty-year-old tree on the school grounds. Taffy was booked at Juvenile Hall and ordered to pay a $320 fine before she could collect her diploma.

Despite a desire for knowledge, Taffy did not go on to college. She started touring the studio casting offices and landed a few television roles, then a small role in a feature, *Tammy Tell Me True.* A role in Blake Edwards' 1962 *Experiment in Terror* helped land a contract at Bill Holden's old studio, Columbia, then in its post–Harry Cohn period.

By the time she was twenty-three, Stefanie Powers—she had chosen the name for herself—had appeared in a dozen movies. She had established herself as a reliable young actress and one who attracted publicity. There was the question of whether Tallulah Bankhead had slapped her more than the script called for in *Die! Die! My Darling!* There was the rumored engagement to Eddie Fisher, rebounding after being discarded by Elizabeth Taylor. There were the bullfight lessons in Mexico and her honorary membership in the bullfighters union.

Tired of ingenue roles, Stefanie Powers became star of a television series, *The Girl from U.N.C.L.E,* which attempted to duplicate the formula and success of *The Man from U.N.C.L.E.* The James Bond spoof, which made full use of Stefanie's athleticism, lasted one season. While filming the series, she married Gary Lockwood, a half-Polish actor born John Gary Yoursek who had starred in a series called *The Lieutenant* and in *2001: A Space Odyssey.* His career declined as hers ascended, and after eight years of marriage they were divorced in 1974, the year Stefanie met Bill Holden.

Bill was fifty-six, Stefanie was thirty-two. Bill had never known a woman quite like her. She had enormous energy and a man's strength, yet she could also be passionate and tender and totally feminine. She cussed like a marine sergeant, but she looked radiant in an evening gown. Self-educated, she could speak seven languages and converse intelligently about European art. She became an ideal companion for a wandering Bill Holden.

"It's tough to find a woman who can travel with you, who will put up with all the problems and hassles," he told interviewer Roderick Mann. "Stef does it wonderfully. I've taken her out on safari, sleeping under the stars, and she's loved it. Most of my life I've had to take care of people, but with her I haven't had to do anything. How many women would accompany a man upriver in northern New Guinea and wind up with dengue fever and not complain? Not many."

The trip to New Guinea resulted from a request of the U.S. State Department for Holden to conduct a mission to the newly established nation of Papua New Guinea, which was released from the Australian mandate on September 16, 1975.*

Bill and Stefanie made an expedition up the Sepik River, where he had already explored the prospect of establishing a sanctuary for birds that were being hunted to extinction by natives who treasured their plumage. This time his search was for native art. Michael Somare, the new prime minister of Papua New Guinea, had asked Holden to help

---

*This was not the first mission performed for the United States government by Holden. During the 1950s and 1960s, when Holden traveled widely, especially to nations that were undeveloped and caught between the great powers of the East and West, rumors persisted that he fed information to the CIA. UPI Hollywood correspondent Vernon Scott once asked Holden point-blank if he worked for the CIA. "Bill was absolutely thunderstruck," Scott recalls. "He denied it, but I suspected from his reaction that there was something there."

establish a cottage industry for the aboriginal artists. Bill and Stefanie collected enough masks and sculpture for an exhibition in Los Angeles and eventually formed an import company to bring New Guinea art to America.

Impressed by the rich movie star from America, the prime minister asked for a $250,000 donation to endow a crafts program. "I'm afraid you've got it all wrong," Bill replied. "I'm not your man. You've got to go to our State Department if you want some money."

After the New Guinea adventure, Bill and Stefanie went on to Bali, Australia, and Malaya, where they rented a car and drove 470 miles to Kuala Lumpur and then Penang. Later they flew to Kenya, and Stefanie accompanied Bill as he and Don Hunt captured animals for a game refuge in Nigeria. They lived in pup tents on plains where lions, rhinos, and elephants wandered. Bill lassoed rare zebras from a speeding Land Rover, and Stefanie helped wrestle the animals to the ground. Then on to Ethiopia, where Bill had obtained permission to capture wild asses that were nearly extinct.

Bill and Stefanie traveled together five months during 1975, to the detriment of her acting career. "Opportunities to travel and learn and be with a man like Bill were more important," she told an interviewer.

The journeys with Stefanie were also a tonic for Bill Holden. He stopped drinking. As he said: "I was drinking because I was bored. Then I met Stefanie, who is an entertaining young lady. So when it came to drinking or being able to accomplish a few things and have the company of Stefanie—well, there was no contest."

Going along with the new candor among celebrities, Holden in interviews sometimes referred to Stefanie as "the woman I live with." But they continued to maintain their separate homes, his in Palm Springs, hers in Benedict Canyon. She often spent a few days in the desert, lying beside the pool or motorcycling with Bill over back roads. When he came to Los Angeles, he sometimes stayed overnight at her house. But they never shared a common home.

They were insatiable travelers. Stefanie visited Bill when he was filming *21 Hours at Munich*. When she was appearing in *Escape to Athena* in Greece with Roger Moore, Telly Savalas, David Niven, and Claudia Cardinale, Bill appeared at the location. He even made an unbilled appearance in the film as an American prisoner of war.

Stefanie's travels were restricted in 1977 when she was cast in another series, *Feather and Father*. But the series lasted only half a season.

She had no children from the marriage to Gary Lockwood, but Stefanie had adopted as a foster son a boy she had seen when she was eighteen and on a promotion trip to Italy. Silvano Rampucci was nine.

She later recalled, "It was really strange. Silvano and I looked at each other and something happened between us. Years before, I had been told by a clairvoyant that I would meet such a child. And long after we'd met, Silvano told me that in his earliest dreams he'd seen someone like me, who wasn't his mother but was important to him. So we just stood staring at each other, and then he took my hand."

She supported the fatherless boy for years, visited him whenever she could get to Rome. She lost track of him, then found him again and helped him finish his education. Silvano, now in his mid-twenties, came to live with Stefanie and found work as a greeter in a Beverly Hills restaurant. Bill Holden took a fatherly interest in the young man and bought him a motorcycle. Because he could not acquire a work permit, Silvano was forced to return to Italy, where Stefanie helped him start a business.

Interviewers found good copy in the global May-December romance of William Holden and Stefanie Powers, and the question of marriage often arose.

Stefanie commented, "I once heard a psychologist say something that made great sense: 'God save us from relationships based on need.' How often do you hear 'Oh, well, opposites attract; she needs what he has'? What about *adult* choice? What about two people who decide to be together who don't really need each other? They can get along very well by themselves; they *choose* to be together because they *want* to be together, without this interdependence that eventually creates a weakness, because one or the other outgrows that dependency, and that's it."

Bill answered the question more succinctly: "Marriage isn't a consideration at all. Why ruin it?"

31

Network

When Bill Holden was visiting Stefanie Powers on *Escape to Athena* in Greece, he gave this advice to Roger Moore: "Take any picture you can. One out of five will be good, one out of ten will be very good, and one out of fifteen might get you an Academy Award."

By 1976, Holden had made thirty films since his last Academy recognition: the Oscar for *Stalag 17*. Then came *Network*.

The script had flowed from the Olympian rage of Paddy Chayefsky, appalled by the greed and misuse of the television medium which he had graced in its early history with his brilliant teleplays. He was joined in *Network* by Sidney Lumet, whose reputation as a director had been established in the era of live television drama. MGM agreed to finance the film. It would be produced by Howard Gottfried and Chayefsky, who insisted on complete control lest his words be altered.

The words were plentiful and brilliant, with long speeches by many of the characters, especially the world-weary news executive Max Schumacher and the messianic anchorman Howard Beale. At first Chayefsky and Lumet considered William Holden as Beale and Peter Finch as Schumacher, then they decided to reverse the roles, provided the Australian-born Finch could master an American accent. He studied tapes of Walter Cronkite, Howard K. Smith, and John Chancellor and arrived at an acceptably American pattern of speech, influenced mostly by NBC's Chancellor.

Bill Holden was overwhelmed by Chayefsky's audacious script. Two matters concerned Bill. The other co-star would be Faye Dunaway, his nemesis on *The Towering Inferno;* the script called for him and Miss Dunaway to perform graphic sex while she ranted on about network matters.

Bill was aware of Lumet's speedy, no-nonsense approach to filmmaking and believed the director could control Miss Dunaway.

Lumet also had exhibited good taste, and Holden assumed Lumet would direct the bed scene for its comic value.

Two weeks of rehearsals began in March of 1976 in the chilly ballroom of the Diplomat Hotel at 43rd Street and Sixth Avenue in Manhattan. All major members of the cast and crew were there, and they watched expectantly for the meeting of William Holden and Peter Finch. The success of *Network* could hinge on their relationship, on the screen and off.

To the relief of everyone, the two actors became immediate pals. Both had been through the mill: battles with producers; romances with famous women; wild alcoholic sprees; the sorrows and triumphs of long acting careers. Both were superb storytellers, and through the weeks of filming they delighted each other and members of the company with adventurous tales.

With their newfound friendship, the actors' sense of competition remained. Bill realized that Howard Beale was a great bravura role with which Finch could march over everyone else in the cast. Ever the competitor, Bill was determined not to let that happen. He always performed best when faced with actors in more colorful roles: Swanson in *Sunset Boulevard,* Holliday and Crawford in *Born Yesterday,* Guinness in *The Bridge on the River Kwai,* Crosby and Kelly in *The Country Girl.*

Bill established his equality with Finch in the opening scene of *Network,* when the two drunken comrades in the TV wars talk boisterously on a Manhattan street corner at night. The two actors performed the scene totally sober; neither drank during the filming.

MAX

Must've been 1950 then. I was at NBC. Associate producer. Morning News. I was just a kid, twenty-six years old. Anyway . . . anyway, they were building the lower level to the George Washington Bridge. We were doing a remote from there. And nobody told me.

(Both men are convulsed with laughter. Max has to shout the rest of the story.)

Then after seven in the morning—I get a call—"Where the hell are you?—You're supposed to be on the George Washington Bridge?"—I jump out of bed—throw my raincoat over my pajamas—I run down the stairs—I run out in the street—Hail a cab —And I say to the cabbie, "Take me to the middle of the George Washington Bridge!"

(More spasms of laughter. Tears stream down Max's cheeks.)
—And the driver turns around and he says, he says—"Don't do it, buddy!
                    (So weak he can barely talk.)
You've got your whole life ahead of you!"

The scene shifts to a bar at 3 A.M. Any bar. Mostly empty. Max and Howard in a booth, so sodden drunk they are sober.

HOWARD
I'm going to kill myself—
                    MAX
Oh, shit, Howard—
                    HOWARD
I'm going to blow my brains out right on the air, right in the middle of the seven o'clock news.
                    MAX
You'll get a hell of a rating, I'll guarantee you that. Fifty share easy—
                    HOWARD
You think so?
                    MAX
Well sure, we could make a series out of it. Suicide of the Week. Well hell, why limit ourselves? Execution of the Week!
                    HOWARD
                    (Beginning to get caught up in the idea)
Terrorist of the Week!
                    MAX
They'll love it! Suicides . . . Assassinations . . . Mad Bombers . . . Mafia Hit Men . . . Automobile Smash-ups . . . The Death Hour . . . Great Sunday Night Show for the whole family. We'll wipe that fuckin' Disney right off the air!

A key scene in *Network* was Max Schumacher's confrontation with his wife, who discovers his affair with the fiercely ambitious Diana Christensen (Faye Dunaway). Beatrice Straight was cast as Louise Schumacher, and although her role was brief, she attended rehearsals with the rest of the cast.

The *Network* company moved to Toronto for television studio sequences, then returned to Manhattan for the remainder of the film. When the time arrived for the scene between Max and Louise Schumacher, Holden complained to Chayefsky, "There are just too many words; I think we should cut them down." Surprisingly, Chayefsky made no protest. But after attempting a shorter version, Holden admitted, "We can't cut it; all those words are important."

As the husband confessing infidelity, Holden was sure and affecting —perhaps because he had already played the scene with Ardis. Beatrice Straight responded with the same intensity. Even though the scene entailed only three pages of dialogue, it was enough to win her the Oscar as supporting actress.

Bill Holden realized that with *Network* he had done his best work in fifteen years, and he was willing to contribute his efforts to help publicize the film. He said so to Michael Mazlansky, partner of the publicity firm of Mazlansky-Konigsberg which had been hired by MGM to attract attention to the film, especially with Academy voters.

Mazlansky told Holden, "I want to be honest with you. I'm handling Peter's publicity on a personal basis, as well as working for the picture. Does that present a problem for you?"

"No," Bill answered, "I trust you to be fair. Peter deserves every honor he gets. I just don't want to be left out of the picture."

Bill consented to everything Mazlansky suggested. He was always punctual, drank only coffee or soda water (not Perrier, as was the Hollywood ritual), generally maintained good humor. Only rarely did he become testy. When Mazlansky told him that a *New York Post* reporter complained that Holden had held back in their interview, Bill snapped, "What does he expect me to do—put on a performance for him?"

Holden even allowed himself to be photographed at his Palm Springs house, something he had rarely permitted. He was in the living room when *The Proud and the Profane* appeared on the television screen. The photographer quickly set up his camera to shoot Bill Holden watching one of his old movies, but Bill said firmly, "Oh, no." He understood the photographer's plot: to compare the young Holden with the man who was fifty-eight and looked it.

When I interviewed Bill at Ma Maison in early 1977, he seemed more excited about his career than he had been for years. He drank soda water and sat at a table in a remote corner of the restaurant, as was his custom. I asked him about the bedroom scene with Faye Dunaway.

"If nobody had been in bed on the screen before, I might have hesitated," he said. "Such scenes are not to my liking. I believe lovemaking is a private thing, and I don't enjoy depictions of it on the screen. But I have to go by what the audience accepts as normalcy in today's world. And *Network* is no *Deep Throat.* The scene was not meant to be pornographic. It was meant to disclose a character flaw; the fact that Faye talks all the way through it tells more about her. It was Paddy's way of getting the dialogue out. But I do agree that the scene was meant to be more amusing than it came off."

He seemed more than a little embarrassed by having done the scene (in which Miss Dunaway assumed the top position and talked business throughout the copulation). He made one rather surprising comment about how Diana struck back at Max by criticizing him as a lover. Bill said in passing, "Isn't that true of women? When they really want to hurt a man, they tell him how lousy he is in bed."

Bill hungered for the Oscar, to signal his return to first rank in the movie world. He wanted *Network* to sweep the awards, and when he received a ballot as a member of the Academy of Motion Picture Arts and Sciences, he marked everything for which *Network* was eligible. "Here, you fill in the rest," he told Frank Schaap. The accountant was amazed. Bill had always thrown away his Academy ballot before.

Peter Finch also wanted the Oscar. He learned that MGM was planning to promote him for supporting actor and Holden for lead actor, a strategy that had helped the studio acquire an Oscar for George Burns in *The Sunshine Boys* in the previous year.

"Absolutely not!" Finch insisted. "Howard Beale was *not* a supporting role!" He campaigned even more strenuously than Holden; Mazlansky estimated that Finch did three hundred interviews during the Academy race.

Peter Finch was on his way to another television interview when he collapsed and died of a heart attack in the lobby of the Beverly Hills Hotel. Two months later, his widow accepted the Oscar for best performance by an actor in 1976.

Months afterward, Bill Holden muttered in jest to Frank Schaap, "If the son of a bitch hadn't died, I coulda had my second Oscar."

32

Anecdota

In 1975, Bill Holden began planning a new house in Palm Springs. After more than twenty years of maintaining homes on four continents, he felt the need for a single residence.

"I found myself being too spread out," he explained to an interviewer. "Sometimes I'd be in one of my homes discussing a topic with friends and I'd reach for a pertinent book I needed to illustrate a point. But it was sitting on a shelf in another house. Frustrating. I finally decided, This is nutsy. You gotta have one place where everything is there."

The one place he was drawn to more than any other in the world was Palm Springs. He once explained his reasons:

"Because the air caresses you here. It's like velvet. And this desert reminds me of Kenya—raw and beautiful, but without the animals."

His collection of art had outgrown his home in the Deepwell area, and he wanted a place big enough to display the sculptures, paintings, and artifacts he had found all over the world. Also land where he could grow trees and plants he had brought from Africa. He had been trying to introduce African flora to the Coachello Valley, contributing thousands of Naivasha yellow fever thorn trees, African acacia, baobobs, and Abyssinian umbrella trees for environmental groups to plant on the barren desert.

Holden had bought property in the exclusive Southridge district overlooking the full sweep of the desert and the hills beyond. He worked closely with his architect, Hugh Kaptur, to design a 7,000-square-foot house that would be partly an art museum, partly a bachelor's quarters.

An essential part of the planning for Holden was security. One day he proposed to Frank Schaap, "I want to install a laser-beam alarm system that would go on when any son of a bitch breaks into my house."

Schaap was appalled. "Bill," he protested, "that could kill a man."

"Fine. That's just what he would deserve."

Schaap was able to convince Holden that a laser-beam alarm system would be unlawful.

With his acting career prospering at last, Jack Nicholson decided to buy himself a luxury automobile. He shopped at several dealers, and he was attracted to the Mercedes 500 touring sedan. One day Nicholson was paying a visit to a friend at the Cedars of Lebanon Hospital in Hollywood, and he saw a well-polished Mercedes 500 in the parking lot. As he was studying the car, he noticed a figure rummaging in the back seat.

Nicholson decided to question the owner about the merits of the car. He tapped on the window, and a face appeared. It was unmistakably William Holden's.

"Oh, hi," said Nicholson.

"Hi," replied Holden, responding in the familiar way that movie stars extend to each other, even when they have never met before.

"I'm thinking of buying the same car as this one," Nicholson said. "How do you like it?"

"I recommend it highly," Holden replied. "I've tried them all— Bentley, Rolly, Jag. For an all-around touring car, Mercedes 500 is the best."

"What are you doing here?" Nicholson inquired.

"Oh, I'm going in for a two-day drying-out period," Holden answered. He finally located what he had been trying to find in the back seat—a six-pack of Heineken beer.

"Come on up to my room and we'll talk," Holden offered.

Nicholson was eager for the chance to talk to William Holden, who had been a longtime idol, and the two actors spent an hour conversing in Holden's hospital room. Although they met only a few times thereafter, they always felt like old friends.

Holden agreed to be one of the on-camera hosts for a television restrospective produced by the Motion Picture Academy as part of its contract with the ABC network. Bill's scenes were photographed in front of the grillwork gate of Paramount studios, which he had first entered almost forty years before. The publicist for the Academy was Art Sarno, who had worked on early Holden films at Paramount.

"Remember me?" the publicist asked.

"Sure, you're Art Sarno," Holden replied immediately. "How's

Jimmy?" He referred to Sarno's cousin, who had also worked in Paramount publicity.

"Jimmy died a few years ago."

Bill sighed. "That's the trouble with coming back to Paramount. That's the third story like that I've heard today."

Holden had lunch in the Paramount commissary, visiting the manager, Pauline Kessinger, and the few other oldtime Paramount hands who remained. As he left the commissary, he encountered Richard Webb, who was appearing in a television movie. The two old friends had been contract players together and had become close friends in the army.

"You old son of bitch!" Bill exclaimed, embracing the blond-haired, tan-faced actor. "You look great! How do you do it?"

"Well, Bill, I'm an alcoholic," Webb replied. "I haven't had a drink since I joined AA fifteen years ago, when I went crazy and tried to have a shootout with the cops."

Bill seemed uneasy. "Gee, that's swell, Dick," he said. "Great to see you again. I gotta go."

Holden was talking to reporter Roderick Mann about the difficulty of finding privacy in America:

"Nobody's safe here. The other day I drove into the garage of my Palm Springs house with some groceries. Suddenly one of those tour buses pulled up and a voice said, 'This is William Holden's house, and I think I just saw him pull in.' I flattened myself against the garage wall —the garage is separate from the house—and tried to hide. But the bags got heavy so I finally thought to hell with it, and walked out.

"And the voice said, 'There he is, folks, I told you he'd come out sooner or later.' "

Red Buttons and Bill Holden had been friends ever since Bill visited the African location of *Hatari*, starring his old pal John Wayne. Buttons delighted in meeting Bill in airports or on movie lots. Bill's eyes always lighted up with warm anticipation, and Buttons always obliged with a few of his latest jokes.

One night Red and his wife Alicia arrived for dinner at an Italian restaurant on Pico Boulevard in West Los Angeles. "Look, there's Bill Holden in the rear," Alicia said. At the same moment, someone in Bill's party called Bill's attention to Buttons. The two friends started toward each other.

To the comedian's astonishment, Bill took Red in his arms, bent him backward, and gave him a kiss full on the lips.

"*Now* where's your one-liner?" Bill grinned.

For once in his life, Red Buttons was without one.

During a trip to Bill's game ranch in Kenya, Mary Beedle fell and broke her hip. She was flown home to California, and her condition became critical. Faced with the possibility of losing his mother, Bill told Frank Schaap he wanted no funeral for her. Bill had already endured his father's funeral, which he considered ghoulish.

"Dammit, isn't there a better way?" Bill asked.

"Yes," Schaap replied, and he produced a card from his wallet.

"What's that?" Bill asked.

"That shows I'm a member of the Neptune Society. You pay twenty-five dollars for membership, then after you die they collect your body, cremate it, and scatter the ashes over the oceans, the mountains, or the desert."

"That's not all they charge."

"No, your survivors pay another two hundred and fifty dollars for the cremation. Since you're a veteran, the government would pick up the expense."

The procedure appealed to Bill's passion for privacy, as well as his sense of thrift.

"Sign me up," he said.

Fifteen naked men stood in the shallow end of the swimming pool.

"Hands on hips!" ordered the instructor. "Now bend your knees until your chin touches the water. Ready, down . . . up!"

The fifteen men were undergoing part of the health treatment at La Costa resort. One of them was the comedian John Belushi, who had come to the spa after another of his manic binges on alcohol and drugs. He had had much to celebrate. His first starring film, *National Lampoon's Animal House*, despite scathing reviews, was proving to be the most successful film of the year. Belushi was visiting La Costa with the film's director, John Landis.

"Now, arms over your head and reach up as far as you can. That's it—stretch!"

Belushi, who detested any form of discipline, was bored. He glanced toward the man at his side, and his eyes widened. The man looked like William Holden. It *was* William Holden.

"You're William Holden!" Belushi exclaimed.

Holden smiled at the beefy young man and continued exercising.

"Do it for me!" Belushi urged.

"Do what for you?" Bill asked.

"The opening scene from *Sunset Boulevard!*"

Bill laughed. "Sorry, friend. I've already done that picture."

Holden befriended Belushi and Landis, and the three of them shared meals together. "I haven't seen your picture yet, but I will," Bill said. "Don't take the bad reviews personally. The critics will knock you down, but you'll get up. Then you'll be a hero all over again. The press, most of them, are scum. They'll be good to you when you're on top. But if you start to slip just a little, they'll try to tear you down. You guys are hot now. You've got a hit picture. Just wait, they're gonna get you."

Before they parted, Landis mentioned that he was preparing another comedy, *The Incredible Shrinking Woman,* to star Lily Tomlin. "I'd sure like you to play the President of the United States," the director said.

Bill thought for a moment and said with a grin, "You know, I'd be good at playing the President of the United States. I really play distinguished characters at this stage of my career."

He added, "I want you to know something, John. If you don't call me for the part, I've been around long enough that I won't be angry."

Gloria Swanson and Bill Holden rarely met after *Sunset Boulevard,* but a bond of deep affection continued between them. Bill told this story to reporter Bernard Drew:

"A couple of years ago, Gloria was in Palm Springs, and she told Edie Adams that she'd like to visit me. So they came to my house and were told by the couple who care for the place that I was in Africa. Gloria said she'd like to look around, and, of course, they showed her through.

"When I returned, they told me Gloria had left a message for me in my bathroom. Sure enough, there on the toilet seat was this note:

" 'Dear Joe'—that was the name of the guy I played in *Sunset Boulevard*—'I'm leaving this note where I know you'll find it. Where is Max? Where is De Mille? Where is Hedda? Where has everybody gone?

" 'Love, Norma Desmond.' "

33

"Bill Holden Is Ready"

"How can they do this to me?" Bill Holden demanded. "How could they ever think I could accept a picture like this?"

He had finished reading the script of *The Omen*. The story of a modern anti-Christ had been written by David Seltzer and was being produced for 20th Century–Fox by Harvey Bernhard; both men had worked intimately with Bill on the television documentary for David Wolper.

"Bill, I think you ought to take it," urged Jack Gordean. "You're hot again after *Network*. Fox is willing to pay you seven hundred and fifty thousand. Maybe the subject matter isn't your cup of tea, but it's the kind of thing today's audiences are going for."

Bill was adamant. "I'm not doing any picture in which a wolf is the mother of a child."

Gregory Peck took the role of the father-victim of the anti-Christ, and *The Omen* proved to be one of the most successful films of 1976. Peck collected a million dollars in salary and percentages of the profits.*

The success of *The Omen* prompted a sequel, and Holden was offered the role of the anti-Christ's uncle. This time he accepted, although Gordean warned, "*Omen II* is not as good as the first one."

Damien: Omen II started on a sour note. The director, Michael Hodges, was fired after ten days of locations in Chicago. When the producer, Harvey Bernhard, broke the news to Holden, Bill was not upset.

"This isn't the first time I've had this happen on a picture," Bill said. "Who's the replacement?"

---

*Once before Peck had profited from a Holden turndown. Holden declined *The Guns of Navarone* because Columbia would not pay the $750,000 fee he had established with *The Horse Soldiers*.

"We're thinking about Don Taylor," said the producer.

"Oh, my God, that's marvelous!" Bill exclaimed. "Don and I made a couple of pictures together. We're old buddies."

When Taylor arrived in Chicago, Bill was waiting at the hotel. The new director declined the suggestion that he begin filming the following day, and Holden supported him. "Why don't I give you the inside dope on this picture?" Bill suggested, and he provided a lengthy and incisive analysis of the production over lunch.

Holden remained sober during *Damien,* as did Don Taylor, who also had a reputation as a drinker. During a break in filming, they reminisced about their days as young actors, when they came to Chicago on publicity tours and drank and ate lavishly at the famed Pump Room.

"Hey, that was fun," Bill enthused.

"Why don't we go there tonight, for old times' sake?" Taylor suggested.

"Great idea! Let's do it!"

After a long day of working with fog and special effects, they returned to their hotel. "So it's the Pump Room tonight," Taylor said wearily.

"Yeah," Bill sighed.

"Do you really want to go?"

"Hell, no!"

"Good. Neither do I."

They had dinner together in the hotel dining room.

Bill finished *Damien* in a state of depression. He realized Jack Gordean had been right: the sequel was not as good as *The Omen.* Although he enjoyed working with Don Taylor, Bill found the script somber and depressing. He was physically drained, having started the film thirty pounds underweight, following an extended drying-out and a severe case of flu.

Two other matters contributed to his depression: Stefanie had not visited him on the location; Ray Ryan had been murdered.

Jovial, fun-loving Ray had always delighted in skirting the edge of danger. This time he went too far.

Ryan, who had often done business with mobsters, testified in 1964 that Marshall Caifano, a Chicago hoodlum also known as Johnny Marshall, had tried to shake him down for $60,000 a year in protection money. Caifano was convicted and sentenced to ten years in prison, and he didn't forget Ray Ryan.

On October 18, 1977, Ryan finished a two-hour workout at the Olympia Health and Beauty Resort near his home in Evansville, Indiana. He went to the parking lot to start his car, and a bomb blew his life away.

Fedora reunited Bill Holden and Billy Wilder, but the circumstances were not as happy as during their collaborations of the 1950s. Wilder and I. A. L. Diamond had adapted a Thomas Tryon story about a faded movie star living in seclusion in Europe and a shoestring film producer who tries to hustle her into a comeback. Many of Wilder's friends suggested he was attempting *Sunset Boulevard Revisited,* but he indignantly denied it.

The script was developed for Universal Pictures, which decided against producing it. The rights were sold to Wilder, who found German tax-shelter money to finance the film. Bill Holden was delighted to work again with Wilder; Bill's first two Academy nominations supported his belief that Wilder had been the best director for him. Wilder realized that he needed a personality of magnitude to portray the onetime movie queen, and he had hoped to enlist Greta Garbo, for whom he had co-authored her last hit, *Ninotchka.* His effort failed, and he cast the German actress Marthe Keller to play both the star and her look-alike daughter.

Fedora was filmed in Munich, on Corfu, and in Paris. Holden was on his best behavior—sober, punctual, hardworking. As he waited while technicians concluded endless details before a shot, he often cracked, "Bill Holden is ready." It was a custom he had learned from Robert Mitchum, and it bespoke professionalism as well as impatience.

To old acquaintance José Ferrer Bill seemed inexpressibly sad. To Marthe Keller he was boring. She avoided dinners with him because she claimed he repeated stories she had already heard.

Fedora had a vogue in Europe, where Wilder's literate cynicism was still appreciated. The film languished without an American release until United Artists gave it brief distribution in 1978. A few critics applauded *Fedora*, especially for its acid-etched views of the New Hollywood, as voiced by Holden: "It's a whole new business now. The kids with the beards have taken over. They don't need scripts—just give them a hand-held camera and a zoom lens."

Ashanti was one of those adventure movies of the 1970s that international promoters assembled with multiple stars, bizarre financing, and wretched scripts. Michael Caine admitted that he accepted the film because of the money; he had just purchased a million-dollar house in Bel Air. He couldn't fathom why William Holden, a rich man, would agree to appear in *Ashanti*. Finally Caine concluded, "Now I see: he wanted a trip to Jerusalem."

Holden was cast in the small role of a helicopter pilot who helps Caine in his pursuit of a modern slave trader (Peter Ustinov). Omar Sharif and Rex Harrison were also in the cast.

Prior to the Jerusalem sequence, Richard Fleischer directed action scenes in the Sinai Desert. By the end of the desert filming, Fleischer had suffered heatstroke in the 130-degree temperatures. He remained behind to recover in the Ashkalon hospital while the rest of the company moved to Jerusalem.

At noon of the second day of his hospitalization, Fleischer was awakened from a nap by a familiar voice saying, "Hi, Dick."

The director opened his eyes and saw the unmistakable figure of William Holden. "Hello," Fleischer said. The two men had never met.

"I'm Bill Holden," said Bill. "I heard you weren't feeling well. Brought you some newspapers and magazines."

Holden remained to chat, and Fleischer was deeply touched by his gesture. The director had been visited by no one else from the *Ashanti* company.

Stefanie remained with Bill during the two weeks he worked on the film, and they dined nightly with principals of the company. Both Bill and Stefanie drank only mineral water, and he expounded on the merits of the various brands and how to find restaurants with the best mineral water.

Holden enjoyed the companionship of the other actors, especially Peter Ustinov and Michael Caine. Ustinov provided amusement with his comments about the Italian crew. When he heard the assistant director give instructions over the public address system, Ustinov remarked, "Whenever I hear Italian spoken over a loudspeaker, I have the feeling it's time to abandon ship."

The Indian caterer consulted Ustinov about whether to serve curry to the Italians. "I don't advise it," said Ustinov. "They weren't in Abyssinia long enough."

Michael Caine and Bill Holden became friends through *Ashanti* and met a few times afterward in California. Caine observes:

"Bill always looked and talked as though he had a secret. Was he connected with the CIA? He would have been ideal. He traveled everywhere, and actors are in a peculiar position to learn secrets. They meet all kinds of high officials who are willing to confide in them, figuring no harm will be done.

"To me, Bill seemed the picture of the disillusioned American boy, just as Jean Seberg seemed the disillusioned American girl. Both were Middle Americans lost in a sea of sophistication."

34

Through the Sound Barrier

"When the dark moods came, Bill tried to get through them by drinking," says Harvey Bernhard. "He was like a pilot trying to break through the sound barrier to get to the comfort zone."

The dark moods oppressed Bill Holden with greater regularity starting in 1978. He remained close to Stefanie Powers, but she had realized that her career had suffered during the travels with Bill. She was striving to reactivate her career with a new television series, *Hart to Hart*, co-starring with Robert Wagner. Although he still visited the game ranch in Kenya and made expeditions to rescue endangered animals, Bill's passion for Africa was waning. The political regime had changed; Kenya was becoming more westernized. Bill's visits to Africa had become more routine, rather than the adventures they had once been.

Bill and Stefanie had been among the first Americans to travel to China, where a deranged Chinese attacked their party with a knife. But traveling itself had become more tedious for Bill: the security checks, the waits for delayed flights, the downgrading of service by the airlines. Bill was sixty years old, and his tolerance of such things had diminished.

The relationship between Bill and Stefanie was beginning to erode. She was in her mid-thirties and realized that her chances for real success as an actress were diminishing with each year. Her ambition was even stronger than when she was a contract actress at Columbia. Friends noticed that she was increasingly impatient with Bill, often mentioned his age to him, complained that his friends belonged to the previous Hollywood generation while hers were the doers of today. Most of all, she could not tolerate his drinking.

The idyll with Pat Stauffer had ended a few years before, largely because of Bill's alcoholism. She had tired of nursing him through the binges, of helping him to seek medical treatment, only to see him fall off the wagon again. Pat's daughter Mindy was twelve, and while Bill and Mindy adored each other, Pat was concerned about the impressions on a young girl of a movie star reeling around the living room.

When the Stauffer home in Corona Del Mar was burglarized of thousands of dollars of equipment, including recording sets Bill had given Pat, a handsome, intelligent young detective arrived to investigate the burglary. Pat was attracted to him, and a romance began.

Bill became intensely jealous, and he came to her house for a showdown. "It's all over, Bill," she told him.

He realized she was serious. He sat down in Mindy's bean-bag seat in the living room and remarked sadly, "I drank us away, Winker."

"Yes, you did, Bill," she said.

With Pat Stauffer out of the picture, the responsibility for Bill during his black periods was assumed by Frank Schaap.

Schaap tried everything. He took Bill to Alcoholics Anonymous meetings. When Bill drank himself into a stupor, Schaap drove him to a sanitarium or hospital. But Bill would only stay until he was sober. Afterward he would never admit the reason for his confinement, claiming that he had the flu or a bad throat. "Yeah, alcoholic laryngitis," commented Schaap.

Frank tried subtle means to convince Bill of his alcoholism. After David Janssen died, Schaap commented to Bill: "You know, everybody tried to get Janssen to stop drinking—his wife, his fellow workers, his friends. He wouldn't listen to any of them, and he drank himself to death. He must have had a death wish."

Holden responded hotly: "Goddammit, he knew what he was doing. It was *his* life, not theirs. He could do anything he wanted with it."

During the drinking periods, Bill became almost paranoidly secretive. Once Deane Johnson telephoned Schaap: "I'm afraid Bill is drinking again. I can't get him to answer the phone." Schaap agreed to go to Palm Springs and investigate. Bill was drinking but had not become incapacitated. Frank went to the servants' quarters to ask Jean and Ben Rodé about Bill's behavior. Bill watched Frank and was furious.

A few days later, Bill stormed into Schaap's office and read him a formal letter forbidding Schaap any investigation into his personal life. Schaap was accustomed to such outbursts and replied, "Look, Bill, I don't give a damn who you sleep with. I'm just trying to take care of your business affairs. If you don't like what I'm doing, then I'll quit."

It was one of many offers or announcements of Schaap's resignation, but always he relented.

Bill Holden was bored. The promise of *Network* had not been realized, and most of the scripts he received were meaningless films to which he lent his still-valuable name for a high price. The success of *Animal House, Grease,* and other youth-oriented films persuaded the major studios to aim for the young market, and there was little work for an aging star. For the first time in his forty years as a star, Bill was forced to seek out his own film projects.

Blake Edwards had told Bill about a script he had planned about the new Hollywood. It was called *S.O.B.* (for Standard Operational Bullshit), and Blake wanted Bill for an important role. On a Concorde flight from Paris to New York in 1978, Bill encountered Tony Adams, Edwards' young assistant. "Any chance of getting *S.O.B.* going?" Bill asked. He often called Edwards or Adams to ask about the project's progress.

Bill was making one film a year, and with his interest in Africa and travel lagging, he had little to do. He belonged to no clubs, played no golf. His principal diversion was solitary: riding his motorcycle in the desert. He greeted old friends with warm cordiality, but he rarely sought them out for dinner or a weekend in the desert.

He was constantly being asked to be the guest of honor at dinners honoring his film achievements and his contributions to conservation. He always told Frank Schaap: "Give them the same answer—I'll be out of the country or making a picture."

With the completion of his Southridge house in January of 1977, Bill Holden had a magnificent refuge in which to withdraw from the world.

Southridge is Palm Springs' most exclusive residential area, a safe haven for millionaires, protected by a guard gate, electronic detection devices, and regular patrols. Bill had bought four acres of rocky land on a hill that afforded a breathtaking view from the granite thrust of Mount San Jacinto to the date groves of Palm Desert. Planning and construction had taken three years, and Holden oversaw every detail. He wanted the house to be part gallery, part home, but no monument that could be pointed out to tourists on the desert floor. The house had to blend into the landscape that he loved.

Holden was repeatedly frustrated by delays. Digging the site and building steel and concrete foundations took months longer than anticipated and proved enormously expensive. So did the house itself. Bill specified a flat roof so he could see the mountains as he drove up to the house, and he wanted picture windows that would reveal the vastness of the desert. The swimming pool was designed so the water flowed over the brink of the lot. Bill wanted to hear the waterfall sound and to float in the water and have an unimpeded view of the desert.

When construction changes created space below the living quarters, the architect and builder suggested converting it to another room.

"Great!" said the delighted Holden. "I always wanted a secret room when I was a kid." The long space was made into an art gallery and a screening room, the entrance through a hidden door upstairs. Sculptures and paintings were placed throughout the house, and Bill constantly moved them for what he considered the best effect. He was intensely proud of the house and meticulous about its appearance. As soon as two cigarette butts were placed in an ashtray, he quickly dumped it. The garage floor had three coats of sealer and was as clean as most people's kitchens.

Despite his pride in the house, he invited few guests. Among his favorites were his only close new friends, Gail and Chuck Feingarten; he was the dealer who exhibited the art that Bill and Stefanie brought back from New Guinea. The Feingartens tolerated the presence of Bertie, Bill's pet python, and were amused when it became jammed in an African sculpture. It became a crisis when Bertie was unable to wriggle free. As they struggled to free the snake, Chuck said, "Don't hurt the sculpture; it's delicate." Bill said, "Don't hurt Bertie; his scales are tender."

Stefanie often came to Bill's house for the weekend, and Ardis was a frequent visitor. But Bill spent more and more of his time alone in the 7,000-square-foot house, rearranging his artworks and trying to drink his way to the comfort zone.

Another disaster movie with Irwin Allen.

The genre had been exhausted, as Allen had proved with *The Swarm* and *Beyond the Poseidon Adventure*. But he still had a contract with Warner Brothers and a film left to make. Everyone agreed it was unwise to proceed with *The Day the World Ended*, but Paul Newman and Jacqueline Bisset were committed, and the production kept moving forward, like a juggernaut impossible to stop.

The novel was based on the Mount Pélée eruption on Martinique in 1902 in which 30,000 were killed. Carl Foreman modernized the story, then Stirling Silliphant did a rewrite, but neither could give it life. Irwin Allen shrugged: "The way to make this picture is to plaster it with names." To Newman and Miss Bisset were added Red Buttons, Edward Albert, Barbara Carrera, Valentina Cortese, Burgess Meredith, Ernest Borgnine, James Franciscus, Alex Karras—and William Holden.

Production began at Kona on the island of Hawaii. The director, James Goldstone, insisted on rehearsals before filming began, and they were held in a conference room at the Kona Surf Hotel. The rehearsals were largely devoted to reworking the script in order to inject characterization. Goldstone found Holden to be amenable to changes—up to a point. When the changes became unintelligible, Holden said firmly, "What I'm going to do is . . ."

The actors clung to each other out of the hope and desperation that springs from a doomed endeavor. Weary of restaurant food, they gathered nightly for dinner at their condominium building. Miss Bisset made an Italian dinner one night, then Miss Carrera prepared a vegetarian meal, Newman cooked hamburgers, and Bill proudly served a chili that scorched the mouths of his guests.

Congenial during the social times, Bill seemed tentative and uneasy on the movie locations. His morale leaped when Stefanie arrived in Hawaii. Jacqueline Bisset recalls watching Bill and Stefanie when they met: "He took her in his arms, then led her out to a patch of grass in the middle of the condominiums. He stood and admired her, his face filled with joy."

After Stefanie returned to California, Bill seemed to withdraw into himself, cloaked in melancholy. About three in the afternoon, he became edgy and snappish, anxious to have the day's filming end. His fellow workers feared his impatience meant he wanted to return to his condominium and drink. After the company moved to the east side of Hawaii, Jacqueline Bisset saw Bill in a bar with a glass of wine in his hand. Her heart sank. Was he starting one of his legendary binges?

Not yet. He retained his equilibrium, even during the tedious physical sequences of the trek of the disaster survivors. The weather was humid, and rainstorms caused long delays in shooting. Bill remained patient and professional. Goldstone admired how Bill without any coaching knew exactly how to keep within range of the three cameras and how to pitch his voice to be heard over the wind machines.

While filming hotel scenes, the company hired beefy Hawaiians to keep tourists from invading the production area. One morning Bill was called to the set, and he responded immediately, as was his custom.

"Can't go in there," said a burly Hawaiian guarding a rope across the lobby.

"I'm Bill Holden," Bill said.

"I don't care who you are. Nobody goes in there that I don't know. And I don't know you."

"You damn fool!" Bill shouted. "They need me in there. Now get your fat ass out of the way!"

The guard remained firm, and the two men shouted at each other until the assistant director, Andrew Stone, Jr., hurried over to pass Bill through.

Holden was seething. "You know," he said to Stone, "if some African talked like that to me, I would have taken out my gun and shot his foot."

Irwin Allen heard about the incident and ordered the guard fired. Holden wouldn't allow it. "He was doing what he was told to do," Bill said.*

Bill's drinking worsened. He spent hours alone in his dressing room. When he emerged, he was uncharacteristically loud and boisterous. He arrived on time and knew his lines, but his diction was blurred, his movements unsure. One day when the company was filming atop a cliff, Bill playfully pushed two of the actors toward the brink. No one fell, but the incident sobered everyone present, except Bill.

James Goldstone grew increasingly concerned, not only for the progress of the production but for the safety of Bill and other members of the company. Ava Ready, who was playing a role in the film, told the director about a close friend who was an expert in crisis counseling and the treatment of alcoholics and drug addicts. He was Michael Jay Klassman, a psychologist and therapist who was also an expert in psychodrama and had conducted performances in Los Angeles theaters.

"Call him," the desperate Goldstone told the actress. "Get him over here. The company will pay for it. We've got to get some kind of help for Bill."

Michael Klassman flew from Los Angeles to the island of Hawaii.

---

*Such an incident was certain to infuriate Holden, as had happened at Paramount in his early years. A few years after selling his interest in the Mount Kenya Safari Club, Holden approached the gate in his Land Rover. The guard refused to allow him entrance because his name was not on the guest list. "Goddammit, I built this place!" Holden exclaimed, and he crashed through the barrier.

Producer Allen asked him not to identify himself to Bill for fear of upsetting him, and for the first two days, Klassman merely observed on the movie set. By the third day he had made his conclusion: William Holden was in a severe stage of alcoholism. He was able to deliver his lines, but his heart wasn't in it. Klassman's overwhelming impression was not that Holden seemed to be a roaring drunk, but that he was a "little boy lost."

Holden failed to notice the young man, whose thick black hair, full beard, and inquisitive eyes gave him the look of a film student. Then one evening at a cast and crew party, Klassman found himself sitting next to Holden.

"I'm Bill," Holden said with his familiar smile.

"I'm Michael," replied Klassman, and they shook hands. They engaged in friendly conversation, and Klassman made no effort to identify himself. Holden seemed cordial, but Klassman noted an underlying depression.

Their relationship remained casual for the remaining two weeks of the Hawaii location. The company returned to Hollywood for additional sequences at the Burbank Studios and MGM. A crucial part of *The Day the World Ended* was scheduled for three and a half weeks on MGM's Stage 30, known as the Esther Williams stage because its sub-floor tank was used for her musical numbers. All of the principal actors were required for closeup scenes on a bridge thirty feet above the stage floor, with smoke bombs and light flashes to simulate molten lava.

It was dangerous work, for which doubles could not be used. Everyone was concerned whether Bill Holden could manage. Especially Michael Klassman, who remained on the set to observe Bill. The psychologist's fears were almost realized one day when Bill shoved a couple of fellow actors on the bridge. Again, no one fell.

Realizing the extreme danger, James Goldstone tried for a showdown with Bill. They had lunch together in the commissary's Oak Room, and at first they avoided mention of what weighed heavily on both their minds. Bill talked about the perils of Africa, the constant sense of mortality, the thrill of roping wild animals, his pleasure in teaching Stefanie how to do it. Goldstone agonized about how to broach the subject of Bill's drinking, then finally settled on a way.

"That opening scene you did in *Network*, Bill," said the director, "it was so powerful, so effective in allowing the audience to see the agony of a man. Alcohol can be a very dramatic and human tool, don't you think?"

"I did that scene cold sober," Bill remarked. He realized what

Goldstone was aiming toward, but Bill simply could not discuss his alcoholism.

A crucial scene was scheduled for a Monday on Stage 30, with Newman and Holden walking across a girder, leading a group of native children. Bill had gone to Palm Springs for the weekend, promising the assistant director, Andy Stone, that he would return in time for the 8 A.M. start of filming.

The entire cast gathered on the set at eight. No Bill Holden. Goldstone became uneasy. The first shot was a complicated setup that required Bill's presence; there was no possibility of filming without him.

Stone waited before calling Bill's house. He had learned about Bill's exaggerated sense of professionalism; it upset him to be reminded when he was late. At 8:20 Stone telephoned Palm Springs. "Mr. Holden left at six o'clock," the butler said.

The cast and crew waited amid mutual embarrassment for Bill and concern for his safety. Nine o'clock and no Bill. Finally, at 9:45, the stage door was flung open, and the unmistakable figure of Bill Holden was silhouetted against the harsh sunshine.

He strode to the makeup table and put a few touches on his face. Then he hurried to his motor home and reported to the set in his costume. Goldstone began the scene immediately. As soon as the director said "Cut!" Bill turned to the other members of the cast and to the crew.

"Ladies and gentlemen, I owe you all an apology," he said in anxious tones. "I left the house at six o'clock, which would have given me plenty of time to get here. But there was an accident on the freeway near Ontario. The traffic was totally stopped. I apologize."

Goldstone quickly announced: "Okay, folks, you can relax for a while. It'll take two or three hours to set up this next shot."

Midway through the morning, a second assistant director whispered to Andy Stone: "I think we've got a problem with Bill Holden." Stone went to Holden's motor home and found him totally drunk.

Michael Klassman stepped forward, telling producer Allen and director Goldstone: "I won't continue unless you let me take over. This man is a danger to himself and to the rest of the company. He must be hospitalized—now."

Goldstone said he could film scenes without Holden, but Allen was reluctant to disrupt the shooting schedule. He was convinced when Klassman emphasized the risk to others in the cast, including Allen's wife.

Bill needed convincing. It came from sympathetic members of the cast: Jacqueline Bisset, Edward Albert, Red Buttons, Pat Morita. Most importantly, Stefanie Powers came to the studio to persuade Bill to enter St. John's Hospital in Santa Monica. She met Michael Klassman for the first time and said tearfully, "Thank God I've finally found someone with the balls to do what I know needs to be done for Bill."

On the first night in the hospital, Klassman identified himself to Holden, fearing the star would rage about being spied upon. Instead, Bill merely grinned. "You're good," he said. "You know what I'm about, don't you?"

"Supposing I had walked up to you in Hawaii," said Klassman, "and I had said, 'Hi, I'm Michael Klassman, I'm a psychologist and drug counselor, and I'm here to help you.' What would you have said?"

" 'Go fuck yourself.' "

"That's what I thought."

Holden willingly entered St. John's detoxification unit, but the following day he telephoned Klassman and raged, "I want out!" He was persuaded to stay three days, during which he was a miserable patient.

Goldstone found work for the company to do at Burbank Studios. He telephoned Bill: "I want you to know that we can wait until you're ready to come back. I don't give a damn about the studio or insurance or anything."

"Don't worry, James," Bill replied, "when I come back, you'll know exactly what I can do."

He returned to Stage 30 in six days. First he met privately with Goldstone and told him: "I want to apologize for letting you down."

"Your apology accepted," the director replied. "Now let's go to work."

Says Andy Stone: "It took a lot of guts for Bill to return to the set that day. He knew there would be eighty people staring at him over their styrofoam cups, remembering what had happened and wondering if it would happen again. It didn't."

"The curious thing," recalls Paul Newman, "is that nobody was pissed off at Bill. With any other actor, that wouldn't have been true. But such was the reservoir of good will that Bill had established, everyone just felt concerned for him."

35

The Inner Door

"I'll tell you right now there are certain areas of my life that I can't talk about," Bill Holden said to Michael Klassman at the outset of their therapy sessions. "Over the years I have done certain things, performed certain missions for the government that are so secret that I can't talk about them to anyone, even you. So don't ask me."

The CIA connection. Shortly after Klassman began treating William Holden for alcoholism, the psychologist was visited at his Beverly Hills office by two well-dressed, fully credentialed men from the federal government. They explained that Holden was a public figure who had performed certain international services for the United States, and they inquired about Klassman's association with him. Klassman explained he was a licensed marriage, family, and child counselor, and he outlined his proposed treatment of the actor's drinking problem. The government men seemed satisfied, and they left.

Holden maintained his secrecy on governmental matters during the months of therapy.

"I'm telling you intimacies that I have never shared with anyone," Bill often told Klassman. But drunk or sober—and Klassman saw him both ways—Bill never talked about the CIA. On a few occasions he mentioned memories that seemed to cause him great pain. He spoke of being in the Congo and witnessing the beheading of two black leaders he had known. He started to mention a tragedy in Kuala Lumpur, then said, "But I can't talk about that."

He had traveled to countries of Asia and Africa before they were approved for American tourists, and was able to meet heads of state wherever he went. It seemed logical that he could have been the carrier of official information. But Holden was too much of a patriot to divulge such things to anyone. Klassman believed that the hoarding of those painful secrets contributed to Bill's unrest.

225

Bill Holden had tried psychoanalysis, but had been repelled by the sterile atmosphere of oak-paneled Beverly Hills offices, the Olympian attitudes of the psychiatrists. Michael Klassman was something different. He had been a football player at California State University, Northridge, and had studied five years in England. With his background in psychodrama, he had an understanding of the actor's life. Divorced, father of a young son, a diabetic, he understood vulnerability. Also, he had experienced alcoholism in his own family. Bill was able to view through Klassman's eyes what Bill's own sons had undergone living with an alcoholic.

The therapy sessions began after the conclusion of *The Day the World Ended* and continued intensely for the next four months, sporadically therafter. The pair met at Bill's Palm Springs house and sometimes talked for sixteen hours at a time. When Bill was in Los Angeles, Klassman visited him at the Beverly Hillcrest Hotel. They rode motorcycles together, walked on the desert, swam in Bill's pool.

Klassman was thirty-two, almost half Bill's age. Bill challenged him: "What the hell do you know? I'm old enough to be your father. I've traveled all over the world. I've seen things you'll never even dream of seeing. What makes you think you can tell me anything?"

"Maybe I'm younger than you are," the psychologist answered calmly. "But if I don't know anything and you know everything, why am I in this chair and you in that one, needing help?"

Holden proved to be a formidable adversary. "I'll submit to this treatment, but you'll find that I'm going to be a tough son of a bitch," he warned.

"I'm not worried," Klassman replied. "Your tough-guy role doesn't bother me."

In their early sessions, Holden was indeed elusive. Klassman learned to recognize the star's "automatic face," the one he could flash so winningly in movie roles and television interviews. During their encounters in Palm Springs, the therapist purposely worked long hours, realizing that he needed to break down the barriers that Holden had created during a lifetime of denial. Often the breakthrough came at three in the morning.

One afternoon in the office of Bill's Palm Springs home, Klassman asked him pointblank: "Are you an alcoholic?"

"No," Bill replied. "I realize that sometimes I drink to the extent where I have problems. But no, I am not an alcoholic."

"I think you are. You exhibit every sign of alcoholism, including the denial that you are an alcoholic."

"What do you mean? I go to work every day."

"No, you don't. You missed a few days on that last picture. What do you say to that?"

Bill ignored the question. "I believe I have a predisposition to alcohol."

"I don't. I believe that you have a lot of emotional problems that you're trying to hide. I believe that you're a very famous person who is caught up in the dilemma of fame and security. I believe also that you're probably very lonely. You're not with the lady you want to be with because she wants no part of you until you clean up your act."

Bill jumped out of his chair and exploded, "Who the hell do you think you are? You've only known me a few weeks. Get the fuck out of here!"

"Okay," Klassman said calmly. He walked out of the office, closed the door behind him, and walked to the kitchen for a snack. Fifteen minutes later, Bill shuffled into the kitchen with a small boy's chastened look. "Hey, look, you're not half bad," he said. "You might be right. Let's talk some more."

Klassman realized he had touched a nerve by referring to Stefanie. Bill had talked fondly of her, told how great she was to travel with and make love to. He had helped her, financially and professionally, and he was pleased with the success of *Hart to Hart*, though disturbed that it made her less dependent on him. He had wanted to marry her, but she had refused. Too many times he had failed her; in China he had been too drunk to attend a state dinner and she had had to deliver his speech. On many other occasions she had been forced to cover up for him. She would never marry him until he got his alcoholism under control. Not in a three-week hospital cure or even six months on the wagon. She had told him he had to undergo intensive therapy with someone like Michael Klassman. He had reluctantly agreed.

Bill found support for his "predisposition" argument when he heard Dick Van Dyke claim the same thing during a television interview with Dick Cavett. As soon as he stopped drinking, Van Dyke declared, his problems ended.

"Bullshit!" Klassman retorted. "I'd like to talk to Van Dyke's wife and children and find out if his problems really stopped with his drinking. I don't think so. The problems come first, then the drinking."

Klassman was able to see what forty years of steady drinking had done to Holden's body. In his twenties and thirties, his remarkable physique had been able to withstand the binges. No more. Bill was given a medical examination at the health institute with which Klassman was affiliated in Beverly Hills. The results showed an enlarged liver, probably the source of backaches Holden suffered. His kidneys were in poor condition, and his blood sugar had risen and fallen precipitously during periods of drinking and abstinence. The result was a condition approaching glycemia, causing periods of intense depression. Bill, who learned early about chemicals from his father's business, took pills to assuage the depression. But he also suffered from chronic insomnia, and that led to another round of booze or pills.

His drinking was reflected in his face: the deep lines, the ruddy complexion, the red nose, the puffy eyes. For an actor, such an appearance could be destructive. For a man like Bill who was proud of how he looked, it was devastating.

Aging frightened him. He wanted to appear as strong and virile as he had in *Picnic* and *The Bridge on the River Kwai*. Klassman tried to point out how alcohol had prematurely aged Bill's face and body—and his sex life.

"Goddammit, I can still jump in the sack with any woman and give her a great time," Bill declared.

"Maybe for an hour," Klassman suggested. "But how long were you able to last when you were younger?"

Bill admitted that after long periods of drinking he was impotent. That disturbed him. He disliked anything that interfered with his macho view of himself. Although he was not contemptuous of homosexuals and indeed worked harmoniously with many in films, he considered homosexuality a wrongful failing. Yet he was most comfortable in the company of men. He admitted that one of his best film experiences was *Network*, because of the hearty companionship with Peter Finch.

"I'm a whore," Bill Holden remarked. "All actors are whores. We sell our bodies to the highest bidder. I had practice being a whore. When I was a young actor starting out in Hollywood, I used to service actresses who were older than me."

This self-deprecatory analysis was part of a pattern that Michael Klassman recognized in his patient. Despite the adulation he had received throughout his career, despite all the romances, Bill believed he was incapable of being loved.

Klassman saw firsthand Holden's resistance to the adoration of fans. One day they took a break in therapy and drove down to Palm Springs for hamburgers at Bob's Big Boy. As soon as Holden walked inside, Klassman remembers, the scene was like the E.F. Hutton television

commercial. Everyone stopped to stare at the famous visitor. The host-
ess came up to him and immediately asked for an autograph.

"Could we have a quiet booth in the rear?" Holden asked. For the
next forty-five minutes, patrons trooped to the table to ask for autographs. Holden obliged, muttering under his breath, "Why can't they
leave me alone?"

Bill was still upset when he returned to the house, and Klassman
decided to provoke him: "You know, I watched that whole scene down
there at Bob's Big Boy, and I think you're full of shit."

Holden was startled. "What do you mean?"

"You grumble about people bothering you by asking for your autograph. But you wanted to be a star, and you love being a star. Why don't
you just accept the fans as part of your profession?"

As Klassman had hoped, Bill became incensed, and soon they were
shouting at each other.

"Look—I'm somebody who just saw you come into Bob's Big Boy,"
the psychologist said. "I say, 'Jeez, there's William Holden, a man I've
always wanted to touch and see! For twenty-five years I've been paying
money to see him. Now I can see him for nothing!' Why shouldn't I be
'intrusive,' as you call it?"

"Because it's none of your goddam business!" Bill shouted. "I'm just
like you or anybody else. It's none of your goddam business who I am."

"Oh, yeah?" said his inquisitor, continuing his role as fan. "You're
a star because I paid money to see your movies. Tell me why I shouldn't
ask for your autograph."

"Because I'm entitled to my privacy!"

Klassman lowered his tone. "Can't you see, Bill? When you go into
a restaurant and people recognize you, part of you wants acceptance
and part wants them to stay away. You're sending double messages:
'Love me, but leave me alone.' You say you want love and acceptance,
but even the public can't give it to you."

During four months of total involvement with Holden's life, Michael
Klassman saw the actor in every mood.

"This is the only script I've ever read that I really wanted to do,"
Bill said of *First Monday in October*. "I think it's going to get me an
Academy Award." He talked excitedly of playing the flinty Supreme
Court justice—obviously patterned after William O. Douglas—in the
film version of the play Henry Fonda had starred in. Bill's agents at
William Morris were working on a deal, and Bill had invited Ellen

Burstyn, who was to be his co-star, to come to the Palm Springs house to talk over the script. Then Bill learned that the ailing Fonda had his heart set on recreating the role. Klassman heard Holden telephone Fonda that he would not be a candidate for *First Monday in October.* In the end, the producers chose Walter Matthau, who was deemed to be a better box-office name.

On the morning of June 11, 1979, Holden sat in his living room watching television when an announcer reported that John Wayne had died. Holden said nothing; he merely stared at the screen as images of Duke appeared. So many memories. Those early years when he and Duke were Charlie Feldman's favorite clients. The drinking bouts in Melrose Avenue bars. The half-hearted rivalry for king of the box office. The fun they had on *The Horse Soldiers* until John Ford and the whole movie turned sour. Bill started to cry.

"God, poor Duke," he said softly. "I'm glad he's dead. He suffered too much."

"John Wayne meant a lot to you, I guess," Michael Klassman said. "Yes."

"Then right now is a chance to achieve that intimacy that you would like to have with people. Do something about it. Pick up the phone and call the Wayne family right now, and tell them how you feel about him."

Bill tried to call the Wayne family but was unable to get through. He sent a telegram. Wayne's death disturbed him profoundly. Bill had known Duke during forty tumultuous years and had known Duke's limitless appetite for life. Now he was gone, and Bill felt the burden of his own mortality.

Holden seemed most alive when he spoke of Africa. All his life he had had a mystical relationship with animals. He was gentle and tender with them, and on his game ranch and in the wild he sometimes had to make painful decisions on some that had to be eliminated for the good of the species. He understood animals, and they respected him.

Bertie was an example. Klassman noted that when Holden entered the house, the snake became agitated. The excitement increased when Holden walked into the room where Bertie was kept in a glass cage. Often as he talked with the therapist, Bill allowed the snake to slither around his neck. "He would say things to it, and Bertie would make love to him," Klassman recalls. "It was funny, tender, loving, hysterical. It was wonderful to see Bill that way."

Klassman pointed out that Bill could relate to animals in a way that he couldn't to people.

"Animals can sense when you're sincere," Bill replied. "People often can't. I've been sincere a lot in my life, and people haven't taken that as sincerity.

"In Africa, life is simple. And death. There is a smell of death that the natives are aware of, that the animals are aware of. You can smell the death on humans, you can smell it on animals. They emit an odor when they find themselves in a life-and-death situation. I kinda like that, being able to know where you stand. Not like here."

Klassman noted how Holden's entire personality changed when he spoke of Africa. It was his extended family, the surroundings in which he felt alive and useful. He could go for days, weeks, without feeling the need for a drink.

"Go back there," Klassman urged. "Go back to Africa. Forget about being a movie star. Forget about that next picture. Stay there six months, a year. You'll change your whole life if you do."

"Yeah, I really oughta go back," Bill said. But he made no move to do so.

"One of your big problems," Michael Klassman told Bill, "is that everybody surrounding you won't bring up the fact that you're an alcoholic. The people you work with on movie sets, they whisper about it. But they never mention it to you. They're afraid they'll hurt your feelings or you'll stop being their friend. Or they'll rock the boat and you'll hold up production.

"Your family is afraid to mention it to you; they pussyfoot around it. Stefanie is the only one who will stand up and say: 'You're an alcoholic. You need help. I'll never marry you until you come to grips with your problem.'

"What the others around you should say is: 'You're a drunk. You're no better than some skid row bum.' *I* know. I work with the alcoholics on skid row. I teach the counselors. I work the streets. You should come with me some day and see what it's like."

Holden agreed. One morning he and Klassman drove back to Los Angeles from Palm Springs, and they toured north Main Street and Los Angeles Street in Bill's Mercedes station wagon. They bought coffee at a taco stand and watched the human wreckage pass by. A toothless little man in tatters stared at Bill for a moment and muttered, "I *know* you. I know you just as sure as I'm standing here." His bleary eyes stared at the familiar face, but he couldn't make a connection. He shrugged and lurched down the sidewalk.

Back in the car, Bill laughed and said, "I'm like those guys sometimes." He was amused, but he was also disturbed. He disliked the indignity that those men faced.

Holden was edging toward the point of admitting that he was an alcoholic, but he hadn't reached there yet. At Klassman's urging, Bill attended a national convention of Alcoholics Anonymous and sat on the dais with Betty Ford and other celebrities at a dinner. But, unlike others who were present, Bill could not stand up and say, "I am an alcoholic."

Bill Holden betrayed a degree of paranoia in the therapy sessions. He nursed long-ago grievances: against Harry Cohn for holding him to a slave contract; against Paramount bosses for treating him like a hired hand; against the many people who had used him for his money, his fame. He had seen every approach of the favor-seekers, and sometimes it amused him to play a cat-and-mouse game with them. Mostly he was angry because so many people sought his friendship for what they could get out of him, not for who he was.

Klassman saw evidence of Bill's paranoia one day when the therapist mentioned that his nine-year-old son Joshua had won his yellow belt in judo by breaking a half-inch board.

"Oh?" said Bill. "Do you have any experience in karate?"

"As a matter of fact, I just got my brown belt in kempo karate," Klassman replied.

"Have you ever had to use it?"

"Only once, when I was being attacked by an outraged alcoholic husband. I just subdued him. What about you? Do you know judo?"

"No, I never learned."

"You never had to use it in a movie role?"

"No."

"Wouldn't it be handy in crowds, in case somebody tried to attack you?"

"No, I don't need it. I've got something else."

"What do you mean?"

"I'll show you." Bill left the room and returned, wearing his familiar khaki bush jacket.

"Okay, come at me," he said.

Klassman assumed his karate position and started toward Bill in slow motion. Bill lifted his arm and suddenly a snub-nosed pistol was pointed at his attacker.

"Bang, bang, motherfucker," Bill said with a grin.

After Klassman recovered from the shock, Bill told him: "I don't need to know karate. You tell me how you're going to stop this bullet."

Bill demonstrated the spring that produced the gun in an instant. He explained that he had acquired the device so he would feel safer on the streets of New York.

Although he didn't say so, there are indications that Holden in his later years always wore the concealed gun in public. There is no evidence that he ever had occasion to use it.

In probing Holden's personal relationships, Michael Klassman found a recurring pattern of guilt. Bill felt guilty that he had not been close enough to his brothers, that both Bob and Dick had died without really knowing that he loved them. He realized he had treated Ardis wretchedly during the time they were married. He felt sorry for the pain and sorrow he had caused Capucine.

Most of all, he considered himself a failure as a father. West and Scott had experienced the hazards of young people in the 1960s and 1970s without a father to give them help and counsel.

"Look what I did for those kids," Bill declared. "I gave them the best education that money could buy. They traveled all over the world with me. When they turned twenty-one, they came into a lot of money. And look at the troubles they got into."

"Bill, I'd love to be able to give those things to my son, too," said Klassman. "Any father would. You're telling me that your children had all the best things you could give them. Now take a step back, Bill, and tell me what your relationship is with the boys now."

At Klassman's instruction, Bill rose from his chair and actually took a step backward, then gazed at two imaginary chairs.

"Tell me what you see."

Bill's face grew more solemn. "I see them doing nothing."

"*Why* are they doing nothing?"

"I should know. You need a father to be there for you. I should know. But *I don't know how to do it.*"

At such moments, Klassman lost his clinical detachment, and his heart grieved for Bill. The man simply didn't know how to be intimate with anyone. But why?

Klassman once asked Bill, "Were you really cared for as a child?"

"Yes, I was," Bill replied. "But not in the way that I wanted."

Through probing, Klassman learned that Bill had great respect for his mother, whose strength kept the family together. She was the dominant figure in the household, since her husband spent long hours at the laboratory. Bill was proud that he was able to provide for her in her widowhood. Klassman perceived her as an "enabler" in Bill's alcoholism, since it was too painful for her to confront him with it. And Bill would never confess it, since that would diminish his manhood in the eyes of his mother.

Bill viewed his father as a brilliant chemist, a firm believer in the Protestant ethic. He was a man who rose early, went to the lab, worked a long day, came home and ate dinner with his family, read the newspaper, and went to bed. For a time, William Beedle maintained tight control over his eldest son, but during most of Bill's boyhood, his mother held the reins. Bill loved his parents and believed they had given him the upbringing they felt was best for him.

"But," he remarked, "I cannot remember my mother and father ever telling me 'I love you.' I cannot remember my mother and father ever hugging me. Especially my father."

Klassman noticed that Bill's cheeks were bulging. "Instead of chewing on your teeth, Bill, why don't you say what your teeth are saying?"

Slowly, hesitantly, Bill began. "I loved my father very much. I respected him very much. But there was always something missing. I never felt that anything I ever did was good enough for him. When I did the play at the Pasadena Playhouse and got the contract at Paramount, my father was very disappointed. He felt my acting was just a frivolous pastime, and I'd come to my senses and become a chemist. No matter how much money I made, no matter if I won the Academy Award, it wasn't enough for him. It was never good enough!"

To his astonishment, tears began streaming down his face.

"Look, it's okay to cry," Klassman said reassuringly. "Nothing has changed. You're still William Holden, you're still charismatic. You're not losing control, you're no less of a man for it. You're able to cry, you're able to feel something that was very important to you. That was your father. Why shouldn't you mourn the fact that you loved him and he loved you but because of the family situation and the times you lived in he wasn't able to give you what you now consider important? It's okay to cry over that. I think you realize now that how you treated your own sons is tied up with how your father treated you."

"Yes, it's true," Bill sighed.

Klassman considered it a major breakthrough, but his experience with alcoholics had taught him there were no simple solutions. Bill Holden would require many more months, perhaps years of therapy before he could control his alcoholism.

36

The Earthling

The Earthling concerned an embittered loner facing his own death, lost in the Australian wilds with a pampered city boy to whom he teaches the lessons of survival. Bill Holden realized the script was imperfect, but he felt it could be improved when the company went on location. He began a series of meetings about the film at the Beverly Hillcrest Hotel, his regular stopping place in Los Angeles.

Bill was especially pleased that Ricky Schroder would be the co-star. The boy had made a sensational debut in *The Champ*, and Bill found him to be bright and cheerful, with no trace of the precocity of most child actors. Bill had reservations about the director, Peter Collinson. The Britisher had a reputation for being a sadistic martinet on his movie sets.

"Look, I know I have a bad reputation, and deservedly so," Collinson admitted. "But I can assure you I will be different on this picture. I love the script, and I know it can be a brilliant film. I need one at this stage in my career."

Bill also needed a good picture. He was willing to take a chance on Collinson and on Filmways Pictures, which was attempting more prestigious films after its conversion from American International Pictures. He discussed the script with Collinson and the producer, Elliot Schick, and Bill pointed out the scenes he considered too flowery and melodramatic. "I can't cope with those things."

During his conferences with Schick, Collinson, and the executive producer, Bill Sharmat, Holden drank only mineral water. He understood the questioning in their eyes, and he volunteered, "I'm not drinking these days."

The final arrangements for *The Earthling* were concluded, and filming was scheduled to start in Australia in June of 1979. Bill Holden was confident and expectant. He looked forward to the locations in the

Australian wilderness, and he felt certain that script problems could be licked and that Peter Collinson would behave.

Holden returned to the Palm Springs house, alone. He decided to undergo a hernia operation he had long postponed. "Let me go with you," Michael Klassman urged by telephone. "No," Bill replied.

He was adamant. Ava Ready, Pat Morita, and others who had become friends with Bill on *The Day the World Ended* also offered to visit Bill. He declined. He was following a lifelong pattern. On every movie, Bill and his fellow workers became close, almost like family. He could even manage an intimacy that he found impossible with his real family. The end of each movie was like a death. Farewells were said, along with vows to continue the relationships. But Bill never did.

Holden entered Eisenhower Medical Center in Rancho Mirage. He had the hernia operation, returned home in a few days, and got drunk. He had not told the hospital that he was being treated for alcoholism, and he had been issued a supply of painkillers. He combined them with vodka to become totally oblivious.

The servants telephoned Michael Klassman, who hurried to the desert. He found Bill out of control. Bill was aware enough to realize that he had to leave soon for the Australian location. Klassman persuaded him to enter Care Manor, an alcoholic rehabilitation center in Orange, near Disneyland.

For the first time in his long history of drying out, Holden remained for more than a few days. He underwent group therapy, but he was constantly bothered by patients who were aware that he was William Holden. One of them stopped him in the hallway to ask for an autograph. Bill exploded: "Listen, you son of a bitch, I'm in here for the same reason you are. Now leave me alone!"

Holden remained at Care Manor two weeks. He left abruptly one day when he looked out his window and saw a photographer. Another patient had tipped off a scandal tabloid.

Bill emerged from Care Manor with clear eyes and steady hands. Two days later he flew across the Pacific to begin *The Earthling*.

Broderick Crawford arrived in Sydney for a stopover on his way to Perth, where he was appearing in *That Championship Season* on the stage. During the drive from the airport, the taxi driver told him, "That other American actor, William Holden, is here in Sydney, too."

"No kidding!" said Crawford. "Do you know what hotel he's staying in?"

"No, I don't."

When Crawford arrived at his hotel, he asked the desk man: "Is William Holden staying here?"

A mellow voice behind him said, "You bet your ass he is!"

The two old friends whooped and fell into each other's arms. They hadn't seen each other in twenty years, and the conversation flew as they lunched in the hotel dining room. They talked about their current assignments, but mostly about the good times they'd enjoyed together: bedeviling Harry Cohn with their race bets, running up the hotel tab in Washington, working with Ronald Reagan in the Screen Actors Guild. And they remembered that night in 1965 when Bill telephoned from Switzerland and finally reached Brod on a location in Spain. Bill had heard the news that Judy Holliday had died of cancer in New York, and he wanted to share his grief with Crawford.

The Earthling company filmed for two weeks in Sydney, then moved to remote locations, first in Royal National Park, finally in a wilderness near the tiny town of Dungog. It was the first American movie to be filmed in Australia since *The Sundowners* twenty years before, and crew members worked hard to show the visitors their professionalism. They did everything to make the Americans comfortable, but there were few luxuries on the locations. At Dungog, only one house was available for rental, and Bill Holden insisted that it go to Diane Schroder and her children, Ricky and Dawn.

"You take it," Bill insisted. "There are three of you, and I'm alone. I can sleep in a camper. I do it all the time in Africa."

Elliot Schick's son Ben was part of the crew, carrying the camera and performing other menial duties. Holden was intrigued by the relationship of the producer and his son. One day on location, the tall young man leaned over and planted a kiss on his father's bald head.

"I envy you," Bill said to Schick.

"You kidding? You envy me!" said the producer. "You're rich, handsome, famous. How could you envy me?"

"I envy your relationship with your son," Bill replied. He said to Ben: "I'll bet you have no trouble saying 'I love you' to your father."

The young man smiled. "No. And he has no trouble saying 'I love you' to me."

Bill turned to the elder Schick. "That's what I mean. That's why I envy you. I could never do that to my sons. Nor could they to me."

Bill seemed fit. Location scenes required much climbing, which he did with little effort. He sublimated his craving for alcohol by eating ice cream, and Elliot Schick provided him with a variety of flavors. Bill was captivated by Ricky Schroder, who called him Billy Willy and idolized him. They played pool together in Dungog's principal place of entertainment, the pool hall, and they organized frog-jumping contests. They had barbecues at night, and Bill roasted marshmallows for Ricky over the glowing coals. Bill was amused by Ricky's wonderment about a large kangaroo. "I wonder what would happen if I grabbed his tail," the boy said. "Why don't you try it," Bill suggested. The kangaroo leaped into the air and gave Ricky a bumpy ride.

The sixty-one-year-old star and the ten-year-old boy drew close, partly out of loneliness, partly in defense against Peter Collinson. Despite his claims of reform, he behaved abominably.

The director knew better than to challenge Bill Holden, so he aimed his vitriol at Ricky. During a scene the boy complained that he couldn't play it according to Collinson's directions.

"You can't!" the director exploded. "What do *you* know, little boy? You're not a good actor. You'll never be a good actor. Today you're doing everything wrong. You're impossible!"

Bill Holden didn't intervene; his code prohibited challenge of a director's authority in front of the cast and crew. He drew Collinson aside and suggested, "You're not going to get a performance out of the kid by browbeating him. Now there are two different ways to do this scene: your way and the way Ricky wants to do it. Why don't you shoot it both ways and decide later which is better?" Collinson reluctantly agreed. The Schroder version ended up in the film.

Collinson found other targets for his abuse. He constantly berated the Australian crew, saying within their hearing, "You can't be soft with these natives. You have to show them who's boss." The Australians, independent and burly, grumbled among themselves but held their tempers.

Producer Schick and Bill Holden talked about the Collinson problem. "Shall we get rid of him?" Schick suggested.

"Forget it," Bill replied. "No director worth his salt is going to fly down here to direct half a picture. We'll just have to stick it out."

The worst damage Collinson was doing to *The Earthling* was in his interpretation of the script.

Bill argued his view of the story: "It should be joyful, a celebration of life, a culmination of manhood. Sure, the man is dying, but even dying can be a positive experience. When a man passes on that part of life which is necessary for a boy's survival—morals, integrity, vulnerability—it is a gift of life, a joyful gift."

Collinson refused to see it that way. He infused both characters with hatred and scars, without qualities to redeem them. He was spewing forth his bitterness over his own fate. Before *The Earthling* began, he had undergone a gall bladder operation, and doctors discovered that he had cancer. Like Patrick Foley, the character Holden played in *The Earthling,* Peter Collinson was dying.

Bill Holden finished *The Earthling* with the same feelings he had after every film: relief, exhilaration, regret, hope. He was pleased to be rid of the demonic Peter Collinson, but sorry to part with Ricky Schroder and the amiable Australian crew. Bill felt that he had done good work for the film, and while he regretted the morbid tone that Collinson had applied to the script, he clung to the cautious optimism that a miracle in the cutting room would save the film.

Instead of returning directly to California, Bill decided to spend a few days in Hong Kong. That was a mistake.

Sitting in a hotel bar before dinner, Bill ordered a glass of wine to celebrate the completion of the movie. The wine tasted good, and he had another. He ate his dinner, went to bed, and enjoyed the best sleep he had known in months. On the following evening, he had a glass of wine before dinner.

Days later, he awoke in his hotel bed. He remembered nothing that had happened after the glass of wine. He discovered later that he had purchased several expensive Buddha statues, which arrived after he returned to California.

Bill was in wretched condition as he flew across the Pacific. He told no one of his arrival except his butler, who met him at Los Angeles International Airport and took him immediately to Palm Springs, where Bill continued drinking.

Irwin Allen desperately needed Bill to record lines of dialogue so *The Day the World Ended* could be completed and released. Allen telephoned Australia and Hong Kong and couldn't locate Bill. Allen sought help from Harvey Bernhard, who had remained close to Bill after *Omen II.* Bernhard called Pat Stauffer.

Bill and Pat had reconciled after four years of not seeing or talking with each other. In July of 1979, Bill learned that Pat had entered Hoag Hospital at Newport Beach for emergency removal of a melanoma. Pat was emerging from the anesthetic when the telephone rang. It was Bill. By the time she had recovered, their relationship had resumed.

Pat had established a code to reach Bill when he had made himself incommunicado. She called his number, waited two rings, then hung up. Then she called again. Bill always answered, no matter what condition he was in.

When Bill answered the phone in November 1979, Pat knew immediately that he was helplessly drunk.

"How dare you do this to yourself—and to me!" she exploded. "Irwin Allen has been looking all over the world for you so he can finish his picture. And I've got my own problems. My mother is dying, and so is my father. Dammit, Bill!"

Bill pulled himself together to make the voice tracks for Allen. In December he delivered the eulogy at the funeral of Pat's father, Emerson Morgan, an ordeal because Bill disliked funerals. Later that month he was scheduled to attend Stefanie Powers' Christmas party.

"Where's Bill?" people kept asking.

"Oh, he'll be along," said Stefanie with a fixed smile.

She was worried. Bill had promised to come on time and help entertain the guests, who included her co-workers on the *Hart to Hart* series, young actors and directors, as well as some of Bill's contemporaries.

"Audrey and I have to leave for my friend Walter Reisch's house," Billy Wilder told Stefanie. "We've had Christmas together for fifty years, first in Berlin, then Paris, now here. I'm sorry we missed Bill. What happened to him?"

Stefanie shrugged her shoulders.

As the Wilders were walking toward their car, a silver Mercedes drove up in front of Stefanie's house. Bill Holden was behind the wheel, and Wilder waved to him. Bill looked the other way. He was too ashamed to have his oldtime mentor see him totally drunk.

Chuck Painter, a publicist friend of Stefanie's, went out to the Mercedes and offered to help Bill out of the car. As Bill tried to move, his glasses fell, and they crunched under his shoe.

Bill was too immobilized to leave the car. Stefanie was furious. She ordered a limousine and had him driven back to Palm Springs. The event signaled the end of their relationship as lovers.

37

The Last Picture Show

In January of 1980, Bill Holden took Pat Stauffer to New York for an exhibition of wildlife photographs by a friend, Claude Parfet. Bill and Pat returned to Palm Springs, and she endured what she recalls as "the worst two weeks of my life."

Bill's drinking was out of control. No matter how Pat tried to watch him, he managed to find something to drink. She puzzled over how his bottle of vodka remained full. Then she tasted it—water. He had been filling the bottle with water and drinking vodka from a secret source. At times he was incoherent and hallucinatory. Pat prayed that he would lose consciousness so she could summon help. But he never passed out, and he refused her pleadings to go to a hospital.

Finally she could stand no more, and she left the Southridge house. She telephoned Bill's Palm Springs doctor, Bart Apfelbaum, and told him the situation. Apfelbaum immediately placed Bill in Desert Hospital. He emerged two days later, miraculously recovered.

Holden continued therapy with Michael Klassman, with interruptions. When a business associate claimed to know details of the therapy, Bill fired Klassman in outrage over the alleged breach of privacy. He discovered the associate's report had been false, and the sessions resumed.

During a heated exchange, Klassman accused: "I know what you are doing. You *want* to drink. You think everybody in the world is against you, so you're just going to shut them out with booze."

"Who the hell do you think you are?" Bill demanded. "You're always taking Stefanie's side against me. I never should have called you. Fuck you! Get out!"

Again Bill relented, and every time a fierce argument developed, Klassman cracked, "Are you going to fire me again?"

Klassman continued therapy sporadically through the spring of

1980. He saw the best of times and the worst of times. The worst came when Klassman arrived at the Southridge house and found Holden in an alcoholic stupor. He was unshaven, disheveled, sometimes soiled by his own waste. One day Bill disappeared. The frantic Klassman searched the house and found him sitting helplessly in the bedroom closet.

Bill's moods altered drastically as his blood sugar rose and fell. During drunken periods he wept, "I wish I could have been close with my father, I wish I could have been close with Ardis, I wish I could have been close with my sons." At other times his anger was volcanic. Or he lapsed into periods of deep depression.

He admitted his alcoholism, but he would not take the ultimate step of recognizing it. Klassman urged him to "go public," citing the good accomplished by Betty Ford, Dana Andrews, Billy Carter, and other public figures who had admitted their alcoholism.

"Why don't you tell the world that you are an alcoholic?" Klassman asked.

"Because it's nobody's damn business," Holden snapped.

"If it's nobody's business, look what you do to make it everybody's business. You're William Holden. You don't think if William Holden is picked up for a five-oh-two [drunk driving arrest] it isn't going to become everyone's business? You don't think if you enter a hospital for a 'cure,' people won't know about it? You say you want to remain private, but everything you do is negative. You are perpetuating your image as an alcoholic."

"Bullshit! The newspapers do."

"No, it's you. Bill, if you would only *accept* the fact that you are an alcoholic, and then, at your own chosen speed, tell the public about it, you could help a lot of people, as well as yourself. In one television interview you could reach a half-million people with the same problem."

With deep sadness, Bill replied, "Part of me really wants to do that. But I'm afraid. I'm afraid of how people will react, what they will think about me, what they will say about me. I'm afraid I will lose the affection of people I love."

He reflected for a moment and added: "You're probably right. If I sat down and talked intelligently about my alcoholism, people would understand it better. But as long as I'm alive, I won't do it. I just won't do it. Not only because I'm afraid of the reaction. I'm also afraid that people will take advantage of me."

Klassman believed that Holden was not only concerned about what a public confessional would do to his movie-star image, but he felt it would be a disservice to his country, which he had served in many ways. "*You* do it," he told Klassman. "After I'm gone you can tell the story."

Like others who treated alcoholism, Klassman realized he could achieve no lasting results with Holden without the reinforcement of those who were close to him. Klassman pleaded with Bill to invite Ardis, West, Scott, or Stefanie to play roles in the therapy. Bill absolutely refused.

Bill's deterioration was noticeable. His lapses of memory became more pronounced. The lines in his face grew deeper. His hands shook, even during periods of sobriety. Klassman tried to reassure him: "Look what you did to your body; it will take time to recover." Bill was disturbed by a further sign of aging: he could no longer bounce back from binges.

Klassman feared that nothing could sway Bill from the suicidal course he had been following. "Bill," he demanded, "why do you want to die?"

Bill looked startled. "I don't want to die. I love life."

"Then why are you doing everything to destroy it? You don't drink for pleasure; you tell me you don't even like the taste of liquor. You don't just sip a drink, you guzzle it. You *want* that high. You *want* to get fucked up. You *want* to get away from this world. On the surface, I've known you for years. I've seen all your movies; when I first met you I told you how much in awe I was. Everyone is. You're a millionaire, you're handsome, you're talented, you have all the women you need. But you're killing yourself. Why? Why?"

Bill grimaced. "I'm *tired.* I've been everywhere, I've done everything. There isn't much left for me to do. I'm tired."

"I'm afraid you're going to die, Bill."

"I know how it's going to be."

"How?"

"Lonely, alone, without dignity."

The fortunes of Blake Edwards had been restored with the successes of the *Pink Panther* sequels and *10,* and Lorimar and Paramount agreed to finance his long-planned satire of the New Hollywood, *S.O.B.* The first actor to be cast was William Holden. Edwards reasoned that Holden's role as the battle-hardened director was "the glue that would keep the film together—a pillar of strength amid a pack of lunatics."

It was a good time for Bill Holden. He felt fit. He drank only beer, although he started before breakfast. He was working with Blake Edwards, with whom he could communicate almost wordlessly. The location was uncommonly pleasant; he could ride his big new motorcycle from his Santa Monica apartment up the Pacific Coast Highway to Malibu. The other actors were congenial and stimulating.

Two were old friends. Bill had known Bob Preston since their Golden Circle days at Paramount, and although their careers and lives had diverged, they remained like comrades from a long-ago war. Craig Stevens also dated back to early Paramount; he and Bill had both worked in *I Wanted Wings*. The Stevenses, Bill, and Stefanie Powers had traveled together in Iran when they attended the 1976 Tehran Film Festival.

The younger actors were awestruck by Bill Holden: Loretta Swit, Richard Mulligan, Larry Hagman, Robert Webber. Bill put them totally at ease during the first script reading at MGM studios. The entire cast was present, including Julie Andrews and Shelley Winters.

The relationship between Bill and Shelley was civil but distant. Her autobiography had just been published, and she had written that for several years she and Bill Holden had met every Christmas Eve for a tryst. Privately he scoffed: "Can you imagine a married man with three children being able to get away for a quick bang on Christmas Eve?" To Shelley he merely smiled and thanked her for the publicity.

Filming of *S.O.B.* began at a Malibu beach house with Richard Mulligan working alone in a mad scene. Besides the usual nervousness about starting a film, Mulligan was embarrassed about behaving so crazily in front of the crowd of strangers. He looked at the film crew and suddenly saw a familiar face: Bill Holden.

Bill approached Mulligan, his smile growing wider. Bill embraced Mulligan, muttered words of encouragement, turned him around, and gave him the actor's ceremonial kick in the rear at the beginning of a performance. "You can do it, kid," said Bill with the reassurance of an old friend. Mulligan, who had known Holden for two weeks, entered the scene with renewed confidence.

Tony Adams, who was producing the film with Edwards, was surprised to find Holden on the location. "But you're not on call today," said Adams.

"I just came for the free lunch." Bill grinned.

He came every day, no matter whether he was working, and other members of the cast followed his example. That pleased Blake Edwards, who liked to have actors available in case he made changes in the filming. As with *When Time Ran Out,* Bill's casual dignity made him the spiritual leader of the large and divergent cast.

Andrew Stone, Jr., was assistant director, as he had been on the Irwin Allen film. At first Bill was uneasy about seeing Stone, who had been witness to his disgrace. But after a week of filming they were able to resume an easy relationship.

Bill set the example by standing in line for the location lunch and eating at a long table with others of the company. He and Preston reminisced about their days as contract players at Paramount, and Bill drew from his endless store of Harry Cohn stories. After a day's shooting, he joined members of the *S.O.B.* company for beer at the Baja Cantina in Malibu. Many times he invited ten or twelve people—actors, secretaries, gaffers, grips—to his Santa Monica apartment for drinks, then took them to dinner on the pier. Their company seemed vital to him. They were the people with whom he had shared his filmmaking life for more than forty years, and that life, however transitory, provided the only continuity he had ever known.

Bill couldn't always maintain his air of equanimity. Julie Andrews saw him slip into dark moods of melancholy silence: "He seemed to be a man who was hurting a lot and trying not to let it show."

Miss Andrews watched her husband direct a scene with Holden, Preston, Mulligan, and Webber. Observing Bill with a trio of stage-trained actors, she feared he would be unable to compete. But when she saw the scene on film, she realized that Holden, with his innate integrity and presence, had not only competed but prevailed.

Holden had played filmmakers before—in *Sunset Boulevard, Paris When It Sizzles, Fedora.* His Tim Culley in *S.O.B.* seemed to come closest to Bill Holden, as when he tried to dissuade Felix Farmer (Mulligan) from suicide.

CULLEY

Felix, if you're going to kill yourself, there are a helluva lot better ways of doing it. For the last fifty years, I have lived a life of dedicated debauchery. I have consumed enough booze to destroy a dozen healthy livers, filled my lungs with enough nicotine to poison the entire population of Orange County and indulged in enough sexual excesses to make Caligula look like a celibate monk. I have, in fact, conscientiously, day in and day out, for years more than you have been in this best of all possible

worlds, tried to kill myself—and I never felt better in my life.
So if you really want to end it all, I can show you a half-dozen
great ways to do it.

During the filming of *S.O.B.*, Warner Brothers released *When Time
Ran Out*, and most of the stars, realizing that it was a turkey, declined
to make any appearances to publicize it. Not Bill Holden. He felt an
obligation to help the producer and the film, no matter how bad it was.
He agreed to appear on the Johnny Carson show.

Tony Habeeb, publicist for Irwin Allen, had made arrangements
for Holden to be released from the Malibu location at four-thirty in the
afternoon, which would allow enough time to reach the NBC Burbank
studio in time for the telecast. But filming had been delayed, and
Holden didn't finish until five. Then Habeeb couldn't find the limousine
driver.

"C'mon, we'll take my car," Holden said, motioning Habeeb to the
four-door Mercedes. The fastest way to Burbank was through Malibu
Canyon, but it had been closed by floods. Bill chose to go down the
Pacific Coast Highway to Sunset Boulevard, then follow its winding
route to Hollywood.

By the time they reached Hollywood, the Carson show had already
started. Bill encountered the usual evening traffic jam on Highland
Avenue, which led over the Cahuenga Pass to Burbank.

"Hold on," he told Habeeb, and Bill drove the Mercedes along the
sidewalk until he passed the crowd of cars at a signal. He walked
through the curtain of the Carson show just as the last segment began.

Ricky Schroder cried out of bitter disappointment when he saw the
final version of *The Earthling*. Bill Holden reacted with anger and
frustration because of how the dying Peter Collinson had subverted
what Bill had hoped would be a film of hope and inspiration (Collinson
died in December of 1980). Filmways was ready to write off *The Earthling* as a $4 million loss. Producers Sharmat and Schick argued success-
fully that the film might be salvaged by judicious editing and recon-
struction.

John Strong was the man chosen to work the magic. Bill had known
him as an actor on *Alvarez Kelly* and had given him advice on his
career. Strong turned to filmmaking and earned a reputation as a "film
doctor," salvaging failed movies as play doctors did in the theater.
Strong had helped prepare *The Earthling* and had scouted locations in
Australia, but had withdrawn from the project before filming.

"I need help and Bill needs help," Sharmat told Strong when Film-ways was deciding whether to shelve *The Earthling*. Bill also told Strong, "I need you."

Strong screened the film and found it a bitter treatise on dying. Both the man and the boy lacked redeeming features, and their relationship ended on a grim note. The actresses in the beach and harbor scenes had been so intimidated by Collinson that the sequences had to be scrapped.

Strong reviewed every foot of film that had been printed, seeking alternative shots. He filmed a new ending with the old Huntington Hartford estate in Hollywood doubling for the Australian jungle. Holden, Ricky Schroder, and the entire crew worked for no pay.

Every line in the film was rerecorded. Strong persuaded David Shire and Carol Connors to write a song for the film, and Maureen McGovern recorded it at her own expense. Because of a musicians' strike, a new score was recorded in Germany.

Strong poured $66,000 of his own money into the reconstruction of *The Earthling*, which was 90 percent changed. He took a videocassette of the final version to Palm Springs to play for Holden. At the finish, Bill put his arm around Strong's shoulder, an unusual gesture for a man who rarely touched other people.

"John, I really want to thank you," Bill said fervently. "You don't know how much this means to me."

Despite the improved version, Filmways remained unenthusiastic about *The Earthling* and gave it a halfhearted release. Another stinging disappointment for Bill Holden.

"You promised to take me to Africa," Stefanie Powers reminded Bill Holden in September of 1980. Because of an actors' strike, her *Hart to Hart* series had been suspended, and she was available to travel. Bill had no film plans.

Bill and Stefanie flew to Kenya for an expedition to capture eight giraffes to transport to a Nigerian zoo. Bill was in good condition, and he roped the animals himself, hanging out of a Land Rover racing across the uncertain terrain. He and Stefanie were companionable, and he still admired her ability to endure life in the wild. But the passion of their physical relationship had ended.

Stefanie returned to Hollywood to resume the series, and Bill stopped in Geneva to visit Scott, who had married a Swiss girl and was operating a limousine service. Bill decided to fly to Hanover for a consultation with Dr. Hans Nieper, whom he had met in Hollywood through Red Buttons. The comedian, who believed that the German doctor had cured his wife Alicia of cancer, had given a reception to introduce Nieper to film people. A dispatch appeared in American newspapers:

> New York (AP)—Oscar-winning William Holden, the star of *The Bridge on the River Kwai* and scores of other films, is expected to fly to West Germany later this month to consult with a doctor recognized as a cancer expert, the New York Daily News reported.
>   But the doctor, Hans Nieper, told the newspaper, "I don't think he's seriously ill."

When Bill arrived in Hanover, he was besieged by reporters. His mother telephoned from Leisure World with grave concern, friends called from California, London, Paris. After three days of examinations, Bill took an unusual step for him. He called a press conference in Hanover and read a statement from Nieper: "I have examined William Holden and found him to be in excellent health." Holden later told Billy Wilder that he had gone to Nieper to "cleanse my lungs"; Bill remained a heavy smoker.

Bill returned to California to find the cancer rumors still prevailing. Then he was appalled to read a story in the *National Enquirer* blaring, "William Holden's Agonizing Battle to Save His Longtime Love." The scandal paper alleged that Holden had sought a cure for alcoholism from Nieper in order to keep Stefanie Powers from abandoning him.

Holden called a few friends in the Hollywood press to make denials. But the rumors would not go away, and Bill fell headlong into another pit of depression.

The drinking spells were worse than ever. He went through days when his memory was totally blacked out, and he seemed to be undergoing brain damage. Finally in December, Frank Schaap managed to get Bill to a hospital. Schaap could take no more. The accountant found himself too emotionally involved with his client, and he feared for his own sanity. He notified Bill that he was quitting the Holden account. Schaap never heard from Bill again.

38

The Final Year

In November of 1980, Bill Holden's old friend Ronald Reagan was elected President of the United States. Bill had not voted for him, but then, Bill never voted. He was totally apolitical. Because of Reagan's political activities and Bill's travels, they had seen little of each other for several years. There had been indications that friends had advised Nancy Reagan not to invite Bill to dinner because his drinking might be an embarrassment.

The deep friendship between Bill and Ronnie remained steadfast, and Bill was given a special invitation to attend the Inauguration on January 20.

Bill resisted going. He felt pride in his friend's accomplishment, but he was concerned that he might drink too much and disgrace himself. He found a reason not to attend.

Dick Delson, publicity chief of Filmways, suggested to Bill, "We need something that will help call attention to *The Earthling*. To my knowledge, you've never had any publicity on your Kenya game farm. I think we can get some good coverage if you would let a TV crew go down there with you."

Bill was reluctant. "You know, my work in Africa has always been something very personal for me. I prefer to keep it apart from my film career."

"I know, Bill," Delson reasoned, "but you won't be around forever. Maybe it would help for others who care about animals to see what you've been doing. Then they might get the idea that they can do something to help."

"I'll think about it."

Two days later, Holden telephoned Delson and said, "Okay, I'll do it."

NBC Magazine sent a camera crew and interviewer Jack Perkins to Kenya in late January, providing Bill with the excuse not to attend the Inauguration. Bill flew to Kenya by way of Hong Kong, where he terminated some business interests. Having found that east-west travel required less adjustment for jet lag, he usually scheduled his trips to Africa and Europe via Asia.

Bill Holden was at the gate of the Mount Kenya Safari Club when the NBC crew arrived. He greeted them warmly, made sure they had comfortable accommodations, joined them for drinks and dinner, spinning funny tales of his long career. His conversation was full of references to Stefanie Powers, his visitors noted.

Perkins and others in the crew puzzled over why Holden, an intensely private man, would allow himself to be photographed and interviewed in the place that meant so much to him. Did he want to sell out his interests and end his involvement with Africa? Was he seriously ill and winding up his affairs? Holden himself provided no hints.

During the bar conversation, Perkins recalled a recent interview with Sophia Loren and how she paid special attention to the cameraman. Bill chuckled, relating how he and Carol Reed had vied for Sophia's affection on *The Key,* but only the cinematographer had succeeded. Bill added, "The first rule for an actor is to make friends with the cameraman; he can remove the wrinkles and shadows and make you look good."

Bill demonstrated his professionalism during the interviews. At one point he leaned forward for emphasis, and Perkins remarked later how effective the move had been. Bill smiled and said, "That's my lean-forward sincerity look."

Any suspicions of a Holden illness were allayed when he took the television people into the wild for a giraffe catch. The sixty-two-year-old actor stood on the jolting Land Rover and lassoed a galloping giraffe, then helped pull it in, providing an exciting piece of television footage.

Bill intended to help launch *The Earthling* at its opening in New York, but he was delayed in Switzerland by a recurrence of malaria. He returned to California and gave some interviews for the film, but it was a futile gesture, since the film was attracting no business.

Bill Holden returned to Palm Springs and started drinking.

From a window of her Palm Springs house, Pat Stauffer could see Bill Holden's place on Southridge Mountain. She was visiting the desert in mid-March and had tried to reach Bill. Whenever she called, the butler told her, "Mr. Holden is out riding his motorcycle." She knew that was a lie, and she told the butler, "If you need help for anything, call me." No call came, and Bill's household help went on vacation.

Pat saw the light at Bill's house one evening, and she dialed his telephone number. She called four times before Bill's groggy voice answered. He was happy to hear her voice and invited her to come to the house.

She was appalled by what she saw. The kitchen was a mess, littered with moldy food and empty bottles. Bill's bed was stained with blood. He had gone for a ride on his motorcycle, and it had fallen on him. The wound was not serious, but it had gone untreated.

Bill was incoherent and hallucinating. Pat made him something to eat and telephoned Dr. Apfelbaum. "Bart, you've got to get up here right away!" she said. Apfelbaum placed Bill in Desert Hospital, and in two days he had recovered. Without admitting why he had been hospitalized, he said to Pat Stauffer, "Bart told me that you called him. I want to thank you."

Bill entered a period of well-being that lasted through the spring and summer of 1981. He was content to spend most of the time at Palm Springs with Pat, rearranging his artworks, swimming in the pool, watching the sunset from the Jacuzzi, talking about future trips. Pat, who found the Southridge house cold and cheerless, urged him to entertain some of his old friends. Bill finally agreed, and he arranged a dinner with an actor and his wife, old friends from the time when Bill and Ardis were suburbanites in Toluca Lake. But the actor was also an alcoholic, and he drank too much before dinner. The evening proved an embarrassment, and Bill told Pat, "See? No more company."

Bill left Palm Springs occasionally. In June, he flew to Dallas to discuss an exchange with Don Hunt's brother Brian, who operated a wild animal ranch in Texas. Hunt was to send Arabian oryxes to Bill's ranch for breeding and eventual return to Arabia, where they no longer existed in the wild. In return, Hunt would receive rare Grévy's zebras that Bill had been breeding.

Sometimes Bill drove to Los Angeles to discuss projects with his agents at William Morris and review business matters with his new accountant, Richard Comstock. Bill dropped in at the Century City offices of Blake Edwards and chatted with Edwards, Tony Adams, and the secretaries, as well as James Stewart, who maintained an office in the same suite. Bill dined with a few old friends: Richard Quine, Barbara Stanwyck, Ray Stark. Bill and Stark vowed that they would finally take that trip on the Trans-Siberian Railroad they had long planned.

Bill was having a business dinner at Mr. Chow's in Beverly Hills when he saw his goddaughter, Patti Davis, daughter of Ronald and Nancy Reagan. Bill and Patti embraced, and he told her, "I've been keeping up with your progress as an actress, and I'm very proud." They had rarely seen each other since Patti was a small girl, and they parted with promises they would remain in touch.

It had been almost a year since he made *S.O.B.*, and Bill was eager to return to work. The two most promising projects were *Dime Novel Sunset* and *That Championship Season*.

Sherwin Tilton was in his late twenties, had left Riverside, California, to study photography in Los Angeles, had become seduced by film, had been allowed to observe movies directed by Roman Polanski, John Schlesinger, and Alfred Hitchcock. Tilton believed that by making a dramatic fifteen-minute film with Karen Black and a volunteer crew he would establish a reputation in the film world. But the film didn't accomplish his goal.

The young man decided to try another avenue. He and a friend wrote a script, *Dime Novel Sunset*, about a greenhorn who goes west in search of the heroes he had read about in pulp novels. He finds two aging desperadoes and tries to enlist them for a final big job. Tilton designed the major badman to be played by his favorite actor, William Holden.

Aware of the hazards of submitting a script to a star, Tilton slipped past the guard at the studio gate and walked onto the stage where *S.O.B.* was filming. He introduced himself to Holden and asked, "Can I have five minutes of your time?" Holden agreed, and Tilton made his pitch about *Dime Novel Sunset*.

"I'll take the script, and I'll read it," Bill agreed. "I promise you I *will* read it."

"If you think it's a piece of shit, tell me," said Tilton.

"Don't worry, I'll level with you."

Two weeks later, Holden left a message with Tilton's answering service: he was still considering *Dime Novel Sunset*, was seeking other opinions. Holden showed the script to Blake Edwards, who liked it. Bill invited Sherwin Tilton to Palm Springs to discuss the project.

The young man was awed to spend a day with William Holden, who conducted a tour of the house with a running commentary on the artworks. Tilton found the house impressive, yet curiously impersonal. He saw no photographs of Holden's family. Aside from the Oscar* in the den, the only evidence of the star's Hollywood past was a portrait in the bedroom of Gary Cooper and his wife.

Tilton, who had seen most of the Holden films, tried to persuade his host to reminisce about them. But after a few comments about career matters, Holden shifted to topics that interested him more— animals, Africa, art. In one respect he remained the movie star: he made it plain that it was Tilton's responsiblity to find the means to make *Dime Novel Sunset* a reality.

Holden suggested Sam Peckinpah might be interested in *Dime Novel Sunset.* He wasn't. Bill proposed a reteaming of himself and Glenn Ford, using flashbacks from *Texas* to show the two oldtimers in their prime. Ford was intrigued. Burt Kennedy, who had directed John Wayne westerns, met with Holden, Ford, and Tilton and agreed to join the project.

Tilton believed his dream was going to happen. He borrowed money from a relative to finance the drafting of a budget, a script rewrite to accommodate Ford, the search for financing, location scouting in Mexico.

"I'm not sure I want to work in Mexico again," said Holden. "I'm sixty-two years old. Maybe I could do it on *The Wild Bunch,* but I don't feel like sleeping with scorpions and falling off horses anymore."

"We've got to shoot in Mexico; it's the only way we can make the picture for a price," Tilton argued. "Supposing the location was Cuernavaca."

Holden's eyes brightened. *"Now* you're talking. *That's* civilized."

But Glenn Ford didn't want to work in Mexico. He dropped out. Holden suggested Robert Preston. Preston was interested. With Holden, Preston, and Kennedy in the project, Tilton was able to find backers. He made another trip to Mexico. He informed Holden of every development, striving to keep Bill's interest alive. They discussed the script on the telephone, sometimes for an hour or more. Bill wanted more humor in the script, more characterization of the two old desperadoes. He suggested making one of them deaf, the other with failing

---

*Perhaps a duplicate for the one he claimed to have thrown into the Bay of Naples. The story may have been fanciful. Holden later denied it, and Sam Spiegel points out that his yacht took Holden and Capucine from the South of France to Barbados, and Naples was not on the way.

eyesight. "And let's have the two old guys do something to show the kid that their way of life was not good for him," Bill proposed.

"One more thing," he added. "I think my character should die at the end of the picture. That makes it much more dramatic."

Jason Miller had tried for ten years to realize his dream of filming his play *That Championship Season.* After it had won Tony and New York Drama Critics' Circle awards and a Pulitzer Prize, Universal Pictures had paid $300,000 for the screen rights, but no film was made. Miller regained the rights and tried to interest many filmmakers and production companies, never with success. In March of 1981, Miller sent his screenplay of *That Championship Season* to William Friedkin, who was recovering from a heart attack.

"I like it, I'll do it," said Friedkin.

Friedkin had seen the play when it was first produced. He had recognized Miller's failed Catholicism in the writing, and had cast the playwright-actor as the doomed priest in *The Exorcist.* Such was Miller's faith in Friedkin that he transferred the film rights of *That Championship Season* to the director without payment.

George C. Scott was Friedkin's first choice as the basketball coach reliving old glories and remembered bitterness at a reunion with his players. Scott, Friedkin, Miller, and their respective advisers met at Scott's Bel Air Hotel bungalow. Friedkin was so offended by Scott that he walked out of the meeting vowing never to work with the actor.

Friedkin and Miller next sent the script to William Holden. A month later came word from William Morris: Holden passed. Paul Newman, Lee Marvin, and Burt Lancaster declined, although Lancaster would have accepted at his regular price. Friedkin reasoned that the major actors would have to reduce their normal salaries in order to secure financing.

Bill Holden reconsidered. He had first read the script when he was depressed over the deaths of Chuck Feingarten and Paddy Chayefsky, and he could not consider working, especially in a highly dramatic role. He reread *That Championship Season* and decided it was worth considering.

Holden, Friedkin, and Miller met for dinner at Madame Wu's in Santa Monica. Holden voiced his concerns. He was offended by the coach's bigotry and felt audiences would be, too. Friedkin observed that the coach was not really a bigot, but that his thinking had become archaic. "He was a product of his times, when winning was very American," said Friedkin. "The passing of time made him obsolete." The director added that he saw the film as "the dark side of Norman Rockwell" and he wanted to achieve a Rockwellian look in the locations.

In talking about the only woman he ever loved, the coach remarked that she "could hump like a hundred-dollar whore." Said Holden: "You have him talking lyrically about the woman, then you destroy what you have set up."

"You're right," said Miller. "The line goes out."

Friedkin cautioned that every studio had turned down *That Championship Season* and its only chance of being made was if the five major actors worked for $200,000 apiece plus a percentage of the profits.

"That's fine with me," said Bill. "When do we start?"

With the $5.1 million budget guaranteed by the John Hay Whitney Foundation, Friedkin started preparations in October of 1981. He rented space at the Goldwyn studio, scouted locations in Scranton, Pennsylvania, Jason Miller's hometown and the place he had written about. The rest of the cast was assembled: Nick Nolte, Martin Sheen, Paul Sorvino, and Miller himself.

During his tranquil summer of 1981, Bill Holden grew more enthusiastic about *That Championship Season.* He calmed all his concerns about the coach's bigotry and saw him, in Billy Friedkin's term, as a mythic character. It was a powerful role, Bill decided, perhaps his best since *Sunset Boulevard.* It was one to go out on.

39

End of Golden Boy

The blowup between Blake Edwards and Paramount Pictures had been predictable. They had battled fiercely over *Darling Lili* a dozen years before. Edwards had experienced foreboding when Lorimar Productions made a deal to release *S.O.B.* through Paramount in 1981. Paramount refused to finance Edwards' plan to premiere the film with a press junket in the oldtime Hollywood style. Furious, Edwards announced he would pay for the premiere himself.

A full weekend of events was planned for June 27 to 29, and Bill Holden participated enthusiastically, along with the rest of the *S.O.B.* cast. He explained to an interviewer: "An actor shouldn't accept a part he doesn't believe in. When he accepts a picture, he has the responsibility to help sell it. You have no obligations except those you willingly assume, but once you assume them, you see them through to the end."

Holden attended a screening of *S.O.B.* at a theater in Malibu, then met with members of the visiting press at a supper at Jean Leon's La Scala West. He looked tan and fit, as good as I had seen him in many years. He was the first to arrive for the press conference with the film's stars at ten the following morning in the Beverly Hills Hotel. Throughout the day he submitted to individual interviews with print, radio, and television reporters.

A dinner dance was held in the Crystal Room of the Beverly Hills Hotel on Saturday night. Bill brought Gail Feingarten, widow of the art dealer, and he maintained an air of gaiety. After Shelley Winters entered the ballroom, conversation at Bill's table centered on her book, about which several of the women expressed shock. Bill refused to take Shelley's account of their Christmas trysts seriously. "Ardis loved reading the book," he cracked, "because she found out where I had been all those years."

Bill danced with several of the guests, including Loretta Swit. She delivered a message from Shelley: "I think Bill is angry with me. Tell him I didn't mean anything with my book." Bill laughed, and he danced Loretta to the bandstand. After a brief conversation with the leader, Bill resumed dancing, steering toward Shelley's table.

Suddenly the music stopped, and the band started playing Irving Berlin's "White Christmas." Bill stood in front of Shelley and bowed with arms outstretched. Her face turned deep red.

Bill Holden was the ringleader in enlisting cast members for the three-day tour of eight major population centers to publicize *S.O.B.* "Let's do it for Blake," he urged. The junket started in San Francisco on July 9, with Holden, Julie Andrews, Richard Mulligan, Loretta Swit, and Robert Webber attending group and individual interviews. They departed that afternoon for New York in two small chartered jets, stopping in Lincoln, Nebraska, for refueling and planeside interviews. In New York they were joined by Robert Preston, and the tour continued by bus to Philadelphia, then by air to Washington, Boston, Toronto, and Chicago, with a brief stop in Denver.

As he had during the filming of *S.O.B.*, Bill Holden became the unofficial leader of the junket. He was always punctual, never complaining, and with his innate dignity he fielded the difficult questions posed by reporters at the press conferences.

"Why are you making this tour?" a television reporter asked. "Is it because the picture is a bomb?"

"*S.O.B.* is not a bomb," Holden answered patiently. "It's a unique, even outrageous comedy, and it has to be explained to the public. Paramount isn't willing to spend the dough, so we decided to pitch in."

"Isn't it demeaning for 'Mary Poppins' to expose her breasts for her husband's movie?" another reporter asked.

"Miss Andrews is an actress, and she is required to do many things in her career," Holden replied in a calm, fatherly voice. "The topless scene is one of them. When you see the movie, you'll recognize that the scene is not exploitive. It is an important part of the plot, and Blake plays it strictly for laughs."

Holden was reflective on the *S.O.B.* junket, both with interviewers and with his fellow travelers. When a reporter at a press conference observed that his Tim Culley was the only character in *S.O.B.* with a semblance of integrity, Bill responded that he always looked for a degree of integrity in the characters he played, though they needn't be virtuous. Joe Gillis in *Sunset Boulevard* finally came to the decision to leave Norma Desmond; Shears in *Kwai* agreed to return for the fatal mission. And the key to Tim Culley came in an exchange with the demented Felix Farmer (Richard Mulligan).

CULLEY

Felix, have I ever lied to you?

FELIX

No.

CULLEY

Well, I have. And now that I have told you that, you can trust
me.

During their journeys together, Holden and Bob Preston enjoyed long
conversations, talking with the ease of reunited old friends. On the
bus trip from New York to Philadelphia, Bill rhapsodized about the
African experience: "You feel something very special there, something very basic. Africa is where man began, that's where our roots
are. Going to Africa always makes me feel so alive. When you realize
that the next breath you draw may be your last, then everything
heightens. You savor the tastes, the smells, the sights. You can even
see the blades of grass."

Yet to Richard Mulligan, who had made a film in Kenya, Holden
admitted Africa is "a young man's game." He had lost his enthusiasm
for Africa, which was no longer so unspoiled and challenging. With its
emerging nationalism, Africa had changed. So had Bill Holden.

On the flight back to Los Angeles, the junketeers were in an exuberant mood, believing their three strenuous days had demonstrated
their dedication to *S.O.B.* and their devotion to Blake Edwards. Holden
was enjoying the last hours of closeness with his fellow players. He
began drinking white wine, which was in abundant supply on the chartered jet.

As the plane approached the immense glittering carpet of Los
Angeles, Holden grew contemplative. He talked with Tony Adams,
Edwards' co-producer, about something he rarely discussed: death. He
was not at all morbid, only realistic:

"I've got it all settled. It cost me twenty-five dollars to join the
Neptune Society. They'll cremate my body and scatter the ashes at sea.
I'm not going to waste my money on some big monument or a damn
Hollywood funeral. I've got more important ways to spend my money."

The euphoria stemming from the *S.O.B.* junket continued through
Bill Holden's 1981 summer. He spent most of July and August in Palm
Springs with Pat Stauffer. He made a few trips to Los Angeles to at-
tend to business matters and discuss *That Championship Season* with
William Friedkin and Jason Miller. Filming had been scheduled to

start in Scranton in October, and Bill was probing into the character of the coach, whose bigotry had disturbed him in the beginning.

"Bill was worried that the coach might emerge in one color," Jason Miller recalls. "He talked about the mythology of the man, what had made him a legend to at least four men. Bill discussed where the coach had come from and where he was going. He wanted to use the full palette of the man, not show him simply as a bigot. He thought the bigotry should be shown in the proper perspective, not emphasized but in throwaway lines."

Holden also had several conversations with Sherwin Tilton about *Dime Novel Sunset*. They talked about script revisions, casting, and production elements; and Tilton said he thought he could have the film ready to start in February. But in order to make final arrangements, he needed a letter declaring Holden's intention to participate in the project. Bill provided the letter.

Holden had continued his association with Michael Klassman, but never with the intensity of those four months in 1979. The psychologist had made trips to Palm Springs when Bill was drunk and depressed, and they had met for therapy sessions in Los Angeles. But Bill was often gone on business trips and locations, and Klassman traveled, too. Klassman left their meetings with a sense of helplessness and frustration. Nothing he could do seemed to halt Bill's downward spiral.

In August, Bill asked Michael to meet him at a coffee shop in Santa Monica. Bill was sober but like a tightly wound spring. Michael urged him to enter the alcoholism unit of the Good Samaritan Hospital, where Klassman had been clinical director of counseling. Bill shook his head.

"I don't have the heart for it," he said. "I'm not going to lick this thing."

Once more Michael urged: "Go back to Africa, Bill. It'll save you."

"Yeah, I really should go," said Bill. But he didn't.

Over Labor Day, Bill and Pat Stauffer went to La Costa for his health ritual before the start of a movie. When he returned to Los Angeles, he was dismayed to learn that the start of *That Championship Season* was in jeopardy. Nick Nolte was balking.

A meeting was held on September 24 in Friedkin's office at the Burbank studios. Seated on the couch and chairs before the director's desk were the proposed cast of *That Championship Season:* William Holden, Nick Nolte, Martin Sheen, Paul Sorvino, Jason Miller. Friedkin outlined the situation:

"We're ready to go. I've finished the budget, we've got a model of the set that will be built at Goldwyn studio, I've hired the crew. I've been to Scranton to pick the locations, and we're ready to start in a couple of weeks. We've *got* to start. If we wait any longer, winter will hit Scranton, and there'll be nothing to photograph but snow. You won't see anything of Scranton. The forecast is for rain and snow all winter."

He directed his gaze to Nolte. "Nick, everyone in this room is ready to go—except you. Why can't you give us an answer?"

"I've told you, Billy," Nolte replied. "I've got this other picture on the fire."

Holden turned to Nolte and snapped, "Come on, man, stop fucking around. All of us here have agreed to go along with Billy's plan. Are you going to make this picture or aren't you? We deserve an answer."

"Give me until next week," Nolte said. "By then I'll be able to make a decision."

Nick Nolte made up his mind the following week: he would do *That Championship Season.* It was too late. Friedkin decided he couldn't risk the Whitney Foundation's investment on the Scranton winter. Besides, he had the opportunity to direct a play in New York in November. He proposed postponement of *That Championship Season* until March of 1982. All of the participants, including Nick Nolte, agreed.

The postponement was a crushing disappointment to Bill Holden, who had come to grips with the character of the coach and believed he could deliver a performance that would crown his career. When he returned to Palm Springs, Pat Stauffer eyed him cautiously, fearful of signs he would break his six-month sobriety. She recognized that he was depressed, and she suggested a vacation trip to Sun Valley, Idaho.

"No, let's do something exciting," he said, and he opened an atlas.

"There!" he said, pointing to the tip of South America. "Let's go to Patagonia and watch the whales. Then we'll fly to Italy and get Mindy [Pat's daughter, enrolled in a Rome school], then end up at the Safari Club on our anniversary, New Year's Eve. We'll hire a witch doctor and get married. How about it, Winker?"

Pat laughed at his boyish enthusiasm. "We'll see how you do," she said.

The following morning, October 6, 1981, Bill Holden was alone at the Southridge house, staring incredulously at the television screen. Scenes of horror unfolded before him: assassins leaping out of a military vehicle to spray bullets into a grandstand of dignitaries, including Anwar Sadat; wounded and dying scattered among the upset chairs. Bill changed channels to another network and saw the scenes enacted again. He turned on the radio, seeking more recent news of whether the Egyptian president still lived. The government said nothing.

Bill telephoned Pat Stauffer: "Jesus, Winker, have you been watching television?"

"Yes, Bill," she replied. "It's terrible."

"God, I can't believe it. Sadat. A man of peace. Let's hope he's still alive."

"That doesn't seem likely, Bill."

"Yes, but there's still hope, Winker."

He clung to that hope until the networks announced that Anwar Sadat had been murdered. Bill was stunned. He had never met Sadat, but he had admired the Egyptian's boldness, his decisiveness, his risk of new enemies in order to make peace with Israel.

Pat Stauffer realized the tragedy would contribute to Bill's depression. He had been oblivious to physical danger all his life, but he had often admitted to Pat his fear of "the three D's—death, divorce, disease." And death had been robbing him of friends: Charlie Feldman, Ray Ryan, Paddy Chayefsky, John Wayne, Chuck Feingarten.

Holden left Palm Springs for Santa Monica the next day.

Before departing, Holden had made arrangements to have dinner with Ray Stark at a new Italian restaurant on Westwood Boulevard and discuss their long-planned trip on the Trans-Siberian Railroad. They agreed to meet at seven-thirty at Stark's house in Bel Air. The producer waited until eight o'clock, then drove to the restaurant, leaving a message for Holden to join him there.

Bill telephoned Stark at the restaurant: "Look, old buddy, I cracked up my Volkswagen driving up from Palm Springs today. I'm in my Santa Monica apartment now."

"I'll come and get you," Stark volunteered.

"No, I don't feel like it tonight. We'll do it again soon."

The long slide had begun.

After October 7, Holden ventured a few times outside the Santa Monica apartment, and he talked with friends and business associates on the telephone. He had frequent conversations, sometimes for an hour and a half, with Sherwin Tilton about *Dime Novel Sunset*. Tilton recalls, "He sounded distraught and tormented, like a man still searching for a meaning to his life and not finding it."

As the days progressed, Holden's voice and attitude changed. His customarily crisp diction slurred, and he dropped his sympathetic, even paternal tone toward the young man. "Now you listen to me, buddy," he began belligerently. At other times he seemed almost maudlin.

"Sherwin, you know that wife of yours?" Holden said. "You know that one minute you spend with her when you arrive home at night? From now on, make that five minutes."

Sherwin Tilton was growing desperate. His dream of becoming a film producer was in danger of disappearing because of an alcoholic star. He tried to keep Holden's interest alive in *Dime Novel Sunset,* but Bill preferred to talk about Africa. He was planning a trip that would take him close to Libya, and he was concerned about the Libyan situation. When Tilton proposed starting *Dime Novel Sunset* in February, Holden said, "I am seriously considering retiring from acting permanently."

Tilton telephoned one of Holden's business associates for advice. "Don't worry about it," Tilton was told. "He makes all those rash statements, but he won't remember what he said. He goes on these binges two or three times a year, and eventually he comes out of them. Then he'll make excuses for being gone. He'll never admit to you that he has been drinking."

Tilton decided to wait. He telephoned the Santa Monica apartment, allowed three rings. If Bill answered in a slurred voice, Tilton hung up, realizing conversation would be useless. Each day he telephoned the Palm Springs house to inquire if Mr. Holden had returned. The answer was no, and Tilton realized the binge continued.

Whenever Holden didn't answer the phone, his familiar voice was heard in a recording: "This is 393-9053. Please leave a message, date, and time, and I'll be in touch with you right away." Now he had recorded a new message, and it reflected his drunken anger: "Well, lessee, this is 393-9053, and there's nobody here but this damn recording machine. So if you want to leave a message, leave your name and number and date and time and I'll try to get back to you."

At 10:30 A.M. on November 2, William Friedkin placed a call to the Santa Monica apartment from his office at the Burbank studios.

After many rings, a blurred voice answered. "Hello."

"Bill, this is Bill Friedkin."

"Oh, hi, Billy."

"I'm leaving for New York to direct a play, Bill, but I wanted to talk to you about starting *That Championship Season* in March."

"I'm not going to do the picture, Billy."

"Oh? Why not, Bill?"

"I'm just not."

"Do you want to talk about it?"

"No."

"Bill, we were depending on you. We have signed contracts with everyone."

"I'll see you in Africa."

"Let's talk about it. Let's get together."

"No, you gotta come to Africa. You belong in Africa. You have no idea what it's like. You've got to come. We'll sit and talk."

"Okay, Bill, I'll see you in Africa. But please think about the picture. I'll call you back and we'll talk."

"Next time I'll see you in Africa."

"Okay, Bill. I'll talk to you later."

"See you in Africa."

During the following week, Friedkin tried unsuccessfully to reach Holden. So did Martin Sheen, Nick Nolte, and Jason Miller. Bill didn't answer the phone. Pat Stauffer tried to reach him, using their code of two rings and a hang-up, then another call. No reply. The apartment manager said that he had seen Mr. Holden and he didn't want to be disturbed. Pat felt reassured because she knew that the maid cleaned Bill's apartment every day. She didn't discover until later that the maid had retired shortly before Bill isolated himself in the apartment.

Once more he tried to crash the sound barrier. This time he failed. On the nightstand beside his body was a revised script of *Dime Novel Sunset*.

William Holden's accomplishments as a film actor were almost obscured in news reports by the curious circumstances of his death. Some critics dismissed him as a popular leading man of little depth. Others recognized his achievements. David Ansen in *Newsweek* wrote of how Holden's physical beauty had made him a star in *Golden Boy* and how he remained a romantic sex symbol in the 1950s. "But the beauty was moral, too: the mature Holden re-emerged with ravaged stoicism in *The Wild Bunch* and became a symbol of hard-bitten decency in *Network* and *S.O.B.* He was courtly, cynical, possessed of a particularly American gallantry that was utterly free of airs."

The Holden will was in character. He made bequests to the three women who had helped in the long battle with drinking: $250,000 to

Stefanie Powers, $50,000 apiece to Capucine and Pat Stauffer. He gave $75,000 each to his sons and stepdaughter, as well as his art, furniture, automobiles, and personal effects. The Kenya game ranch would be given to an organization that would continue his ideals, his primitive art collection to the Palm Springs Desert Museum. The remainder of the estate was placed in trust for his family, including Ardis and his mother.

For months afterward, Bill Holden's friends were still struggling to unravel the cruel puzzle of his death. Billy Wilder offered this explanation: "Here was a most successful man who virtually abandons his profession to take care of endangered species. He does not care about himself, indeed he kills himself. What he didn't realize was that he himself was an endangered species: the beautiful American."

40

Academy Awards, 1982

On March 29, 1982, John Travolta stood before television cameras on the stage of the Los Angeles Music Center. He told the Academy Award audience, "Four years ago, William Holden and Barbara Stanwyck came on this stage to present an award. When they did, Mr. Holden departed from the script to speak from the heart. He said that his career derived from the lady standing next to him. That all he was came from her generosity, her support, her abiding belief in him. Barbara was completely surprised by this. She listened, her public face letting her private face show . . . but only for an instant. The actress in control . . ."

Travolta then paid tribute to Miss Stanwyck, introduced scenes from her film career, and presented her with the Academy's honorary award for her accomplishments.

After thunderous applause and a standing ovation, Miss Stanwyck thanked the Academy's board of governors and the fellow workers she had toiled with during her long career. Clutching the Oscar, she concluded:

"A few years ago, I stood on this stage with William Holden as a presenter. I loved him very much and I miss him. He always wished I would get an Oscar. And so tonight, my Golden Boy, you got your wish."

As she held the Oscar aloft, eyes glistening, many others remembered Bill Holden. The horror of his death had been dulled by the passage of time, and what remained was the image of the smiling, incredibly handsome, unmistakably American Golden Boy.

THE FILMS OF WILLIAM HOLDEN

Title, distributor, year of release, director (in italics), cast

Golden Boy, Columbia, 1939. *Rouben Mamoulian.* Barbara Stanwyck, Adolphe Menjou, William Holden, Lee J. Cobb, Joseph Calleia, Sam Levene, Edward S. Brophy.

Invisible Stripes, Warner Brothers, 1940. *Lloyd Bacon.* George Raft, Jane Bryan, William Holden, Humphrey Bogart, Flora Robson, Paul Kelly, Lee Patrick, Henry O'Neill, Frankie Thomas.

Our Town, United Artists, 1940. *Sam Wood.* Frank Craven, William Holden, Martha Scott, Fay Bainter, Beulah Bondi, Thomas Mitchell, Guy Kibbee, Stuart Erwin.

Those Were the Days, Paramount, 1940. *J. Theodore Reed.* William Holden, Bonita Granville, Ezra Stone, Judith Barrett, Vaughan Glaser, Lucien Littlefield, Richard Denning.

Arizona, Columbia, 1941. *Wesley Ruggles.* Jean Arthur, William Holden, Warren William, Porter Hall, Paul Harvey, George Chandler, Byron Foulger, Regis Toomey.

I Wanted Wings, Paramount, 1941. *Mitchell Leisen.* Ray Milland, William Holden, Wayne Morris, Brian Donlevy, Constance Moore, Veronica Lake, Harry Davenport.

Texas, Columbia, 1941. *George Marshall.* William Holden, Glenn Ford, Claire Trevor, George Bancroft, Edgar Buchanan, Don Beddoe, Andrew Tombes, Addison Richards.

The Remarkable Andrew, Paramount, 1942. *Stuart Heisler.* William Holden, Ellen Drew, Brian Donlevy, Rod Cameron, Richard Webb, Porter Hall, Frances Gifford, Nydia Westman, Montagu Love.

The Fleet's In, Paramount, 1942. *Victor Schertzinger.* Dorothy Lamour, William Holden, Ezra Stone, Betty Hutton, Cass Daley, Gil Lamb, Leif Erickson.

Meet the Stewarts, Columbia, 1942. *Alfred E. Green.* William Holden, Frances Dee, Grant Mitchell, Marjorie Gateson, Anne Revere.

Young and Willing, United Artists, 1943. *Edward H. Griffith.* William Holden, Eddie Bracken, Robert Benchley, Susan Hayward, Martha O'Driscoll, Barbara Britton, James Brown.

Blaze of Noon, Paramount, 1947. *John Farrow.* Anne Baxter, William Holden, William Bendix, Sonny Tufts, Sterling Hayden, Howard da Silva, Johnny Sands, Jean Wallace.

Dear Ruth, Paramount, 1947. *William D. Russell.* Joan Caulfield, William Holden, Edward Arnold, Mary Philips, Mona Freeman, Billy De Wolfe, Virginia Welles.

Variety Girl, Paramount, 1947. *George Marshall.* All-star cast.

Rachel and the Stranger, RKO, 1948. *Norman Foster.* Loretta Young, William Holden, Robert Mitchum, Gary Gray, Tom Tully, Sara Haden, Frank Ferguson.

Apartment for Peggy, 20th Century–Fox, 1948. *George Seaton.* Jeanne Crain, William Holden, Edmund Gwenn, Gene Lockhart, Griff Barnett, Randy Stuart, Marion Marshall.

The Dark Past, Columbia, 1948. *Rudolph Maté.* William Holden, Nina Foch, Lee J. Cobb, Adele Jurgens, Stephen Dunne, Lois Maxwell, Barry Kroeger, Steven Geray.

The Man from Colorado, Columbia, 1949. *Henry Levin.* Glenn Ford, William Holden, Ellen Drew, Ray Collins, Edgar Buchanan, Jerome Courtland.

Streets of Laredo, Paramount, 1949. *Leslie Fenton.* William Holden, William Bendix, Macdonald Carey, Mona Freeman, Stanley Ridges, Alfonso Bedoya, Ray Teal.

Miss Grant Takes Richmond, Columbia, 1949. *Lloyd Bacon.* Lucille Ball, William Holden, Janis Carter, James Gleason, Gloria Henry, Frank McHugh, George Cleveland, Stephen Dunne.

Dear Wife, Paramount, 1950. *Richard Haydn.* William Holden, Joan Caulfield, Billy De Wolfe, Mona Freeman, Edward Arnold, Arleen Whelan, Mary Philips, Harry Von Zell.

Father Is a Bachelor, Columbia, 1950. *Norman Foster* and *Abby Berlin.* William Holden, Coleen Gray, Mary Jane Saunders, Charles Winninger, Stuart Erwin, Clinton Sundberg, Gary Gray.

Sunset Boulevard, Paramount, 1950. *Billy Wilder.* William Holden, Gloria Swanson, Erich von Stroheim, Nancy Olson, Fred Clark, Lloyd Gough, Jack Webb, Franklyn Farnum.

Union Station, Paramount, 1950. *Rudolph Maté.* William Holden, Nancy Olson, Barry Fitzgerald, Lyle Bettger, Jan Sterling.

Born Yesterday, Columbia, 1950. *George Cukor.* Broderick Crawford, Judy Holliday, William Holden, Howard St. John, Frank Otto, Larry Oliver.

Force of Arms, Warner Brothers, 1951. *Michael Curtiz.* William Holden, Nancy Olson, Frank Lovejoy, Gene Evans, Dick Wesson, Paul Picerni.

Submarine Command, Paramount, 1952. *John Farrow.* William Holden, Nancy Olson, William Bendix, Don Taylor, Arthur Franz, Darryl Hickman, Peggy Webber, Moroni Olson.

Boots Malone, Columbia, 1952. *William Dieterle.* William Holden, Johnny Stewart, Stanley Clements, Basil Ruysdael, Carl Benton Reid, Ralph Dumke, Ed Begley.

The Turning Point, Paramount, 1952. *William Dieterle.* William Holden, Edmond O'Brien, Alexis Smith, Tom Tully, Ed Begley, Don Dayton.

Stalag 17, Paramount, 1953. *Billy Wilder.* William Holden, Don Taylor, Otto Preminger, Robert Strauss, Harvey Lembeck, Richard Erdman, Peter Graves, Neville Brand, Sig Ruman.

The Moon Is Blue, United Artists, 1953. *Otto Preminger.* William Holden,

David Niven, Maggie McNamara, Tom Tully, Dawn Addams, Fortunio Bonanova, Gregory Ratoff.

Forever Female, Paramount, 1954. *Irving Rapper.* Ginger Rogers, William Holden, Paul Douglas, James Gleason, Jesse White, Marjorie Rambeau, George Reeves, King Donovan.

Escape from Fort Bravo, MGM, 1954. *John Sturges.* William Holden, Eleanor Parker, John Forsythe, William Demarest, William Campbell, John Lupton, Richard Anderson, Polly Bergen.

Executive Suite, MGM, 1954. *Robert Wise.* William Holden, Fredric March, Barbara Stanwyck, June Allyson, Walter Pidgeon, Shelley Winters, Paul Douglas, Louis Calhern, Dean Jagger, Nina Foch.

Sabrina, Paramount, 1954. *Billy Wilder.* Humphrey Bogart, Audrey Hepburn, William Holden, Walter Hampden, John Williams, Martha Hyer.

The Country Girl, Paramount, 1954. *George Seaton.* Bing Crosby, Grace Kelly, William Holden, Anthony Ross, Gene Reynolds, Jacqueline Fontaine.

The Bridges at Toko-Ri, Paramount, 1955. *Mark Robson.* William Holden, Fredric March, Grace Kelly, Mickey Rooney, Robert Strauss, Charles McGraw, Keiko Awaji, Earl Holliman.

Love Is a Many-Splendored Thing, 20th Century–Fox, 1955. *Henry King.* William Holden, Jennifer Jones, Torin Thatcher, Isobel Elsom, Murray Matheson, Ann Richards, Richard Loo.

Picnic, Columbia, 1956. *Joshua Logan.* William Holden, Rosalind Russell, Kim Novak, Betty Field, Susan Strasberg, Cliff Robertson, Arthur O'Connell, Verna Felton, Reta Shaw, Nick Adams.

The Proud and the Profane, Paramount, 1956. *George Seaton.* William Holden, Deborah Kerr, Thelma Ritter, Dewey Martin, William Redfield, Ross Bagdasarian.

Toward the Unknown, Warner Brothers, 1956. *Mervyn Le Roy.* William Holden, Lloyd Nolan, Virginia Leith, Charles McGraw, Murray Hamilton, Paul Fix, James Garner.

The Bridge on the River Kwai, Columbia, 1957. *David Lean.* William Holden, Alec Guinness, Jack Hawkins, Sessue Hayakawa, James Donald, Geoffrey Horne, André Morell.

The Key, Columbia, 1958. *Carol Reed.* William Holden, Sophia Loren, Trevor Howard, Oscar Homolka, Kieron Moore, Bernard Lee.

The Horse Soldiers, United Artists, 1959. *John Ford.* John Wayne, William Holden, Constance Towers, Althea Gibson, Hoot Gibson, Anna Lee, Russell Simpson, Stan Jones.

The World of Suzie Wong, Paramount, 1960. *Richard Quine.* William Holden, Nancy Kwan, Sylvia Sims, Michael Wilding, Lawrence Naismith, Jacqueline Chan, Andy Ho.

Satan Never Sleeps, 20th Century–Fox, 1962. *Leo McCarey.* William Holden, Clifton Webb, France Nuyen, Athene Sayler, Martin Benson, Edith Sharpe.

The Counterfeit Traitor, Paramount, 1962. *George Seaton.* William Holden, Lilli Palmer, Hugh Griffith, Ernst Schroder, Eva Dahlbeck, Ulf Palme, Carl Raddatz.

The Lion, 20th Century–Fox, 1962. *Jack Cardiff.* William Holden, Trevor Howard, Capucine, Pamela Franklin, Makara Kwaiha Ramadhani.

Paris When It Sizzles, Paramount, 1964. *Richard Quine.* William Holden, Audrey Hepburn, Gregoire Aslan, Noël Coward, Ramond Bussieres, Christian Duvallex.

The Seventh Dawn, United Artists, 1964. *Lewis Gilbert.* William Holden, Susannah York, Capucine, Tetsuro Tamba, Michael Goodliffe, Allan Cuthbertson, Maurice Denham.

Alvarez Kelly, Columbia, 1966. *Edward Dmytryk.* William Holden, Richard Widmark, Janice Rule, Patrick O'Neal, Victoria Shaw, Roger C. Carmel, Richard Rust, Arthur Franz, Donald Barry.

Casino Royale, Columbia, 1967. *John Huston, Kenneth Hughes, Val Guest, Robert Parrish, Joseph McGrath.* Peter Sellers, Ursula Andress, David Niven, Orson Welles, Joanna Pettet, Dalia Lavi, Woody Allen, William Holden, Charles Boyer, John Huston.

The Devil's Brigade, United Artists, 1968. *Andrew V. McLaglen.* William Holden, Cliff Robertson, Vince Edwards, Michael Rennie, Dana Andrews, Gretchen Wyler, Andrew Prine, Claude Akins, Carroll O'Connor.

The Wild Bunch, Warner Brothers–Seven Arts, 1969. *Sam Peckinpah.* William Holden, Ernest Borgnine, Robert Ryan, Edmond O'Brien, Warren Oates, Jaime Sanchez, Ben Johnson, Emilio Fernandez, Strother Martin, L. Q. Jones.

The Christmas Tree, Walter Reade–Continental, 1969. *Terence Young.* William Holden, Virna Lisi, André Bourvil, Brook Fuller.

Wild Rovers, MGM, 1971. *Blake Edwards.* William Holden, Ryan O'Neal, Karl Malden, Lynn Carlin, Tom Skerritt, Joe Don Baker, James Olson, Leora Dana, Moses Gunn.

The Revengers, National General, 1972. *Daniel Mann.* William Holden, Susan Hayward, Ernest Borgnine, Woody Strode, Roger Hanin, René Koldenhoff, Jorge Luke.

Breezy, Universal, 1973. *Clint Eastwood.* William Holden, Kay Lenz, Dennis Olivieri, Marj Dusay, Eugene Peterson, Joan Hotchkiss.

The Blue Knight, Lorimar, 1973. *Robert Butler.* William Holden, Lee Remick, Anne Archer, Eileen Brennan, George DiCenzo, Sam Elliott, Jamie Farr.

Open Season, Columbia, 1974. *Peter Collinson.* Peter Fonda, William Holden, Cornelia Sharpe, John Philip Law, Richard Lynch.

The Towering Inferno, 20th Century–Fox/Warner Brothers, 1974. *John Guillermin.* Steve McQueen, Paul Newman, William Holden, Faye Dunaway, Fred Astaire, Susan Blakely, Richard Chamberlain, Jennifer Jones, Robert Wagner, O. J. Simpson, Robert Vaughn.

21 Hours at Munich, Filmways, 1976. *William A. Graham.* William Holden, Shirley Knight, Franco Nero, Richard Basehart, Anthony Quayle.

Network, MGM, 1976. *Sidney Lumet.* William Holden, Faye Dunaway, Peter Finch, Robert Duvall, Ned Beatty, Beatrice Straight.

Damien—Omen II, 20th Century–Fox, 1978. *Don Taylor.* William Holden, Lee Grant, Jonathan Scott-Taylor, Robert Foxworth, Nicholas Pryor, Lew Ayres, Sylvia Sidney, Leo McKern.

Fedora, United Artists, 1978. *Billy Wilder.* William Holden, Marthe Keller, Hildegard Knef, José Ferrer, Henry Fonda, Michael York.

Ashanti, Columbia/EMI/Warner Brothers, 1979. *Richard Fleischer.* Michael

Caine, Omar Sharif, Peter Ustinov, Rex Harrison, William Holden.

The Day the World Ended, Warner Brothers, 1980 (also released as *When Time Ran Out*). *James Goldstone.* Paul Newman, William Holden, Jacqueline Bisset, Edward Albert, Red Buttons, Barbara Carrera, Valentina Cortese, Veronica Hamel, Burgess Meredith, Ernest Borgnine, James Franciscus, Alex Karras.

The Earthling, Filmways, 1981. *Peter Collinson.* William Holden, Ricky Schroder, Jack Thomas, Olivia Hamnett.

S.O.B., Paramount, 1981. *Blake Edwards.* Julie Andrews, William Holden, Marisa Berenson, Larry Hagman, Robert Loggia, Stuart Margolin, Richard Mulligan, Robert Preston, Craig Stevens, Loretta Swit, Robert Vaughn, Robert Webber, Shelley Winters.

INDEX